G·R·E·A·T
EXPECTATIONS

Becoming a Dad

The First Three Years

John C. Carr, LCSW

STERLING

New York / London
www.sterlingpublishing.com

D0190069

STERLING and the distinctive Sterling logo are registered trademarks of Sterling Publishing Co., Inc.

Library of Congress Cataloging-in-Publication Data Available

10 9 8 7 6 5 4 3 2 1

Published by Sterling Publishing Co., Inc.
387 Park Avenue South, New York, NY 10016
© 2010 by John Carr
Distributed in Canada by Sterling Publishing
c/o Canadian Manda Group, 165 Dufferin Street
Toronto, Ontario, Canada M6K 3H6
Distributed in the United Kingdom by GMC Distribution Services
Castle Place, 166 High Street, Lewes, East Sussex, England BN7 1XU
Distributed in Australia by Capricorn Link (Australia) Pty. Ltd.
P.O. Box 704, Windsor, NSW 2756, Australia

Manufactured in the United States of America
All rights reserved

Sterling ISBN 978-1-4027-5630-6

For information about custom editions, special sales, premium and corporate purchases, please contact Sterling Special Sales Department at 800-805-5489 or specialsales@sterlingpub.com.

Acknowledgments

Without the unconditional support and love of so many people I could not have seized the opportunity to write this book. First and foremost I want to thank my wife, Abby (the true writer in the family), for encouraging me to dream big, for working so friggen hard, for the many weekends of taking the kids so I could write, and for being the best wife I could ever ask for. To my son, Stephen Erickson, who is willing to have a catch with me and has taught me something precious about forgiveness; my daughter Lila Jane who knows how to make me laugh and encourages me to do nails; and to my daughter Mary Sylvia who delights me with her bright curiosity. To my mother, Sylvia Sinclair Berking, who sacrificed herself so many times so that I could fulfill my own dreams, and even dreamed of me on the soap box. Milo J. Berking read the proposal and said, "I wouldn't change a thing." My father, Stephen Kerry Carr, who was willing to enter into the "rooms" and teach me something about second chances. And my first real teachers and models were my beloved sisters Kate, Syl, Deb, Suzy, and Liz, who taught me it was a good and strong thing to feel. My brothers Keb, Matt, and Dan traveled to the land of our father to discover brotherhood. All my brothers- and sisters-in-law, and nieces and nephews. A big shout out to Mrs. Tiegue and to Susanette Blenman, who gave her dedication, courage, firmness, and laughter.

Thanks also go out to my dad friends—Hoppa, Dean, John B, Andy, Steve, Todd, Matt, Evan, James, Ray, David, Doug, Craig, and Joe—and to the many dads I've gotten to know through GVLL and PS-41, as well as the dads who have attended "Downtown Dads." The men and women in my practice dare to examine the tough stuff and amaze me with their tenacity to grow and heal. And the men in my dads' groups: LG, MP, PM, JT, CB, DM, BP, JP, MH.

Charlie was such a firm and tender model and was *with* me through it all. Thanks to my "work" group, Nina, Liz, and Ed, said, "Of course!" Thanks also to my "writing" group: Abigail, AnnaLee, and Dominick.

Acknowledgment is also made to the Blanton-Peale Institute, PPSC (Jenny, Amy, Ruth, Andrew); Soho Parenting (Lisa, Jean); and Everyday Parenting (Ruth, Hannah). The Third Street Music School Settlement, Don Waring, and Grace Church community in New York, Shing-Min, EGPS, the Men's Leadership Alliance (Keith, Tom, Jeffrey), and Anthony Dimeio at Bold Ministries also deserve thanks.

Thanks to my agent, Lauren Galit, for taking a huge chance on me. Thanks also to Michael Fragnito, Jennifer Williams, Melanie Gold, Rachel Maloney, Anwesha Basu, and the whole team at Sterling Publishing. My "other" editor, Christa, burned a lot of midnight oil weeding through drafts and always found a way to say something nice. Elizabeth Browning helped me get in touch with my truth; Dr. Scott Haltzman and Dr. Michael J. Diamond inspired me to write, along with Bob Stein, Kyle Pruett, Jason Gold, Tom Kearns, and Dana Glazer. And I could not forget our doula, Jen Kroll; ob-gyn Dr. Fong; midwife Sylvie Blaustein; and finally, my biggest fan, Debra.

There are so many more people I would like to acknowledge, so to *all* of you who said, "I'm so glad someone is writing about this"—THANK YOU!

Contents

Introduction / vii

Part I. Pregnancy and Delivery / 1

1 Adjusting and Preparing for Fatherhood / 5
Types of Dads / 5
Emotions and Fatherhood: A Primer / 7
Change Is Everywhere / 10
Decision Making: Being on the Same Page / 18
Great Expectations / 19

2 The Trimesters: Finding Your Role / 21
Trimesters Overview / 22
The Best Supporting Role You'll Ever Play / 34

3 Delivery Day: Getting It Done / 35
Getting Prepared / 35
Typical Stages of Labor / 38
Fatherhood: Your Labor Begins / 47

Part II. Time to Adjust: Birth to 12 Months / 49

4 Getting to Know Your Newborn / 51
Baby's Here: Now What? / 51
Primary Needs in the First Year / 64
The First Birthday / 73

5 Striking a Balance: Family, Work, and Self / 75
Trying to Do It All / 75
Division of Labor: Job Responsibilities / 83

6 Getting Gear / 87
Stuff, Stuff, and More Stuff / 87
Gear versus You / 103

Part III. Coming Up for Air: 12 to 24 Months/ 105

7 Transitioning from Infancy to Toddlerhood / 107
Thinking, Walking, and Talking / 107
Safety Precautions: Toddlerproofing / 119
Family Emergency Plan / 121
Toddlerhood Reviewed: Your Growing Child / 121

8 Taking Care of Yourself / 123
What Is Self-care? / 123
The "Me Time" Challenge / 130

9 Nurturing Your Marriage / 131
Focusing on Your Relationship / 131
The Cost of an Unhealthy Marriage / 138

Part IV. Full Engagement: 24 to 36 Months / 141
10 Raising a Toddler / 143
   The Not-So-Terrible Twos / 143
   Family Events and Regressive Behavior / 154
11 Understanding the Importance of Father Play / 155
   Playtime: More Than Having Fun / 155
   A Lifetime Connection / 167
12 Fathering and Discipline / 169
   The True Meaning of Discipline / 169
   Common Discipline Issues / 179
   Firm on Behavior, Tender with Feelings / 182
13 Expecting and Managing Big Feelings / 183
   Real Men Have Feelings / 184
   Unexpressed Negative Feelings / 186
   Big Feelings Happen / 191

Afterword / 193
Index / 197

Introduction

It took twenty-seven hours for my first child to be born, and my wife showed me why the process is called *labor*. When I entered the recovery room soon after the birth, I held my baby, took a deep breath, and immediately felt like I had been promoted. I was shocked by this feeling but I guess it made sense since it was, in a classic sense, a rite of passage into a new realm of responsibility and it came with a deep hope that I could have a positive impact on this little life. And, of course, right alongside hope was dread and fear that I might screw this kid up or—perhaps even more poignantly for me, since my son was born just two weeks after 9/11 and one mile away from the World Trade Center—I feared that I would not be able to protect him adequately. That was my introduction to the role of father as "protector."

Becoming a dad changed me; it also changed my relationship with my wife, and my regard for my own parents. I can confidently say it will change you, too. You will become, in some respects, just like your dad—it's part of the rite of passage. Likewise, you will probably break rank and father quite differently from him as well.

You are fathering under different circumstances than your father did—much more is expected of you. Your father probably became a dad when society had different expectations about the father's role in pregnancy, delivery, and parenting. It's been more than thirty years since dads have been invited into the birthing process. That was a marked change in our culture, from a time when men waited passively outside the delivery room, "boiled water," or waited at the office for news that their baby had arrived into the world, to one in which the majority of men are expected and want to play an active role in preparing for and being part of the birth. I encourage you to take that invitation into the delivery room seriously. You are there—or should be there—for good reason. These new expectations and demands can be confusing and frustrating (to say the least) but, given the proper guidance and support, incredibly rewarding, too. That's where this book will help. My primary goal in writing this book is to help the new dad realize why it is so important that he become physically and emotionally involved, and to give him specific ways to do that. I believe this will make dads better able to manage the great expectations that modern-day fatherhood places on men.

I will cover the most important aspects of the first three years of fatherhood. The first part, "Pregnancy and Delivery," guides you through the trimesters and helps you identify your roles up through delivery. The second part, "Time to Adjust: Birth to 12 Months," helps you identify the key developmental milestones your child goes through during his first year and assists you in striking a balance between family, work, and that mountain of baby gear.

The third part, "Coming Up for Air: 12 to 24 Months," will focus on key developmental milestones of your child's second year as well as the importance of keeping your marriage and yourself healthy. The final part, "Full Engagement: 24 to 36 Months," will look at your involvement through play, discipline, and dealing with feelings. All throughout, I include quotes from real dads, tips for navigating the sometimes choppy waters of fatherhood, and things to consider along the way.

Research shows that children who grow up with a positive father presence are more prone to succeed in work, school, relationships, overall mental health. Kids with absent dads are more susceptible to depression and suicide, are twice as likely to drop out of school, more likely to be violent or aggressive in school, do poorly in academics, abuse drugs and/or engage in criminal activity, and become teenage parents. This book promotes ways for new dads to be emotionally and physically involved and to deepen their ability to adjust to—and therefore manage—the expectations of family, work, and commitment to self.

I write this book to honor the rite of passage into fatherhood and to stress the importance of the father's role in uplifting his family and supporting his children's mother through pregnancy, birthing, and childrearing. I humbly add my voice to the growing body of literature on fatherhood and rejoice in the fact that there is more being written on the subject. I do not have the final word on how to do the job—I have certainly made my mistakes—but each man is dealing with his own personal experience. I have thought a lot about this subject and have counseled many men as they work on becoming the best dad possible.

—John Carr, LCSW
New York, NY

Pregnancy and Delivery

> *"When a child is born, a father is born. A mother is born, too of course, but at least for her it's a gradual process. Body and soul, she has nine months to get used to what's happening. She becomes what's happening. But for even the best-prepared father, it happens all at once."*
>
> —Frederick Buechner, Presbyterian minister and author

Congratulations! You are going to be a father. Maybe you've discovered your "guys" can swim. Or maybe you've been told that the baby you've been working so hard to adopt is on its way. Or maybe you've been through a long in vitro fertilization process and the implantation has been successful. However it happened, fatherhood is slowly sinking in.

For many men, learning that you are going to be a father can ignite a whole new set of expectations, not to mention a wide range of feelings, from delight and excitement to shock and anxiety. All these reactions are all true and normal. On one hand, becoming a father can give you such a sense of virility, strength, and potency, as well as a feeling of excitement and anticipation for this baby. On the other hand, there may be concerns about what sort of parent you'll be, what this will do to your relationship with your partner, and how you are going to financially afford an additional person in the family.

The difficult question for many men is: How do I deal with the positive and negative thoughts and feelings as well as the practical demands of parenting, all at the same time? The answer is (1) by remembering that it is valid to have a variety of feelings, thoughts, and behaviors (sometimes simultaneously) about your partner's pregnancy, becoming a dad, and adding a baby into your life; (2) by working hard at getting "a window" into what's going on for your partner and understanding her emotions, thoughts, and behaviors, and not necessarily taking them on as your own; and (3) by remembering that you can and will adjust to the impending changes and practical demands, even though you may not be physically experiencing symptoms. The more you can remember these three things the more you will be prepared emotionally and practically for the honor and responsibility of becoming a father.

The purpose of this first section is to offer useful advice to help you through the period of pregnancy up through the actual delivery of your baby. More specifically it should:
• help you understand what is happening to your baby, your partner, and yourself during the three stages (trimesters) of pregnancy.

- aid you in figuring out your role during each trimester.
- prepare you both practically and emotionally for delivery day.

As you and your partner begin to digest the reality of what is happening, you both may wonder about a whole range of things. It's quite normal to be inundated with questions that, at least for now, have no answers. For dads in particular, who have become increasingly more involved in pregnancy, birthing, and baby care, concerns have expanded over the last thirty or so years. Because of this, there is a growing need to provide men with support and information. This section will validate and answer some of your questions.

Adjusting and Preparing for Fatherhood

I'll never forget my neighbor saying to me as my wife was about seven months pregnant, "Say good-bye to your life as you know it!" But, even though I wasn't sure what was coming, I was excited about this next stage of my life. After all, I wasn't giving up a great life; I was adding to it.

Today, becoming a father means handling your baby in ways that previous generations of dads didn't: changing dirty diapers, feeding, trimming fingernails, administering unwanted medications, cuddling, and playing. The payoff, of course, is a closer bond with your child from birth. I can't think of anything more worthwhile than that.

Types of Dads

The dad you become will be largely influenced by the dad you had. Your evolving roles reflect, for better or worse, an image of your dad *and* you. It is possible to shift in and out of these roles and to exhibit various behaviors. Consider the six types of dads below, knowing that no man is a pure form of one or the other. Use the descriptions to reflect on what kind of father you want to become, and ultimately being mindful of the father your child needs you to be.

Consider This

A recent study conducted on marmoset monkeys determined that dad monkeys had a higher density connection in the prefrontal cortex—the part of the brain associated with complex personality, social, and cognitive behaviors—than non-dad monkeys.

The Reluctant Dad is hesitant to take on the challenges associated with fatherhood. He originally conveyed ambivalence about having children and when he and his wife first considered having a family he went along with the idea because he didn't want to "rock the boat." His reluctance may be largely due to a sense of satisfaction with life as it is and the knowledge that kids will alter things, from his relationship to his wife, to the amount of time and energy he can spend on his career, to his very sense of self. His reluctance may also come out of unconscious feelings stemming from unmet needs or unhealed wounds. This dad is dealing with the question, "Do I want this change?"

The Driven Dad is primarily focused on work and providing for his family financially. His identity is in his work. He is driven to provide in ways that perhaps his own father couldn't, but, at the same time, has a longing that is often unspoken to be home with his family. Instead he is stuck on the high-pressure, societal-reinforced career track and is determined to stay on it. Once the baby arrives, the stakes will only increase, so he is working harder than ever to provide. He may have a history of getting little to no praise from his own father. This dad is living by the motto, "I can't stop; if I do, our family will fall apart."

The Perfect Dad had a father who expected perfection in all aspects of life, work, family, relationships, and self-care. The perfect is the enemy of the good and it is the good that this dad needs to consider. He idealized his own father and needs to work on exposing and accepting, ever so slightly, his father's imperfections as well as his own. This dad is living by the motto, "I can't settle for less than perfect."

The Unconscious Dad has little to no awareness of the impact he will have on his baby. He sees his presence or absence as inconsequential. His own father did not make time for him and neglected their relationship. He will essentially "let go" of his kids from an early age—it's how his dad did it and he turned out "all right." This dad is living by the motto, "I'm doing the best I can, and everything else will work itself out."

The Overprotective Dad has an overdeveloped protective muscle. He is hyperconcerned about safety issues, whether it's medical concerns or fears for safety. It's possible that he lived with an overprotective parent and is replicating that or a neglectful parent and is overcompensating for what he didn't get. Or he may have lived through some trauma or remembers too keenly some of his own past high-risk behaviors and is overcommitted to prevent his child from doing the same. This dad is living by the idea: "If I don't protect my child, he will get hurt."

If these roles are familiar and easy for you to imagine, I invite you to also consider one more type of father:

The Good Enough Dad is a term borrowed from D. W. Winnicott, the British psychoanalyst and pediatrician who coined the term *Good Enough Mother*. Other writers have since adapted the "good enough father" phrase, which to me means a dad who:

- Is relatively comfortable with making mistakes and is able to ask for forgiveness.
- Sees himself as important to his child's development.
- Feels his kids have a lot to teach him about life, including how to parent.
- Is not wedded to the idea of being just like his dad or totally different from his dad; he's aware that he will be like his dad in some aspects, like it or not.
- Understands the importance of getting help with his own stuff, such as anger, anxiety, unmet needs, and unhealed wounds, and may even be in therapy to work on these things.
- Loves his children unconditionally and gives age-appropriate room for them to make their own mistakes.
- Is able to see his role as more than just financial provider, protector, and disciplinarian.
- Thinks of himself as a model for how to deal with emotions, logic, tenderness, and healthy aggression.
- Is aware that his children will mimic him and tries to make himself worthy of being mimicked.

TIP

The dad you want to be and the dad your child may need you to be may be two different people. Give some thought to your vision of fatherhood, then hold it loosely and be prepared to adjust your vision.

Emotions and Fatherhood: A Primer

It can be hard for men to become active players in the parenting matrix and make their positive presence felt. We'll be discussing this in greater detail in chapter 13, but in large part, men don't necessarily welcome the full range of emotions. It has only been about thirty years or so since men were allowed in the delivery room, so in many ways we are still adjusting to the new expectations and all the emotions that come with being a larger—even integral—part of the process.

When I run groups for dads, I invite them to bring *all* their emotions, including the the negative, the scary, and the shameful. There are very few venues where men can do this, yet it is so important for us to shed light on the whole experience, not just the positive. I am regularly reminded that, when given permission, men tend to be eager to share their feelings and connect with other men. There's an old saying in the therapy community: Ask a man what he feels and he'll tell you what he thinks. The emotional life of men is one of the first aspects of expectant fatherhood that is often overlooked. Here's a primer on the typical emotions that expectant dads experience.

POSITIVE EMOTIONS

For many, finding out you're going to be a father is the fulfillment of a lifelong goal and may be the happiest time in your life. It's important to own those positive feelings. I encourage dads who I see in my practice to name and expound on what jazzes them about having a baby. Usually it's something about wanting their child to experience some of the goodness of their own childhood. Or perhaps it's fantasizing about playing ball with their son or dancing with their daughter at her wedding. Expectant dads often report feeling a sense of enormous pride, joy, and being connected to something bigger. What is it for you?

NEGATIVE EMOTIONS

Even the happiest of dads have some hesitations, reservations, or ambivalence. If there is a predominant "negative" emotion that comes up for expectant dads, it seems to be anxiety from pressure to provide. Even though there is more equality in gender incomes and a significant rise in at-home dads in recent years, expectant fathers still tend to feel the sometimes intense pressure of having to provide and to "suck it up." You may even be feeling anxious as you read this book. Be assured this is common and expected.

If you feel overwhelmed by anything you read in this book, stop what you are doing. Take a break if you need to, and come back to it later. Many men want to preoccupy themselves only with what they *need* to know.

Negative emotions need a safe place to be processed and understood. When this doesn't happen, the emotion(s) can spill out and turn into unhealthy behavior. Spend some time working at getting comfortable with your emotions and begin talking about them, particularly the negative ones. Sharing negative emotions might feel risky, because you're worried they might not be accepted or understood, or you might feel like you are burdening your partner. Men are hardwired to protect, but this does not mean you have to protect your partner from your negative feelings. In fact, keeping your feelings from her may only cause her more anxiety as she will likely be left wondering what is going on in your head and why you can't tell her about it. The only way she will know for certain what you are feeling is if you give voice to it. Likewise, the only way you will know what she is feeling is if she tells you. Neither of you can read minds or anticipate needs.

So here's the charge: Open the lines of communication. Tell your partner what is emotionally and practically going on with you, and vice versa. And—I believe this is critical—you must be permitted to give voice to the full range of issues, even those emotions perceived as "negative." This will allow you to be fully engaged in the process, problem solve if necessary, and ultimately be present in a positive and authentic way.

TIP

It is normal to feel profound pride at being a father, and yet wonder if people see you as anything but a sperm donor. Find a way to celebrate your becoming a father.

Real Dad

"When I first learned that my wife was pregnant, the overwhelming imperative to provide and succeed blotted out the sense of fun work once had. I was attentive to that change and I wanted my wife to intuit everything. My challenge was to let her in on what was going on for me."

—Ryan, 32

ACCEPTANCE AND DENIAL

It would not be strange if you find yourself vacillating between acceptance and denial that your partner is pregnant or that you will have a baby in less than nine months. Because you are not experiencing physical changes, it may be easy for you to fall into denial or forget your partner is pregnant. One of the ongoing challenges for you throughout the pregnancy is to pay attention to the level of denial you experience and gradually shift into the reality that you are going to be a dad and your presence and participation are important.

Ways men deny that they too are experiencing the pregnancy:

- They emphasize that *she* is pregnant and it's all about her.
- They continue to live as if nothing has changed.
- They don't talk about the baby or participate in preparations, like attending doctor appointments or readying the baby's room.
- They don't allow themselves to wonder how things will be when the baby arrives. They put it off "for later."

Suggestions for shifting into acceptance:

- Read more about pregnancy.
- Ask your partner how she is doing.
- Look at pictures of the growing fetus and share them with friends and family.
- Purchase some baby gear or necessities.
- Fill a backpack with a pound or five of sugar and strap it to your midsection; walk around your home for a couple of hours just to experience the physical sensation of what it's like for your partner to be pregnant. Then, at the same time, imagine feeling motion sickness, sluggishness, and pressure

against your internal organs (such as your urinary bladder).

On the other hand, there are many men who experience symptoms of pregnancy just like their wives do (see Sympathetic Pregnancy, below). Even though the root causes of these symptoms are psychic or emotional rather than physical, that doesn't mean they are any less real. This is a common occurrence for expectant dads, and there is nothing wrong with you if you feel some of these symptoms. In fact, you should take it as a healthy sign of acceptance. Let me explain what I mean.

Kevin was a thirty-six-year-old professor with a stable career. He and his wife were expecting their first child within the next six months. Out of nowhere he began experiencing heightened anxiety and difficulty sleeping. Kevin had no history of anxiety or sleep problems and had never been in therapy before. We explored several possible reasons and came to the joint conclusion that his anxiety was at least partly triggered by the impending baby's birth. Just naming this fact was helpful for him and moved him to talk with his wife about some of his concerns—all of which brought them closer and alleviated his worry and sleep problems.

Sympathetic Pregnancy

Men experience Couvade Syndrome (*couver* is French for "to brood" or "to nurture") in ways that closely resemble symptoms of expectant moms, such as back pain, mood swings, food cravings, fatigue, weight gain, depression, and insomnia. Experts believe Couvade is an expression of anxiety in the body, and possibly an expression of ambivalence about fatherhood or a way for the dad-to-be to assert his presence into the pregnancy. If symptoms persist, you may want to consider counseling and/ or biofeedback. (Visit www. aapb.org to learn more about biofeedback and to find providers.)

Change Is Everywhere

CHANGES IN YOU

One of the major contributors to the literature on men's experience of pregnancy is psychotherapist Jerrold Lee Shapiro. His book *When Men Are Pregnant: Needs and Concerns* *of Expectant Fathers* describes beautifully how our culture truly values motherhood and why it's important for the male experience to be honored as well. He writes: "People pamper the pregnant woman. . . . Strangers will offer your pregnant wife their seats on the commuter train or bus. They will stop her on the street or between aisles at the local supermarket to chat about their own pregnancies . . . [in] their sincere desire to connect with someone so close to the beginnings of new life. Our culture loses its paranoia, and its boundaries, in the presence of a pregnancy. This is exactly how it should be. But what about you, the father? Psychologically you are just as pregnant as she is."

Now, more than twenty years after the publication of *When Men Are Pregnant*, the experience of the expectant father still gets overlooked. Men have an emotional, if not physical, experience of pregnancy that is not completely acknowledged, understood, or honored. Nor are there enough studies being done on the subject of fathering—only 2 percent of all studies focused just on fathers while 48 percent focused on mothers and the remainder focused on both parents.

So, what about *you*? It makes sense to ask, since society at large and men in general are still getting used to the idea that you have a role to play beyond breadwinner, provider, and disciplinarian. We are still getting used to the idea that you have needs that must be considered in the experience of pregnancy, birth, and childrearing. You may be expected to be involved, helpful, and handy, not to mention strong and stoic. This might leave you wondering where you'll go for support, and who'll listen to your questions and concerns. Earlier I had suggested talking with

your partner as an option—for some men that may be a bad idea. With no place to go, many men retreat into their work, detach emotionally, and sink into "the cave." To avoid this, consider what kind of dad you might be, what kind of a dad your father was, how he might influence how you father and, ultimately, what kind of impact you want to have on your child's life.

It is never too early to start taking a personal inventory of you, your partner, and some of the dynamics that exist in your marriage. Actually, the earlier the better, because the longer you wait the more stuff there will be to do. For example: How did you find out your partner was pregnant? What was the process of getting pregnant like for you? With so many ways to actually get pregnant, men can feel excluded from the process. How do you feel about the news? If you are happy, great! If you feel ambivalent, worried, coerced, not included, or in any way negative, stop and figure out a way to talk with your partner about it. Work it through and resolve it. If you don't, it will likely haunt you and could contribute to relationship deterioration (see chapter 9 for more on this).

The Dad You Had

As an expectant father you may wonder how your father did it. You will likely compare yourself to your own father. You will be thrown back into your own experience as a child and have all sorts of questions and all sorts of feelings. As we know, there is no "manual" for how to be a parent, yet we all operate with an internal manual that is heavily influenced by how we were parented.

Many dads report that they do not want to be like their fathers. In fact, many commit themselves to the idea that they will do everything in their power not to repeat their dad's mistakes. Often dads come to see me in my practice because they are filled with fears of repeating the same mistakes their dads made. It's also important to remember the good things you did get from your father or learned from your father—it is rarely all one or the other. Take stock of it all and try not to discard the good stuff too.

One way to handle those fears is by reconnecting with your dad, if possible. As long as your father is still alive, it's neither too early nor too late to begin this process. Whether you like it or not, as you father your own child you will be revisiting your relationship with your father. That experience, of being fathered by your dad, is the manual you will use, again either by repeating what he did or by doing the exact opposite. Reconnecting with your father might help you understand more deeply why he made the decisions he did.

Even if your father is deceased, learning about his story and your experience of him can open up the potential for forgiveness, understanding, acceptance, and gratitude. Recover stories, gain insights, and begin healing old wounds. (See the Afterword for resources on healing your father's legacy.)

CHANGES IN HER

You can expect your partner to go through a variety of changes during the pregnancy, but there is no telling exactly what they will be. Some women love being pregnant and some have real difficulty.

Watch for these potential changes in your partner:

- A "glow" of health, vigor, and femininity (noted and mentioned by you, of course)
- Hormonal changes that affect every organ in her body
- Unexpected mood swings
- A heightened interest in sex or a decreased interest in sex
- A repulsion to certain smells or flavors
- A craving for certain smells and flavors
- A "dark cloud" feeling, which may include bouts of irritability or depression (not her fault!)
- A "silver lining" or a positive, life-is-good feeling
- Difficulty sleeping
- Bleeding or spotting during the first three months
- Fears of miscarriage (particularly if there's a history)
- Giving up of alcohol, cigarettes, or recreational drugs

As I've mentioned, many expectant dads will not experience physical symptoms, and many will. This will make it harder for you to tune into what your partner is going through. There are a variety of physical, emotional, and hormonal changes going on, so what's a guy to do? Your job is to learn about what your partner is going through and experiment with what helps.

There are many ways you can show your support for your partner and your new family. Here are ten of them:

1. Read some of the books she's reading on pregnancy. (Try *The Pregnancy Book* by William Sears and Martha Sears.)
2. Ask her what she needs or what she thinks might be helpful. Just having your attention may be all she needs.
3. Listen closely to her answer. It may be different than how she would normally answer. For example, she used to go for a run when she was stressed, but now she likes to eat.
4. Try to imagine what it must feel like for her. For instance, your partner's morning sickness may feel similar to motion sickness.
5. Help her put her feet up.
6. Tell her clearly when you will be able to help and when you are too busy. Don't leave her guessing.
7. Give back, shoulder, and foot rubs; brush her hair; apply lotion to arms or abdomen.
8. Tell her how beautiful she looks.
9. Give her what she craves. (Sorry, it may not be you.)
10. Spend time with her.

When my wife was pregnant with our first child, I showed up late to a doctor appointment. When I finally arrived, my wife was in the waiting room in tears. Through her tears she was able to tell me how disappointed she was that I had missed the all-important, twenty-week sonogram, which showed the baby. She so badly wanted to share this moment with me. We asked the nurse if we could get a second glimpse. They were very understanding and I was really glad we asked. It helped me get a window into what was "literally" going on inside my wife and share in the excitement.

> **TIP**
>
> Hormonal changes are necessary to your baby's development and are not anyone's "fault." You may not be able to fix her mood. Sometimes the only thing you can do is just *be* with her. Be patient and learn along with her what works.

CHANGES IN YOUR RELATIONSHIP

Pregnancy can be fraught with so much planning, anticipation, and preparation that you may forget to laugh, play, and talk with each other. For many couples the shift in focus from "the couple" to "the baby" begins right away, with the news of the pregnancy. This is why it's important not to forget each other and to remember that, with work, focusing on both is possible.

Children can deepen your relationship. Having a child together has a way of bringing two people closer. The fact that you two will have jointly created another human being is an amazing thing. A trusted colleague once told me that the best thing parents can give their children is a healthy marriage or relationship. A strong marriage requires time apart from your children. To maintain your connection, start working on this right away by taking time to be together during the pregnancy. Talk about your values for education, breastfeeding, sleep, etc.; learn more about your partner's childhood and let her learn about yours and discuss collective assumptions, fears, and hopes; and make and keep dates for dining out, movies, or other events.

> ### TIP
>
> Remember that your partner's body is gearing up to bring a child into this world and not (necessarily) to have passionate sex. Her breasts, for instance, are no longer "yours," if, in fact, they ever were yours.

Children can ruin a relationship. When two become three, necessary distractions keep a couple from tending to their marriage or relationship. Many couples in my practice report difficulties stemming from parenting differences. Raising a child is a very personal matter since you are parenting an extension of yourself. Many new moms and dads get into serious conflict because they were parented differently or have different ideas for parenting, and are operating from different manuals. The first year of parenting is a huge adjustment for both of you. As a new parent you gain and lose at the same time. Just as you gain this wonderful new life, you are losing some of your spouse's attention. This means watching your partner direct more of her energy toward the baby and less toward you.

> ### Real Dad
>
> *"I didn't realize that I felt distant from my wife until we were twelve years into our marriage and our oldest child was seven. It dawned on me that I lost a part of her as soon as our firstborn came into the world. I still haven't adjusted to that."*
>
> —Dirk, 45

CHANGES IN YOUR HOME

There is no single correct way to prepare your home for the new arrival. Some parents believe that it's superstitious to buy too much baby gear before the birth while others stock up as soon as possible. More and more parents are finding out the gender and preparing the room with the gender-accepted colors before the baby comes home. By the time we had our third child, I understood just how helpful it was to buy some baby diapers and set up the changing table, just as an external reminder that this was indeed happening even if I didn't physically feel it.

As you prepare your home, keep in mind that you are welcoming a new life into your space. It might help you to think of this as a sacred space. It's much like, but on a grander scale, the kind of preparation that goes into readying your home for an out-of-town guest. As you prepare outwardly, also try to imagine what kinds of new noises you might hear. This, too, helps the new dad who is not feeling things physically begin to internalize the impending change.

If your home is not babyproofed by the time your child arrives, don't panic. After the baby is born you have seven to nine months before he starts to crawl and move around.

The things you will need right away are newborn diapers, wipes, a changing table, a bassinet, and clothes (Onesies and newborn outfits that are appropriate for the time of year). You'll also need a stroller, and baby formula and bottles if your partner is not breastfeeding. (See chapter 6 for checklists of items for years 1, 2, and 3.)

CHANGES IN FINANCES

One of the biggest issues I've noticed in my practice is the degree to which men focus on the financial responsibilities associated with having a child. We know a baby will cost money. And while times have

changed and men are no longer the only providers and breadwinners, providing for a family continues to be a source of anxiety. In fact, with many more women in the workforce, the rise of dual-income households, and also more at-home dads, the question of finances can even be more complicated. You can certainly seek the counsel of a financial advisor, but remember that parents have been raising children for millennia without the need for a profit-and-loss spreadsheet.

Some questions that often come up for men are:

- How long will I/she be able to take off for parental leave?
- How much paid time can I/she take in addition to parental leave?
- How will we afford things without her/my income?
- Do we need a larger home? A bigger car?
- How will money affect our family dynamics and my sense of self?

All these and more questions like them are bound to bring up feelings of anxiety and pressure. The most important thing you can do is talk about the practical solutions and the emotional implications.

The first practical solution is to get a real sense of what the actual costs are. Here are some facts and figures to consider:

Overall First-Year Expenses

Yes, there are many different costs associated with starting a family, so here's an overview of potential fees. Of course, costs vary according to where you live, but here's a ballpark idea of what to expect.

The birth. The cost of a normal vaginal delivery is $5,000 to $8,000; the cost goes up to $12,000 for a cesarean delivery, and much more if there are complications. Of course, medical insurance mitigates the out-of-pocket costs.

The first-year supplies. You can expect to pay $9,000 to $11,000 for diapers, formula, baby furniture, clothing, baby gear, etc.

Food. If the baby will be breastfed, there will be nominal expenses associated with food, though expect some costs for breast-care supplies. The average cost of a breast pump is about $200, and hospital-grade breast pumps may be rented. If not breastfeeding, budget about $2,300 per year on baby formula and $50 per month on jarred food starting at the fourth to sixth month.

Child care. If you and your partner are going back to work right away, a full-time nanny can cost anywhere between $25,000 to $30,000 per year. Placing your child in day care can cost $3,000 to $8,400 in your baby's first year.

Clothing. The cost of a wardrobe depends largely on how much secondhand stuff you acquire, but it can range between $150 and $300 for the first year.

Health insurance. Your health insurance premiums will likely increase. Ask your insurance provider, as cost varies greatly.

Gear and furniture. Cribs cost anywhere from $100 to $400 and up. You can get a good-quality crib for about $250 to $300. A changing table can cost as little as $90 and as much as $700. Strollers cost roughly $200 to $600.

College. Let's not to get too far ahead of ourselves, but the cost of raising a baby to the age of eighteen is somewhere between $125,000 and $250,000, not including college tuition. According to 2007–2008 College Board statistics, the average tuition for a private four-year college education was $23,712. The average total tuition for a four-year public college education was $6,185. The estimated cost for college for the year 2028 (eighteen years from the publication of this book) is more than $90,000 for one year of tuition. Thankfully, you do not have to deal with that bill just yet, but plans that are specifically designed for college tuition savings (called 529 plans) can help you start planning for that eventuality.

In summary, having a baby costs money, but many dads adjust successfully and find ways to not only survive but thrive at supporting their families. Spend some time *before* the baby arrives figuring out what sort of financial shape you're in, talk with your partner about it, and see how a baby is going to fit into your budget. Chances are, it'll cause you more anxiety if you put it off. I've witnessed many dads kick into high gear and do what they need to do to make ends meet. But it's also important to remember not to be so fixated on costs that you forget what your children really need . . . and that is huge doses of love and as much of you as possible.

Ways to Save

A comprehensive study of cost cutting is beyond the scope of this book, so I'll limit my discussion to four key ways you can save money right off the bat: (1) use cloth diapers instead of disposables, (2) breastfeed instead of using formula, (3) accept secondhand items (clothes and furniture) instead of buying everything new, and (4) arrange for one parent to stay at home instead of paying for full-time child care.

Diapers. Expect to spend $1,600 to $2,300 for disposable diapers by the time your baby is potty-trained. Your baby will go through at least six to eight diapers a day on average, which comes out to about $80 to $130 a month. (This is especially the case in the first few months, when diaper changes are more frequent.) Cloth diapering has two advantages: It's environmentally friendly and it costs less. Keep in mind, however, that the cost savings is almost nullified if you use a diaper service, so you'll have to plan on laundering them yourself to really save. Cloth diapering costs approximately $800 to $1,100 by the time your baby is potty-trained, without the diaper service.

Breastfeeding. For the first year of your baby's life, you can expect to spend about $2,000 on formula, depending on whether you use powder or ready-to-eat liquids. You can really cut your costs dramatically if your partner is able to breastfeed for a year or more.

Hand-me-downs. Items from friends or family can also significantly cut your costs. Your baby does not have to wear a whole new set of clothes. If we had wanted to, my wife and I could have probably gotten through the first three years without buying my

son a stitch of clothing. Savings can be had with furniture and gear as well. Many parents are eager to get rid of clunky, space-eating cribs, strollers, and baby gear that they no longer need so take advantage of their generosity.

At-home care. Another way to save big is to plan for either you or your partner to stay home with the baby, or to have some kind of creative arrangement that allows one or both of you to be home at different points. This is, of course, a big decision and has financial and lifestyle implications. Discuss it, and see if it's cost efficient. Unfortunately, the United States is one of few industrialized nations that does not provide paid paternity leave. Although the Family and Medical Leave Act (FMLA) allows parents and other caretakers to take up to twelve weeks of unpaid leave (from jobs at companies with fifty or more employees), most parents feel they can't afford the lost income. Dads who work at companies with fewer than fifty employees are, unfortunately, out of luck, unless they can prevail upon their employers or negotiate directly with their bosses to hold their jobs while they take unpaid parental leave. A few companies allow for a paid paternity leave and it seems like the trend is in the right direction, but still, only a very small percentage of businesses offer the option at all. And of those that do, research shows that ongoing "workplace hostility," or coworker envy, prevents men from actually using the benefit.

If all this talk of baby costs has you confused, by all means seek help from a financial advisor.

Decision Making: Being on the Same Page

There are a lot of decisions that need to be made, which means, obviously, you and your partner have a lot of things to talk about. Beginning the conversation early is important and should continue throughout the pregnancy. Roles and expectations may shift as the pregnancy evolves, but you should check in with yourself and ask regularly: What does my partner need? What do I need? What am I able to provide? If I can't provide something, who can? You need to be clear with each other both about what you want and what you are able to live with. Here are some questions to consider.

What role will I play in doctor visits and do I need to attend all of them? Try to attend as many doctor appointments as possible, particularly if this is your first child. When you go to an appointment, keep your focus on your partner—how she's feeling, what she needs, etc.—but also bring up some of your own concerns or questions. This is a great opportunity to ask questions that will lower your anxiety—write them down ahead of time, so you can jog your memory during the appointment. The key task is to be present as much as possible and to be clear about when you are unable to be there.

Who will deliver the baby? You typically have two choices: an ob-gyn or a midwife. The most important objective is to have your baby delivered by someone you and your partner trust. The birthing process is a very personal experience and it is critically important that you find someone who will respect your partner's wishes first and yours second. Get personal referrals from friends or family members and then interview your prospects. You should come away from an interview with a good sense of the doctor's or midwife's philosophy, how he or she will treat your partner, how well he or she listens to your collective concerns, and whether you're encouraged to ask questions. You also want to be able to imagine your role in the birth. Your opinion should be respected, listened to, and responded to. Do you respect and trust the person who is going to deliver your child? Are your questions being answered and are your concerns taken seriously? The key task here is to develop trust in whomever you chose to deliver your baby.

Here are some key questions to ask your doctor or midwife:

• What is your approach or philosophy?
• Are there any birth plans you're opposed to?
• Are you okay with having a midwife or doula present at the birth (if you and your partner want one)?
• Who is your backup if you are not able to be at the birth?
• Can we meet your backup?
• How often do you perform c-sections?

Is it a good idea to get genetic counseling? Yes. This is standard practice, and all it typically entails is answering questions about your respective health histories and learning your options for other prenatal testing, such as DNA testing and amniocentesis (for more on this see "Getting Prenatal Tests," for each of the trimesters in chapter 2). Genetic counseling may be recommended by whomever you have chosen to deliver the baby. In those cases, you will be asked a lot of questions regarding your ethnic, sexual, medical, and family backgrounds in order to assess the risk levels for abnormalities.

Where do we want the baby to be delivered? Typically you have three choices: a hospital, birthing center, or your home. Again, this is a very personal choice. Things to consider are your partner's age, the degree to which she is considered "high risk" (her doctor/midwife/geneticist will tell her this after the genetic testing and history taking), and what your partner wants. She may want a hospital birth so that she can have an epidural and is better prepared for any potential complications. Or she may opt for a natural birth in a more personal setting. For some moms-to-be, having a baby in a hospital gives them a sense of security; others want the hospital only as a backup. The key task is to stay connected to what you both want.

Who will be present at the birth and how will we deal with visitors afterward? As a new dad, "crowd control" will be one of your primary jobs since your partner will be either in labor, recovering, or caring for the baby. Some moms are okay with video cameras; others don't even want their husbands present. This can be a very sensitive issue and should be handled with intention and care. Reviewing this question speaks to what kind of boundaries your partner needs to feel safe and comfortable with the baby. Assume nothing when it comes to visitors. What your partner wants is primary; what you want is secondary. Knowing what you both want will really help you to know when and where to draw the line.

Great Expectations

Getting ready for fatherhood can be quite remarkable and full of great expectations. This chapter hopefully got you thinking about some of the practical and emotional things to consider as you prepare yourself, your relationship, and your home for the job of becoming a dad. Whether it's the practical job of assembling furniture or the emotional work of connecting with your own father and keeping your marriage strong and durable, there are indeed great expectations laid upon a new dad. Welcome to the club and keep asking yourself the important questions. Here are a few to consider as you and your partner navigate pregnancy.

REFLECTION QUESTIONS

1. What's one thing you can you do on a consistent basis to take care of your partner? What's one thing you can do on a consistent basis to take care of yourself?
2. What was going on for your dad in the areas of work, relationship, and family when you were in your mother's womb?
3. How might you be distinctly different from your dad? How might you be similar to him?
4. What kind of parent do you anticipate your partner becoming? What will she be really good at? What will be a challenge? How might you be able to support each other?
5. Which of you might be better equipped to wake with the baby during the night and/or deal with a hard-to-soothe baby?

②

The Trimesters: Finding Your Role

It can be a real challenge to understand your role(s) when your partner is pregnant.

First, this is new territory: Historically men have played a minimal role in pregnancy and delivery. Because of this many men have little in the way of role models for how to be positively involved.

Second, because the pregnancy is happening to the mom-to-be, the dad-to-be is not connected physically to the process. This makes it harder to tune into what is going on. Many expectant dads are also physically away a lot due to work demands.

Third, many men experience negative emotions during the pregnancy and delivery that are often not welcomed by him, his spouse, many health-care providers, or society at large. I recall a friend of mine asking me how *I* was doing when the birth of my third child was only a few months away. Hesitantly I spoke of the serious doubts and anxieties I was having, along with the positive feelings of excitement and pride. This is normal, expected, and healthy for men to acknowledge and accept that experience.

During the pregnancy men have two primary goals—to take care of their wives and themselves. One of the best ways to begin to do this is to learn as much as you can about your partner's pregnancy. Not only will this help you better support your partner through some big changes, but it can help you process some of your emotions and quell some of the fears and anxieties you might be having.

Real Dad

"Sometimes I wonder how other guys would view me if I am as involved as I want to be."

—Julio, 22

Trimesters Overview

Pregnancy is split into three equal trimesters to mark the development of the growing baby. At the moment of fertilization, the zygote is a single-celled organism. It becomes a blastocyst as it travels down the fallopian tube (it already contains hundreds of cells) until it attaches to the uterine wall. Until week ten it is called an embryo, and then from week eleven till birth it is referred to as a fetus. (Numerous Web sites, such as MayoClinic.com, show the week-by-week progression of fetal development. For more information, consult this book's companion volume, *Great Expectations: Your All-in-One Resource for Pregnancy & Childbirth* by Sandy Jones and Marcie Jones.)

A full-term pregnancy is thirty-eight weeks from fertilization, and any birth before thirty-seven weeks is considered preterm or premature. The due date is determined by what's called Naegele's Rule: Take the date (the first day) of your partner's last menstrual cycle, add a year and seven days, and then subtract three months. For example: April 21, 2009 + 1 year = April 21, 2010 + 7 days = April 28, 2010 − 3 months = January 28, 2010.

THE FIRST TRIMESTER: WEEKS 1 TO 13

The first trimester marks the first three months after conception during which your partner's body will begin showing signs that she is pregnant. Amazingly, women's bodies are like sensors; they may intuit the pregnancy or actually feel a tingling sensation in their breasts or wake up with nausea.

There is no telling how your partner will react to the growing fetus. Some women love being pregnant; others do not. Because hormones are hyperactive, 80 percent of women experience nausea and/or vomiting. Other common symptoms include exhaustion, a swollen feeling, irritability or moodiness, and breast pain. On the flip side, they may also experience an elevated mood, more energy, and an overall positive outlook. My wife, for example, loved being pregnant and it seemed to really agree with her.

During the first trimester the embryo is fragile. Its task is to travel down the fallopian tube and latch onto the side of the uterus, which is where it will receive its nutrients. It starts out as a single cell, but by the end of three months it has grown to about two inches, weighs about an ounce, and has the beginnings of human body parts and organs. It even has ears and may be able to hear.

Because the risk of miscarriage is greatest during the first trimester it's extremely important for your partner to eat well, rest as much as possible, and take prenatal vitamins as prescribed by her doctor. This is where you come into play.

Your Jobs in the First Trimester

- If she's tired, make it possible for her to nap as much as possible. Help her make good food choices (especially foods containing folic acid, as this B vitamin prevents birth defects) and help her with her prenatal vitamin regimen.
- Talk to each other about the news—how it's affecting both of you positively and negatively. Share your hopes and dreams, fears and anxieties.
- Make time to be together. Whether it's going on walks, movies, or out to dinner, be intentional about spending time together. It's good practice for when the baby comes to have a regular time that you can count on as belonging to the two of you.
- Take this as an invitation to slow down—to do less and just *be*.
- Remember that the risk for miscarriage goes down after the heartbeat is heard, so you may want to be selective about whom to tell about the pregnancy. Whenever my wife and I were tempted to shout the news to everyone we saw, we stopped and asked ourselves if we'd be comfortable telling them about a miscarriage too. If the answer was no, we tried to abstain. There was still plenty of time to inform everyone.
- Educate yourself. Become familiar with the pregnancy stages and what's going on for the baby.
- Journal your thoughts and feelings. Think of the journal as something for you.

> **TIP**
>
> Rent the documentary *The Business of Being Born* and discuss your respective reactions with your partner. There is even a 24-hour online rental at www.the businessofbeingborn.com.

Getting Prenatal Tests

Be involved in the decisions about prenatal tests, and whenever possible, be there for their administration and/or getting the results. Most of the routine prenatal tests will be done during the first trimester, during your partner's first prenatal visit. Here are the names of some of the tests, and brief descriptions for why they're done.

Blood pressure. This test is done at every kind of health-care visit, and so it is done at prenatal visits as well. It is a risk-free assessment of a mother's blood pressure. Pregnancy-induced high blood pressure is known as preeclampsia, and can cause complications.

Chorionic villus sampling (CVS). Performed in the first trimester, this test is administered to determine genetic disorders, such as cystic fibrosis, Down syndrome, muscular dystrophy, and sickle cell anemia. A tube or needle is inserted through the abdomen into the cervix to obtain a small sample of cells. The test is 98 percent accurate, but because it causes miscarriage in approximately one out of a hundred women, it is conducted only when needed.

Rh factor screening. Blood is drawn in this routine test to determine whether the mother is Rh positive or negative. If the mother is Rh negative, her blood's antibodies could attack the baby's, if the baby is Rh positive. This test is usually conducted at the first prenatal visit. When a mother and baby's Rh factors are opposite, the mother receives an injection in the third trimester or after any procedure that would cause the mother's blood to come in contact with the baby's blood. My wife's blood is Rh positive and necessary procedures were taken with no complications.

Ultrasound (sonogram). The ultrasound or sonogram has become a routine method for checking fetal heartbeat, confirming the due date, and for ruling out certain types of problematic pregnancy. The first ultrasound is routinely done during the second trimester but can also come during the first trimester. Later in the pregnancy ultrasound is used to determine gender, and to ensure that the baby is in the correct position. Women usually receive at least two ultrasounds throughout a pregnancy, either with a probe inserted in the vagina or a transducer applied to the abdomen that bounces sound waves off the baby to produce an image on a screen. No specific risks have been identified for either the mother or baby in receiving this test, but some experts advise against "recreational" ultrasounds (conducted just to appease your curiosity).

Urinalysis. This is a routine, no-risk test that screens for diabetes. Even women who normally have no diabetic condition can develop diabetes during pregnancy (called gestational diabetes). The test can also test for urinary tract infection and dehydration.

Vaginal swab. Usually performed at the first prenatal visit and then again during the third trimester (usually very close to delivery time), a vaginal swab is a 100 percent accurate, risk-free test for the presence of certain bacteria, such as yeast and Group B strep, which could be passed to the baby during birth.

When Things Don't Go As Planned

It's amazing and remarkable that there are so many successful pregnancies since there is really only one twenty-four-hour period within a month that a woman is ovulating. Not to mention the fact that after the egg and sperm connect, the embryo has to travel down the fallopian tube and successfully attach itself to the uterine wall and begin getting its nutrients. Imagine the odds!

The complexity of this process makes it difficult for many women to get pregnant in the first place, and, once they are, it is the reason why the first trimester is a fragile period. So much has to go right for the pregnancy to endure these early days, and it is in the first trimester that the likelihood of miscarriage is greatest.

Of course, you don't want to be either overanxious or oblivious to the fact that things don't always go as planned.

The Center for Human Reproduction reports that, across the board, roughly 15 percent of all pregnancies result in loss, with that number increasing or decreasing for specific populations. Studies suggest that two-thirds to three-quarters of all miscarriages occur in the first trimester, usually for genetic reasons.

Miscarriage can be difficult to recover from, with expectant parents feeling very alone until they talk about it with others and come to realize that there are support systems out there.

Your partner may feel like she failed. Be tender and forgiving with her. Resist the temptation to try to fix or blame. This is the time to heal and mourn.

Real Dad

"My wife had two miscarriages, and each of them was emotionally taxing for both of us, but particularly for her. We truly experience pregnancy so differently—there is no right way to mourn the loss."

—Dan, 37

Do not try to appease her by saying, "We can try again soon." She may not want to right away. Give yourselves whatever time you need before you're both ready to try again. It can be helpful to figure out a way to mark the loss with a ceremony or ritual that is meaningful to you both. If reading might help, try *Facing the Ultimate Loss* by Robert J. Marx and Susan Wengerhoff Davidson and *Help Your Marriage Survive the Death of a Child* by Paul Rosenblatt. Both are recommended reading by the Center for Bereavement in New York.

THE SECOND TRIMESTER: WEEKS 14 TO 24

By the second trimester things are becoming a little more real. Hopefully the morning sickness is going away. Both of you should have heard the baby's heartbeat if not seen the baby during an ultrasound. The ultrasound is the first opportunity for you to connect with the baby, which can help if the reality has not already sunk in. It also makes you realize what a miracle this baby is and how awesome it is that you are a part of it. This is also the time when most couples become more public with the news of the pregnancy.

You may notice shifts in your partner's normal routines, eating habits, and emotional expressiveness. One dad I worked with recalls thinking, "Okay, what's happened to my wife? When is she coming back?" Your partner's hormonal shifts, work pressures, aches and pains, worries about motherhood and her changing body, and everyday responsibilities could make her irritable and sensitive to criticism. You may not think so if she calls you on the carpet for something, but these vocalizations are a good thing.

Your baby, on the other hand, starts out a cluster of cells and by the end of this trimester turns into a football. He weighs about 1½ ounces at the start of the trimester and by the end weighs more than a pound. All organs are just about fully formed by the end of the twenty-fourth week.

Your Jobs in the Second Trimester

• Take on more of the chores around your home.
• Take stock of all the reasons you fell in love with your partner and remind her of those qualities now; tell her why you believe she will be a great mom.
• Talk about what you're looking forward to (adding to your family) and what concerns you have (the costs) about being an expectant dad.
• Talk with two other new fathers about how they feel as parents.
• Ask your father what it was like for him when you were born.
• Grab some time with a friend and do something fun, just for you.
• Keep other people's perspectives and opinions separate from yours.

The second trimester is an exciting time for several reasons. It is often referred to as "the hump" to get over, the time when you can breathe a sigh of relief because the threat of miscarriage decreases, morning sickness is dissipating, and you're heading into a more placid time of pregnancy. This is generally the time when you can hear a heartbeat and actually see the baby during the big twenty-week ultrasound. Seeing and hearing

your baby will undoubtedly induce feelings of excitement and perhaps anxiety in you. Try to take the day off or at least a couple of hours for the twenty-week sonogram—it's a significant milestone in the baby's development, and it's a good idea not to shoot off to work immediately following this procedure. Give yourselves some time to process what just happened and take your partner out for lunch. It's an important life event and shouldn't be overlooked.

Real Dad

"Visually, an ultrasound is all blurry and muddled. Yet when our doctor arrived to take a look and he explained what we were seeing, it finally began to sink in that there was a new life growing inside my wife."

—Chris, 32

Getting Prenatal Tests

Be involved in the decisions about prenatal tests, and whenever possible, be there for their administration and/or getting the results. Here are the names of some of the tests that could be conducted in the second trimester, and brief descriptions of why they're done.

For more information, consult a good pregnancy book or do some online research.

Amniocentesis. Frequently called an "amnio," this test looks for different kinds of birth defects (such as chromosomal damage) and certain diseases, and can assess a baby's lung maturity. During the second trimester, a needle is inserted through the abdomen to the amniotic sac to obtain a small amount of fluid. There are some risks associated with an amniocentesis, including miscarriage in approximately 1 in every 250 women, so it is not a routine test, but it is a very accurate one.

Glucose tolerance test. When a urinalysis is insufficient, a pregnant woman may need to take a longer test for diabetes, involving the drinking of a glucose-rich liquid during the second or third trimester (depending on family history of gestational diabetes) followed by a blood test. There are no risks, but the liquid is rather nasty and can induce nausea and/or vomiting.

Finding Out the Gender

It's been very interesting to hear about different families' decisions about finding out the gender. It seems to me, at least partially, like an act of taking control of uncertainty by using technology to ease the anxiety of simply not knowing.

Even though you can find out the gender of your baby around the eighteenth to twenty-second week of your partner's pregnancy, it's not a given that you have to do it as early as possible or even at all. According to a recent Gallup poll, 51 percent of people said

they would wait until the birth to find out. Proponents say that it gives you a chance to adjust to the gender and deal with any disappointment. Others say that life is too planned, that this is one of the few genuine surprises left, and that surely expectant parents will adjust just like their parents did. Where do you stand on this?

Real Dad

"The technician informed us we were going to have a girl. We prepared the room, received a ton of girly clothes, and then the baby came and the doctor said, 'It's a boy!' I couldn't believe it. Sometimes you don't really know what you are going to get. My challenge was to embrace the unexpected!"

—Brian, 40

Shifting Your Routines

Aside from the moment of hearing and seeing your baby for the first time, you and your partner will begin to experience some shifts in your regular routines, behaviors, and desires. For example, your partner may become more interested in sex, and you might celebrate this as a pregnancy bonus. For other women, sexual desire decreases and sleepless nights become the norm. All this can lead to heightened anxiety and friction. You may begin to feel like something (someone) is encroaching on your life. It is critical to be aware of this and to talk about it with each other. I have found in my practice that when couples don't talk about their reactions to the impending birth, whether they be positive or negative, conflict, distance, and/or resentment builds. We sometimes try to act as if nothing is different when, really, it is far more healthy and productive to be awake and aware of the impending changes and find a way to honor and cherish these moments and not pretend everything is as it was.

Creating a Birth Plan

The birth plan is one of the greatest tools you can utilize to gain a sense of control. The birth plan asserts what your partner and you want to have happen during the birth. It lays out what your wishes are and communicates those wishes to your birthing team. A typical birth plan will cover topics such as what to do in case of emergency, the position your partner wants to be in during delivery, medications your partner wishes to have or not have, visitor protocols, who cuts the cord, etc. Will you hire a doula (a helping professional who can accompany your partner through labor, delivery, and even at home)? When you both agree on a birth plan, discuss it with your

health-care professional(s) to get any questions answered.

Figure out with your partner where to take birthing classes and how much you intend to be involved. Note that there are three main types of birthing classes: International Childbirth Education Association (ICEA), Lamaze, and Bradley Method. The instruction can vary, and the commitment required for each type of class is different, so you'll both want to be informed before choosing a type. For instance, Lamaze typically requires a six-week commitment, but the Bradley Method is a twelve-week class that teaches husband-coached childbirth with breathing and relaxation techniques. If you're even thinking about taking birthing classes, you'll want to do your homework here, since you'll be a participant in the birth, not just an observer.

In your birth plan you should answer the following questions:

Medication and other interventions. What strategies of pain management are preferred?

What kind of pain medication will your partner need to take, if any?

How strongly is your partner in favor of or opposed to medication?

Under what circumstances is medication okay?

Under what circumstances is induction of labor okay?

Is there a preference with regard to electronic fetal monitoring?

The birth. How strongly does your partner want a natural (vaginal) child birth versus a cesarean section?

What position does your partner want to be in when delivering? On her back, all fours, in a birthing pool, or some other position?

How would your partner like to be coached with regard to pushing? Is it okay to have music on during the delivery?

Any other requests, like: Does your partner want the baby placed on her belly right after the birth? Who will cut the cord? If the baby needs to be taken out of the room, can the father be with him/her?

Postbirth. Is it possible for you to stay in the hospital overnight?

If it is a boy, will he be circumcised?

How will the baby be fed— breastfed or formula? Would you like some assistance in getting either of these feeding routines started?

Does your partner want the baby to sleep in her room overnight or in the nursery?

What is involved in hiring a doula (see further discussion in third trimester)?

TIP

Many expectant parents take birthing classes from their hospitals these organizations:

Bradley Method: www.bradleybirth.com

International Childbirth Education Association (ICEA): www.icea.org

Lamaze International: www.lamaze.com

Sharing the News

Notice how it feels for you when you tell people you're going to be a father. Are you excited? For some men this is a very real expression of strength and power.

Are you cautious? A good friend of mine, Evan, recalls postponing the joy of telling friends because he felt a degree of anxiety at every step of the pregnancy. He attributes this to the having previously gone through a miscarriage with his wife.

Are you deferential? Another dad I've worked with shared that he gave all the honor to his wife and barely felt anything for himself. He almost didn't see himself as a part of the miracle.

No matter how you decide to share the news, the key is to be present to what it is that you are feeling and thinking, and to notice how you behave. This will help you make your positive presence felt.

Other people's reactions are just that: other people's reactions. Sharing the news may elicit a range of reactions, hopefully mostly positive ones, but don't be surprised if you receive some negative vibes as well. One couple I've worked with told me that the expectant dad's father reacted to the news of their first child by saying, "How are you going to afford it? Having a child is a big responsibility." The dad-to-be was hurt by this reaction, particularly since he had wanted a baby so badly and more specifically wanted his father's support. As I previously noted, I recall sharing news of our first pregnancy with a friend, and he equated fatherhood with being shackled.

I couldn't have felt more different. In a way I was open to saying good-bye to my life as I knew it and eagerly looking forward to what life would be like with a baby. You may need to build up a sort of Teflon shield to protect yourself from other people's negative reactions and projections.

THE THIRD TRIMESTER: WEEKS 25 TO 40

The third trimester is characterized by impending change and preparation. Your partner is growing in size and therefore in discomfort, which can be enhanced by extreme weather conditions, such as heat and humidity or the icy cold of winter. Her uterus is now about the size of a soccer ball and she may feel as if the baby is treating her uterus like a soccer ball. The growing fetus impinges on all the surrounding organs—bladder, ribs, and diaphragm. These physical changes mean your partner may be experiencing back pain, foot and ankle swelling, regular trips to the bathroom, shortness of breath, and exhaustion.

There will likely be changes in her psychological state as well. She may become impatient and irritable—wouldn't you? She may be self-conscious of her body, wondering about what kind of mom she will be, and nervous about what kind of birth she will have. Things can get quite emotional for her. She's about ready to burst.

At the beginning of this trimester your baby is slightly more than a pound and by the end it's a six-to-ten-pound little person kicking and protruding from your partner's belly. This is a great time to sing, hum, or talk to the baby and see if it responds.

As a dad-to-be you will have to step up your support and do a lot more chores; you don't want your partner to overdo it and pose a risk to herself and/or the baby. Think of your primary job as taking care of your partner so she can take care of the baby. Now before you start to feel like a "working mule," as one of my dad friends put it, chalk up this extra workload to poetic justice for the fact that you don't have to endure the vagaries of pregnancy or labor. Consider the many times that your partner may have carried an extra burden for your benefit. In today's day and age, with so many expectant moms working right up until their due date, there are many women who can—and do—overdo it. Slowing them down long enough so that they can rest and take care of themselves (or be taken care of) is important. The two of you are, after all, a dynamic team, and this is good practice for the teamwork required for successful parenting.

Your Jobs in the Third Trimester

- Get the baby's room ready. If you are going to paint the baby's room, do it a few weeks before the due date so the paint smell is gone—or maybe better yet, use the earth- and baby-friendly non-VOC paints you can find at most home improvement stores. (Non-VOC paints don't have "volatile organic compounds" or the traditional paint smell. It means you won't have to worry about your partner inhaling those fumes and you could move baby right in after painting.) Stock up on newborn diapers, get the changing area ready, and procure a suitable crib or bassinet. Make sure you have some clothes, especially Onesies, for the baby to wear. Try not to freak out if you don't have it all ready. It will be okay; and in most cases, you'll have more than enough.

- Develop a birth plan with your partner, if you haven't done so already. A birth plan includes your wishes and desires for when everything goes perfectly, but also includes contingency plans for things such as premature delivery or cesarean birth.
- Get a tour of the hospital or birthing center. Be sure that the facility's policies are in alignment with your own philosophy, particularly involving routine medical interventions and the like.
- Check to see how flexible your work schedule will be for the actual birth and afterward. Your partner is likely to need some help when she first returns home. If you can't be there, who will? Family? Friends? A doula?
- Ask two fathers about what stands out in their experience of their baby's birth. Were they surprised by anything?
- Find some time to exercise.
- If you enjoy it, journal your thoughts and feelings.
- Start thinking about child-care options.

Getting Prenatal Tests

Here are the names of some of the tests that could be conducted in the third trimester, and brief descriptions for why they're done. Again, be there and be involved.

Consider This

There are so many things to do, decisions to make, and feelings to manage. Stay engaged, because (1) you will get to know yourself better, (2) you will get to know your partner better, and (3) you will be more fully invested in your baby.

Biophysical profile. Done in the third trimester only if the baby is late or problems are suspected, the biophysical profile is an ultrasound often done in conjunction with a nonstress test to monitor the baby's breathing rate, muscle tone, and volume of amniotic fluid. There is no known risk, but the ultrasound is typically only performed as needed.

Glucose tolerance test. When a urinalysis is insufficient, a pregnant woman may need to take a longer test for diabetes, involving the drinking of a glucose-rich liquid during the second or third trimester (depending on family history of gestational diabetes) followed by a blood test. There are no risks, but the liquid is rather nasty and can induce nausea and/or vomiting.

Nonstress test. Given in the third trimester if the baby is past due or if problems are suspected, this risk-free and pain-free test involves belts being placed around the abdomen and monitors uterine contractions and fetal heartbeat.

Household Chores

For many expectant dads the third trimester is fraught with a lot of doing, particularly in getting the house and the baby's room ready. This is the area where many men are comfortable.

Don't be surprised if you find yourself doing any or all of the following:

- Assembling furniture, crib(s), strollers, car seats, changing table(s), etc.
- Painting or wallpapering the baby's room.
- Behaving as if you were the one about to give birth. Seriously. Maybe your back hurts, you've gained weight, you can't sleep, you're tired, etc. It's a reminder that you have needs too.
- Buying a new car.

Thinking About Fatherhood

You will be amazed at the number of decisions that expectant parents are confronted with. Everything from what kind of birthing experience you want to have, to what, if any, religion you will raise your child with, to what brand of stroller to buy or how to decorate the baby's room. This is where many dads check out and say (to their wives or to themselves), "This is not my domain." You probably won't have to participate in every decision, but be aware that decisions left unresolved have a way of finding you. Besides, your partner may need you to weigh in on certain matters, such as whether or not to circumcise, or may want your opinion to help balance hers, such as whether to purchase the overpriced but very cute baby gear instead of the serviceable and more affordable options.

Don't be surprised if you find yourself thinking any or all of the following:

- This is crazy; what were we thinking?
- Our lives were easier and simpler before.
- How am I going to make more money?
- How did my dad do it?
- How am I going to protect this baby from all the crazy things in this world?

Stay the Course

For many an expectant mom, the more the baby grows, the more uncomfortable she feels. The last few weeks in particular are commonly very uncomfortable for a mom-to-be. You will probably hear your partner say numerous times

> ## Real Dad
>
> *"Men can get squeezed out of the equation. The birth plan brought me in and gave me a role and a voice as to what happens to my wife and child."*
>
> —Joe, 35

how ready she feels to just have this baby already. All you can do is compassionately try to ease the discomfort.

> **TIP**
>
> If you think you might be squeamish during the delivery, tell your partner and or care provider *now* so that she can prepare for it and doesn't think you're bailing on her at delivery time.

Doulas

I am a big fan of doulas. A doula is essentially a labor coach, someone who assists with the labor and delivery of the baby by providing support, primarily to the expectant mom but also to the dad-to-be. She is essentially an extra set of knowledgeable hands and eyes that can apply a woman's touch or alert a hospital staff member to a crisis. The use of doulas in this country are increasing, and for very good reason.

My wife and I used the same doula, Jennifer Kroll, for all three of our children and she was particularly helpful during the birth of our third child. Our first child had been born on the due date and the second had been late by two weeks, so when my wife started having contractions about two weeks before the due date for the third, both of us were taken by surprise (even though we were told it was possible). Eventually the contractions got so intense that we called the doula. It turned out to be a very smart decision.

The great thing about a doula is she comes to you when you need her. In our case, our doula met us in front of our apartment building and rode with us to the hospital. I am convinced that if the doula had not been with my wife in the backseat, I would have either gotten into a car accident or the baby would have been delivered en route to the hospital. She was able to comfort my wife and convince her that the baby was not going to be born in the car. She navigated me through the smoothest and quickest route to the hospital. Then, when we arrived, she took my wife inside while I parked the car. I mention all these details because they ended up being critical. Our third child was born twelve minutes later.

Doulas can also be helpful in providing useful information to you, your partner, and the medical staff. With the birth of our second child, Jennifer was the one who first noticed that our baby was crowning and about to be born. And during our first pregnancy, Jennifer also assisted us in developing a birth plan and, better yet, helped ensure that the birth plan was respected at the hospital. The doula can be a source of wisdom and calm and she can be your best advocate while you're busy worrying about and taking care of your partner and baby. It's a great combination to have.

One caveat: Doulas can be expensive and are generally not covered by most insurance plans.

Expectant Dad's Checklist

Become a student of the pregnancy. Read books and articles, and/or talk to the doctor to find out what's going to happen and when.
- Have your partner teach you about what's going on in her body.
- Teach her about what's going on with you. This could come in the form of bizarre dreams, your own feelings, thoughts, cravings, and urges.
- Ask your partner daily how she's feeling and what she needs.
- Don't assume your negative thoughts and emotions will burden your partner. Instead, ask her. Then, if you need to, find another place to express yourself, either with a friend, therapist, or dads' group.
- Take time off from work to be present for doctor or midwife visits. Make a point of attending at least 50 percent of the time, or more if possible.
- Help create a birth plan and have some of your desires represented in the plan. This will map out, in general, what your partner and you want to have happen and should be shared with the doctor or midwife.
- Start organizing your home. Clear out clutter and prepare the room for the baby.

The Best Supporting Role You'll Ever Play

Pregnancy and birth are incredible things, but the father's role can sometimes be hard to define and claim. This chapter gave you some things to consider as you try to figure out just where you figure into the process. In general, being a dad at this stage means being as supportive as possible and giving voice to your thoughts and feelings. It means knowing what's going on with your partner and baby so you can support her the best way possible. It means taking part in birthing classes and being present in the birthing room.

REFLECTION QUESTIONS

1. What role are you finding yourself playing so far?
2. What positive things can you do to help your partner (and yourself) through this period of unknowns?
3. How do you think this baby will change things in your home?
4. How will the baby influence how you and your partner talk to each other?
5. Are you feeling squeezed out? Talk to your partner about this.

Delivery Day:
Getting It Done

Getting Prepared

With the anticipation and so much going on in the last few weeks of pregnancy, it might be a challenge to remember everything you need for the big event. One of the most common complaints that expectant dads have is that they were caught off guard or they felt unprepared for the baby's birth. This chapter goes into the details of both normal and emergency labor, but always remember: Even the best-prepared father will be (pleasantly) surprised.

Witnessing and participating in your child's birth is unlike any other experience in life. I remember our birthing class instructor telling us, as we were preparing for our first child, that every birth is unique unto itself. Three children later, I can attest that this is indeed true.

The primary sources for the information in this chapter come from my own experience,

examples in my practice, and Penny Simkin's book *The Birth Partner: A Complete Guide to Childbirth for Dads, Doulas and All Other Labor Companions*, a book I highly recommend.

> **TIP**
>
> Don't take a bumpy road to the hospital.

AS THE DUE DATE APPROACHES

Even when you've done everything in your power to maintain control and be prepared, you're still likely to be surprised by something. This is the wonderful world of the unknown. Every birth is different, no matter how many times you've been down this road. Still, here are my top five general tips that may help you figure out your role in these last weeks and days.

- Stay close to home. Think of the month prior and the month after your partner's due date as "home time." Do your best to decrease your workload and travel time. Prepare your boss, clients, and co-workers for the possibility of having to leave work abruptly.
- Expect emotions. Having a baby is the most personal experience that you will ever have. Sometimes big emotions are expressed (by your or your partner) as irritability, anxiety, fear, and sadness, or as excitement, joy, elation, and delight.
- Maintain your supportive role. You are not the lead character in this life event. You are in a supportive role, but possibly the most important one.
- Be present, yet ready to get out of the way. There may be times when you need to back off and allow your partner and/or the birthing team to call the shots. Don't forget that you're needed, but be mindful of being in the way.
- Pre-register your partner at the hospital. Pick a day when you both can go to the hospital with your insurance and payment information. Pre-registering will make it easier to get into the hospital on the day she delivers.

TIP

Don't let others tell you that you're "babysitting." You're being a dad.

Consider This

Quick facts: In the 1960s, 10 to 15 percent of fathers attended births. By the 1980s, 85 percent expected to attend the births of their children.

YOUR ROLE(S)

With the vast majority of dads now attending the births of their children, what are the roles the dad-to-be plays as the due date approaches? What does a father do? Try these hats on for size:

- The valet. If you are driving to the hospital or birthing center, sometimes your job, as it was for me, is to park the car.
- The walking buddy. Leading up to active labor, your partner may need to do some walking or pacing. Be with her as she does this; she may need to hold your hand or physically lean on you. Remember that she's feeling contractions, a pain that you and I will never experience or understand. This can be very scary for her, so it's important to stay with her through this.
- The masseur. Only if it helps and feels good, rub her neck, head, feet, and any other part of her body. Again, only do this if she gives you the okay. Some women in labor do not like to be touched! Listen to her and don't take it personally if she says "no thanks."
- The coach. Tell her how great she is doing and how much you believe in her. Offer words of

encouragement like, "You can do it!" or "I'm so proud of you." But also don't overdo it—you'll know (or you'll soon find out!) the point at which encouragement turns into cheerleading, and how much of it she can take.

- The shoulder. Particularly during labor but also after the birth, your strength is something your partner can use and may rely on. Offer your shoulder, body, and any other part of you that she might need to lean on.
- The labor assistant. If your partner is laboring on her back, the obstetrician may ask you to hold a leg. This may help as she pushes the baby out.
- The rock of Gibraltar. One of your roles is to keep it together. The delivery team isn't looking for another panting or screaming parent. And if something comes up that makes you think you might faint, then calmly excuse yourself. You won't be the first dad to do this.
- The umbilical cutter. This is not a required duty, but most dads are asked if they would like to cut the umbilical cord.
- The gatekeeper. You might recall the scene in *The Wizard of Oz* when the Emerald City gatekeeper says to Dorothy and her companions, "Nobody can see the Great Oz!" Well, for as long as your partner says so (but at least before and after the baby's delivery), that gatekeeper is *you*. You are the protector. Make sure that your partner's wishes are respected with regard to medical treatment, visitors, and the like. You do not owe anyone a visit the minute you get out of the delivery

room. Of course you want to celebrate and share the news, but you also want to savor the moment together and allow the experience to sink in. In short, be mindful of boundary crossings.

PREPARING YOUR HOME

Getting any last-minute necessities before the baby comes home is a responsibility that often falls on dad's shoulders since mom is likely still recovering from the birth. Here's a checklist to help you prepare to bring your baby into your home. Delegate this task to a friend or relative who has offered to help. You'll need:

- Lanolin, breast pads, nursing bras, and a breast pump (if needed) if she is breastfeeding
- Clean and tidy house—it won't stay that way for long
- Fridge full of easy-to-prepare foods
- List of contact numbers of people to call when you could use some help
- List of emergency contacts— pediatrician, hospital, and so on

THINGS YOU'LL NEED AT THE HOSPITAL

Get used to the idea of packing a lot of "what if" essentials for any baby-related excursion, including for labor and delivery. The items in the following list that are a major priority are in boldface text. Other things are secondary and can be gotten at a later date or brought in by a friend or family member. Feel free to shift priorities around, depending on your specific circumstances and preferences. It is also important to consider the hospital or birth center's proximity to home and if trips home to pick stuff up are even possible. In any case, try planning things out ahead so that special trips to rustle up forgotten items is unnecessary.

For Mother-to-be

- A small bag of your partner's belongings—a nursing-friendly nightgown, a change of comfortable clothes to wear home, a robe, slippers, toiletries
- Foot lotion
- Healthy snack food
- Favorite juices (perhaps hospital staff can keep these cool for you)

- Nursing bra
- Hair ties or clips
- Warm blanket

For Father-to-be

- Phone numbers of people to call
- Birth plan
- A watch with a second hand
- Change of clothes and toiletries if you plan to sleep over
- Music CDs, iPod
- Books or magazines
- Journal, camera, or video camera (with your partner's blessing)

For Baby

- Clothing—a Onesie, an outfit to go over the Onesie, and a hat
- Receiving blanket
- Car seat

Typical Stages of Labor

There are three distinct stages of labor and learning about them can help you modulate your expectations and anxieties. Labor can last as few as two hours or as long as two days. It is very typical for first-time births to last longer than subsequent deliveries.

FALSE LABOR

Prelabor (aka false labor) is considered the warm-up phase and not every expectant mother goes through it. It is sometimes referred to as "false labor" but there is nothing false about it. It begins with the first contraction but the contractions are considered nonprogressing, meaning they don't lead to cervix dilation, which is key to preparing your partner's body for delivery. The contractions may come and go for a period of hours or days. These are commonly referred to as Braxton Hicks contractions.

How do you know if your partner is in prelabor? She might produce a thick, blood-tinged vaginal mucus, which is often called a mucus plug, or "show." This is caused by the thinning of the cervix. She might also have a restless night's sleep, complain about feeling crampy, experience soft bowel movements, and/or leak a watery vaginal discharge.

Your Jobs

- Time contractions to see if they are progressing.
- Call the birth team for advice, reassurance, and possible examination.
- Be with your partner. Try to keep her calm and relaxed by giving her a massage, preparing food, or going for a walk. Be reassuring. Do not take her to the hospital unless you are instructed to do so by her caregiver; you will most likely be asked to go home if you do. This can be a very sweet time together and marks the beginning of the birthing experience and your life as parents.

How to Time Contractions

Birthing classes will instruct you on how to time contractions, and you'll need some basic supplies: a piece of paper, something to write with, and a watch with a second hand. On the paper, make four columns with the following headings: start, duration, interval, and comments. In the first column write down the time each contraction starts. Time the duration of the contraction and record its length in the second column. In the interval column you can record the number of minutes from the start of one contraction to the start of the next, but if you accurately record the time when each contraction starts, you should be able to "do the math" to figure out the interval. The final column is for any comments about each contraction, such as the strength of the contraction, your partner's appetite, and how she is coping.

STAGE 1: LABOR AND DILATION (2 TO 24 HOURS)

During this stage, there are three things the medical staff will be concerned about: dilation, effacement, and station. The fetus is held safely in the uterus (or womb) while the cervix (the lower opening into the uterus) thins (called effacement) and opens (called dilation). The fetus's descent into the birth canal or vagina is referred to as its station or birth presentation, which is typically measured from –3 (early labor) to +5 (delivery is imminent) and is determined by the location of the fetal head in relation to the midpoint of the mother's pelvis. When the head is at the pelvic midpoint, it is called 0 (zero) station and the baby is considered to be "engaged" and ready for birthing. (Diagrams of fetal position and station can be found online or in Penny Simkin's book *The Birth Partner*.)

Within the first stage are three phases: the Latent or Early Labor phase (the longest phase, lasting a few minutes to twenty hours), the Active Labor phase (lasting thirty minutes to six hours), and the Transition (lasting ten to sixty minutes).

Signs of Early Labor

- Her water may have "broken," also called ruptured membranes.
- Effacement (cervical thinning) can be as high as 100 percent. (Effacement is measured in two ways: percentages [0 to 100] and centimeters of length: 0 percent

means no thinning and 100 percent means paper thin. The cervix becomes shorter and therefore becomes thinner, so a cervix that is 4 centimeters long is 0 percent effaced; 1 centimeter long means 80 to 90 percent effaced.) First-time moms usually efface before dilating. At this point, the baby may be in –3 station.

- Cervical dilation or opening of the cervix is about 3 to 4 centimeters (as determined by a vaginal exam).
- Contractions progress by being longer, stronger, and closer together, usually lasting about a minute.
- She may be making sounds you have never heard before. This is natural and a sign that labor is progressing. She needs to moan, groan, and make whatever sounds will help her through the contractions. She will be totally focused on getting through the pain associated with contractions.

Your jobs:
- Discourage chitchat or disturbing conversations.
- Time and log at least five or six contractions.
- Use the techniques learned in birthing class, help her breathe through the pain of each contraction.
- Give her praise and support.
- Listen to what she tells you.

Signs of Active Labor

- Cervical dilation is at about 7 centimeters, effacement could be up to 100 percent, and the baby may be in –3 to 0 station.
- Contractions intensify and last

for no more than one and a half minutes, coming 1 to 4 minutes apart, which likely means that her pain level is increasing.
- She has stopped laughing at your jokes and is tired, annoyed, discouraged, and/or scared. There is no turning back.

Your jobs:
- Encourage her to let go of her need to be in control (if she hasn't already).
- Help her bear the contractions, which are a painful necessity to birthing the baby.
- Use all the techniques you learned in birthing class to help her through the pain, whether it's through encouraging words, soothing music, repositioning, or rhythmic breathing.

Signs of the Transition Phase

- Cervical dilation is at about 10 centimeters, effacement is 100 percent, and the baby may be in 0 to +2 station.
- Contractions last for more than a minute, come more frequently, and are the most intense.
- There could be leg or whole-body trembling, nausea or a need to vomit, pelvic or leg cramps, skin that feels sore to the touch, the need to have a bowel movement, or feeling hot or cold. You might wish the labor would stop and fear that it will never end but it does and will.

Your jobs:
- Remember that this is probably the worst she will feel and that it is almost over.
- Hold her hand, rub her head, or do what she likes unless the staff

ask you to back off—but do not expect her to relax.

- Stay calm. If she has requested no medications, don't bring it up unless she or the birthing team does so first. When this phase ends and your partner moves into the second stage, she will feel some relief.

STAGE 2: THE BIRTHING STAGE (15 MINUTES TO 3 HOURS)

This stage is also referred to as "expulsion." As the baby's head presses against the cervix, it triggers faster contractions. Within this stage there are three phases: Resting (ten to thirty minutes), Descent (thirty minutes to three hours), and Crowning/Birth (two to twenty minutes).

Signs of Resting

- She eases into a restful state where there is generally no urge to push.
- She asks questions like: "Have you fed the dog?" or "Does your mother know how to get to our house?"

Your jobs:
- Stay with her and encourage her not to push. This phase can be thought of as a time to regroup and regain the energy necessary to birth the baby.

Signs of Descent

- The baby descends through the birth canal and the top of the head can be seen through the

vaginal opening.
- She feels the urge to push and will either be instructed to do so or asked to wait, depending on whether she's had an epidural.

Your jobs:
- Stay with her and help her get into a position for pushing that she and the team are comfortable with.
- Continue to encourage her.

Signs of Crowning/Birth

- There are only a few contractions, roughly four to seven minutes apart.
- Your partner may feel a burning sensation as the baby's head stretches her perineum to its maximum, possibly even to tearing. This can panic some first-time moms.
- Your partner may be encouraged to pant or blow, to help ease the baby's head past the perineum.

Your jobs:
- Stay close and continue to support her. I was in a different spot for each of my kids' births. For the first I was holding one of my wife's legs, for our second I was at the foot of the bed, and for the third I was holding her hand. Wherever you end up, try to make sure you're being helpful. If you are not sure where to be, ask the birthing team or your partner.

STAGE 3: THE PLACENTAL STAGE (15 TO 30 MINUTES)

Very soon after the baby is born the placenta will come out as well. The placenta is the source from which the baby received its nutrients, and it has been attached to the uterine wall by the umbilical cord. As the placenta detaches from the uterine wall, some bleeding may occur. For some moms, this stage passes by unnoticed; for others there may be intense cramping. Far less pushing is required for the placenta than it was for the baby, but the placenta does need to come out.

Your jobs:
- Cut the umbilical cord (optional). I was surprised at how strong the cord was.
- Help your partner get comfortable.
- Make sure the baby is with her as soon as possible, depending on whether or not there were any complications. Under ideal circumstances the baby will get to lie on your partner's belly, skin on skin, which will offer the most warmth.
- Hold your baby, if your partner is not ready. Your baby needs to sense you too! Take three slow, deep breaths. . . . Your child is finally here!

COMMON QUESTIONS

These are some common questions that come up for expectant fathers leading up to and during the course of labor and delivery. The answers I've provided are not exhaustive and are not meant to replace the knowledge and expertise of your birthing class or labor and delivery team.

When do we go to the hospital? When your partner's contractions last for at least a minute each and are four to five minutes apart. Usually it takes about an hour to determine whether or not the pattern warrants a trip to the hospital. When in doubt, call your birthing team.

How long can my wife stay in the hospital? This will largely depend on your insurance coverage and whether or not there were any complications for your partner or baby. A typical normal vaginal delivery allows for up to two days' stay in the hospital. A cesarean section typically allows for a three-day stay.

What do we do if her water breaks? Check for amount, color, and odor. Call the birthing team, as this is sometimes an indication that you need to get to the hospital. The general medical rule is that birth follows within twenty-four hours after the water breaks.

What do I do in an emergency situation? Although it is rare, particularly with firstborns, sometimes babies don't wait for the hospital or doctor. In these rare occasions it can be important for you to remember a few guidelines. They are:
- Try to stay calm, decisive and authoritative.
- Call 911. Without leaving your partner, get help from neighbors, friends, or even children.
- Make the birthing area warm. It's very important for the baby to maintain its body temperature.
- Get blankets, paper towels, newspapers, or whatever you can find to soak up body secretions (expect blood and mucus) and wipe the vernix (a white, pasty, protective coating comprised

largely of dead cells) from the baby's face and nostrils.

- Wash hands, if possible, without leaving your partner.
- Ask your partner to lie on her side. This might help slow things down.
- As soon as the baby is born, watch and listen for proper breathing.
- If the baby doesn't breathe right away, rub its head, back, or chest briskly or slap the soles of its feet.
- Place the baby on your partner's belly and cover them both with blankets. Remember to keep the baby's face exposed so she can breathe.

Real Dad

"Even though I attended all the birthing classes, I still felt clueless. The most important thing I did was listen to my wife and not minimize her complaints. She taught me that she is the boss of her body."

—Matt, 40

What is a cesarean section (c-section)? Surgical incisions are made in the mother's abdomen to take the baby from the uterus. It is the most common surgery in the United States: In 2008 one in three births in the United States was a cesarean, amounting to about 1.3 million c-sections per year. One of the most publicized reasons for a c-section—or at least an elective one—is to prevent damage to the pelvic floor, which may prevent your partner from being incontinent later in life.

Why would a doctor recommend a c-section? There are many reasons why the procedure is performed. The baby may be too large to deliver vaginally or there may be multiples. The mother's body may not have responded to the induction of labor, or perhaps she has gestational high blood pressure (preeclampsia). There may have been a delay in getting an epidural, or there might be an overdue or arrested labor, or a ruptured uterus. Doctors may also recommend a cesarean when the mother is exhausted from a prolonged labor, there is fetal distress, or there is a need for forceps or a vacuum extractor. In addition, they are performed when there is serious bleeding or hemorrhaging. They are required when there is a prolapsed cord (the umbilical cord exits the uterus before the baby does).

Also, a c-section is frequently called for when the baby's position could endanger its life, such as:

- in breech position, with feet facing the cervix (see page 45).
- in frank breech position, with buttocks facing the cervix.
- in transverse position, or lying horizontally.

While c-sections are medically necessary in some cases, there has been some controversy about their high frequency. Interview your birthing team on this issue. It is very appropriate to ask them what their c-section rate is and under what conditions they perform them. **What should we expect with a c-section?** You might be asked to leave, or you might be prevented from seeing the incision, largely due to concern that you might faint and get in the way. She will be sore for a few weeks.

Real Dad

"I wish someone had told me how bloody my wife's c-section was going to be. The next thing I knew, my wife was in danger. I was treated like an afterthought."

—Bill, 28

What is an epidural? An epidural is used to numb your partner and allows her to rest if the labor is particularly long. It contains a low dose of a narcotic and an anesthetic. It is administered by a specialist directly into your partner's spine with a syringe. There is a fair amount of preparation time required, so your partner needs to request it early enough so that she can be prepped for it. She'll be asked to bend over, curl her back, and relax as much as possible.

Real Dad

"I remember feeling sorry for my wife as she got an epidural. She had labored for quite some time and had not dilated past 7 centimeters. Since her water had broken 24 hours previously, they wanted to deliver the baby as soon as possible. It looked really uncomfortable for her."

—Darren, 35

What is Pitocin? Pitocin is a synthetic drug that is administered intravenously to speed up muscular contractions, so that labor will move more quickly.

What is an episiotomy? This is a surgical cut between the vagina and anus. An episiotomy is administered just prior to the baby being born and is done to relieve pressure at the vaginal opening and to prevent additional tearing of the perineum (the area between the vagina and the anus). A local anesthesia is given so the mother-to-be feels nothing. It does require stitching, which occurs soon after the baby is born, and some professionals believe that natural tearing is faster to heal than a surgical cut.

What is breech? This is when the position of the baby has moved so that its feet, buttocks, or knees are pointing down toward the cervix and the vaginal opening. The ideal position for the baby to be born is head facing down. Although breeched babies can be born safely, it can cause problems during the birth. Your job is to not panic and let the team and your partner do their best to reposition the baby.

What is preeclampsia? This is a condition that affects the liver, brain, and kidneys of the mother-to-be. Symptoms that may indicate your partner is experiencing preeclampsia include: swelling on face and hands (edema), headaches, increase in blood pressure, and protein in the urine. It usually shows up in the last half of the pregnancy and occurs in 7 percent of all pregnancies. These symptoms need to be closely monitored and may require your partner to go on strict bed rest and cut back on work. Your job would be to make sure she gets the rest she needs and to pick up the slack. This can be quite stressful for the expectant dads, so get ready to give and/or get extra support. It also could require hospitalization and, unchecked, could result in preterm birth.

How do I deal with difficult birth, labor, or hospital staff? The ideal situation is that your birthing team is one you've chosen and therefore trust. But when this isn't the case (and it often is not), it is important to work toward building an alliance with them as quickly as possible. First, empathize: It may be that they are working on very little sleep.

Do your best to respect them by referring to them by name. In the sincerest of tones, thank them for their dedication and devotion to your partner and baby. This will improve the likelihood of getting what you need.

If your best efforts fail, speak up for your partner, baby, and self. You have the right to be treated with the utmost respect and care. This is where the hard work of preparing a birth plan can come in handy. Review the plan with the nurse and/or doctor. If a staff member is not adhering to the plan or is not caring sensitively for your partner or baby, complain to the head nurse and request that she or he be removed. Do your best to handle the conflict out of earshot of your partner, who needs to be surrounded by love, kindness, and support.

What is the Apgar score? The baby is observed at one and five minutes (sometimes ten minutes as well) after birth. The baby is scored, based on five criteria: heart rate, breathing effort, muscle tone, reflex activity, and skin color. A score of 7 or above is very good. If the score is below 7, then the baby will need extra attention and observation until the problem is corrected. Try not to make a big deal out of the score—it rarely impacts college admissions.

What is induced labor? The most common way to speed up labor is to use medications such as Pitocin. Labor can also be sped up or, at the very least, helped along by "self-help" methods. These include finger stimulation of the cervix or suppositories that promote softening, thinning, and sometimes dilation of the cervix. Reasons for inducing can vary but it is usually due to going past the fortieth week, fetal distress, maternal exhaustion, and/or prolonged labor.

What is Electronic Fetal Monitoring (EFM) and why is it done? The purpose of EFM is to monitor the baby's heart rate as well as the frequency and duration of your partner's contractions. There are two ways to electronically monitor the unborn child: internally and externally. The internal device attaches to the top of the baby's head while still inside your partner. The external device is a belt that wraps around your partner's belly. Most medical facilities will do this as a part of routine care, but you may be able to request no EFM if there are no complications.

Why is IV needed? The intravenous bag is filled with a combination of water, dextrose, electrolytes, and/or medications. The bag is connected to a tube that extends to a needle, which is inserted into your partner's veins. Feel free to ask why they are doing this, and what's in the bag, but usually it's for one of four reasons: (1) they want your partner to stay hydrated and/or equipped with enough calories; (2) medications like Pitocin are easier to administer; (3) if she's having an epidural, it increases her blood volume and prevents a drop in blood pressure; and (4) to keep a vein open just in case she needs medications later on.

KEY QUESTIONS FOR INFORMED DECISION MAKING

Your doctor or midwife may recommend an unexpected test or intervention that will help your partner deliver the baby. When in doubt, use these standard questions before agreeing to such tests.

- What is the problem?
- Can you explain your reasoning for administering tests?
- Can you explain the risks, benefits, and side effects before administering any unplanned intervention?
- How is the intervention done?
- What's the risk of doing nothing?
- What are the chances of the problem being corrected with this intervention?
- If the problem is not corrected, what are the next steps?
- How can I be helpful?

FOUR THINGS YOU MUST LEARN

Before you leave the hospital, make sure that a obstetric nurse or doctor has shown you how to do the following things (if you don't already know). Get someone to demonstrate first and then ask him or her to supervise you as you do it, to make sure you've got it right. Learn how to:

- Change a diaper (see page 68)
- Swaddle (see page 66)
- Bathe the baby (see page 68)
- Umbilical cord and circumcision care (see page 68)

Fatherhood: Your Labor Begins

This chapter hopefully helped you feel less in the dark about what you can do to prepare for the delivery of your baby. As you may have noticed, you have jobs every step of the way. The primary one is to stay close and be present to your partner's needs. This will go a long way.

Once the baby has arrived, a different kind of work is required: the work of adjusting to this new life. You've waited a long time for this moment and it's finally here. You are a father. Nothing makes it more real than holding your child in your arms, in your home for the very first time. Bringing your baby home can be full of emotions, like pride, relief, fear, and anxiety. After all, you're in charge now. The next section will help you make the adjustment to the first year.

REFLECTION QUESTIONS

1. What can you do or say that will help your partner get through the delivery? What will you want to avoid doing or saying?
2. What do you notice about her that convinces you she will be fine? Tell her why! First-time childbirth can be scary.
3. Post delivery, what objects, moments, or images from the birth were most meaningful? Capture them somehow.

Time to Adjust: Birth to 12 Months

> *"Everything has changed, yet everything is the same."*
>
> —Chris, 44

Welcome home! The moment you enter your home for the first time after the birth of your baby, you will experience it in a different way. There will be new sounds, new smells, new sights, new rituals, new routines . . . all is new in this familiar and yet new home. At times you may experience awkwardness and anxiety, and you may ask: How will I adjust to all these new responsibilities to my baby, my partner, and myself?

Rest assured, coping strategies are forthcoming to make the transition more manageable. Chapter 4 focuses on your baby's developmental milestones in the first year and how you can best support your infant's growth. Chapter 5 delves into some of the never-ending challenges associated with balancing work and family. Chapter 6 walks you through the essential gear to buy that will make your life and your baby's life a little easier and more fun.

Getting to Know Your Newborn

Baby's Here: Now What?

Labor is over, the baby has arrived, and now it's time to whisk home your little boy or girl. It's not uncommon to walk out of the hospital feeling a little (okay, maybe a lot) unqualified. What will your growing baby need and what can you do to help? The answers to these questions are different depending on your baby's age and what works for your particular family. In general, you will want to figure out a way to create what British pediatrician turned psychoanalyst D. W. Winnicott called a "holding environment." This holding environment can be thought of as a safe container for the newborn to explore her capacities and the world around her. Ideally this safe container should be loving, consistent, and somewhat predictable. As you create this space, I recommend you find a rhythm, routine, and structure that serves not only the baby's developmental needs but you and your partner as well.

You've been discharged from the hospital with no instruction manual. This book will give you a sense of what you are in for but even the best-prepared fathers experience elements of surprise and anxiety. This chapter will lay out the key developmental milestones as you and your baby grow. The goal is to engage her on her level. I'll also identify what I believe to be a newborn's primary needs, why they exist, and what a dad can do to help satisfy them.

Every newborn baby has five primary needs: (1) to be held, comforted, and soothed; (2) to be fed, nourished; (3) to sleep, get rest; (4) to be cleaned, diaper changed; and (5) to be cared for medically. I call these the FIVE BIG NEEDS, and you might be able to remember them more easily with these single-syllable words: hold, feed, sleep, clean, care. Or, if you like acronyms, it's HFSCC.

These needs are not always easy to discern since, obviously, she can't just tell you how she's feeling or what she needs specifically. But the good news is that a baby's needs are generally pretty basic. So unless there is something out of the ordinary going on, satisfying these five needs will contribute greatly toward having a content baby.

COMPLETE DEPENDENCE

Your newborn baby is completely dependent upon you and your partner to satisfy her needs. Human beings, like no other animals, give birth to a baby that cannot do anything for itself. A newborn colt, in contrast, can walk on its own within minutes of being born. Human babies have reflexes, like sucking, which helps them obtain milk, and crying, which helps them communicate that they have an unmet need, but it is the parent who has to discern and supply the need. The ability to walk, talk, and grab things and, of course, skills like reasoning don't come until much later. My point is that, at this stage of their development, you have a big role to play in the life of your newborn.

BABY STATES

Your newborn baby will move in and out of emotional and behavioral states. These states are indicators for what your baby is feeling and needs. It can be useful to know what state your baby is in so that you can respond accordingly. For example, if your baby is in the Quiet Alert state, then you know this is a good time to observe your baby and quietly interact with her. In addition, it can also be fun to watch your baby move in and out of these states. I invite you to be curious and study your little one. Birthing instructors typically teach about the different states so this should be just a quick refresher.

Quiet Alert

Your baby's eyes are wide open and alert. His limbs are still and calm. He appears to be taking in his surroundings—spongelike. This is when a baby is most able to learn and absorb. My wife and I used to call it QA for short and would give each other a quiet high five whenever our baby was in this state.

Your baby is in QA when he:
- Acts like a sponge, takes everything in, and absorbs through hearing and seeing.
- Follows objects with his eyes.
- Remains in this state for minutes at a time.

Active Alert

This is similar to quiet alert but with a little more activity. This is a good time to interact and play with your newborn.

Your baby is in this state when she:
- Is more active, using spontaneous arm and leg movements.
- Makes small cooing, gaga sounds.
- Is not crying or distressed.

Crying or Distressed

Crying is your baby's main form of communication. Take it as his way of saying "pick me up" and gently move, sway, or pace around. Swaddle him and keep him close. If he continues to cry, he probably needs one (or more) of the FIVE BIG NEEDS, such as food or a fresh diaper.

Your baby is distressed when he:
• Shows visual or audible evidence of distress. Don't be alarmed if your newborn does not shed a tear, he won't until about two weeks old, which is when their tear ducts start working. He is not manipulating you.
• Flails his arms and legs or moves his head from side to side.
• Cries, even when there is little sound to it.

Sleepy or Drowsy

Your baby is in this state when she is either waking up or on her way to falling asleep. This is a good time to practice the "sleep button," when she is drifting off to sleep and you very gently stroke the skin in between her eyes in a downward motion with the tip of your finger. This is a good time to quiet her surroundings and dim the lights.

Your baby is in a sleepy or drowsy state when she:
• Makes little to no noise or movements.
• Begins to close her eyes.
• Spontaneously and quickly grins.

Quiet or Light Sleep

This is fun to watch and, again, is a good time to keep the surroundings quiet until your baby falls into a deeper sleep. His breathing may become irregular in this state.

Your baby is in this state when he:
• Is about to close his eyes and they appear as little slits—they may not be fully closed.
• Is still but startled easily.
• Shows limb or face twitches.

Active Sleep

This is a very exciting time for sleep-deprived parents, though I don't recommend you make a lot of noise while your baby is in this state. Place her on her back to sleep—it minimizes the risk of SIDS (sudden infant death syndrome).

Your baby is in this state when she:
• Makes minimal or no movements; limbs are limp.
• Breathes regularly.
• Makes sucking motions with her mouth that are very cute.

MEETING YOUR BABY'S DEVELOPMENT NEEDS

When I was in social work school, one of my professors used to say over and over how important it was "to meet our clients where they were at." He didn't mean this literally, although that was sometimes important, too. What he meant was that we needed to meet them where they were at developmentally. At the very least, this means having a firm understanding of what their needs and capabilities are as they relate to emotion, sociability, cognition, and behavior.

The same goes for caring for your newborn. Having a good sense of what you might see and how you can respond is helpful information. Many parenting books and Web sites will tell you what you can expect, but they don't tell you how to respond. The developmental milestones of a baby in its first year are amazing and unique at each stage, and need to be understood in order to meet the child where she's at. Otherwise, you'll be unnecessarily confused, anxious, and frustrated. For example, if you expect your four-month-old to be eating solid food, then you are not meeting her where she's at. I will review the developmental stages in greater detail in a moment, but let's first look at development in a "big picture" way.

"NORMAL" DEVELOPMENT

For the sake of clarity, when I talk about developmental milestones I am describing what "normal" development looks like. I put quotes around the word *normal* because it is such a loaded word that can conjure up anxiety and fear in parents. As a father, I have noticed myself and other parents, within seconds of meeting each other, asking, "How old is your baby?" followed by some developmental statement or judgment. It seems to be human nature to make comparisons to be sure our babies are developing within normal limits, because we all want that for our children.

However, I want to caution you about the use of the word *normal*.

It is meant to describe a wide range of developmental characteristics, but children develop different capacities at sometimes wildly different rates. For example, a child may be walking but not talking, or crawling but not eating solid foods. There are so many variables to consider with respect to developmental milestones—what is within normal limits and what is considered "delayed"—that I question the wisdom and accuracy of comparing children, particularly babies.

When parents learn that there may be a delay in their child's development, it can be a source of great anxiety and concern. In my work with them, I try to help them stay calm first and, after that, work toward making rational decisions about how to handle the situation. A fearful or anxious parent is common but typically

Consider This

Ask yourself if worrying about your baby's development has more to do with you than the baby. For instance, did you grow up with high standards and great expectations from your parents and little in the way of acceptance? Are you concerned about keeping up with the Joneses at playgroup or positioning your child so he or she gets into the "premier" day care?

not helpful in making sound decisions. Whether it's you or your partner who's flustered, work hard at trying to lessen your worry. I am not saying don't be vigilant if you see something that concerns you—by all means investigate it if you feel it would help you—but be mindful and aware of your anxiety. There are coping strategies if not solutions to your concerns.

The developmental milestones presented here focus primarily on "normal" development and only touch upon developmental delays, as it is beyond the scope of this book. If ever you have a question about your child's growth and development, you should consult your pediatrician. In some cases you will be referred to a developmental psychologist for an evaluation.

DEVELOPMENTAL MILESTONES AND YOU

Developmental psychologists and pediatricians generally agree on five development markers or skills to look out for when assessing your child. They are:

Gross motor skills: the use of large muscle groups to stand, sit, balance, walk, change positions, and run.

Fine motor skills: the use of hands and fingers to pick things up, draw, write, dress, and so on.

Language skills: verbal and non-verbal communication as well as understanding what others say.

Cognitive skills: includes learning, comprehension, problem solving, reasoning, and remembering skills.

Social skills: includes interacting with others, picking up on social cues and body language, and having relationships with others where there is cooperation and responding to the feelings of others.

In the following sections, I divide the milestones and skills under the following headings: Physical and Behavioral Development, Emotional and Psychological Development, Cognitive Skills, Language Skills, and Social Skills.

Physical and Behavioral Development

From a physical standpoint, the first year is the fastest period of growth people will ever experience in their lives. Babies begin with more than seventy-five reflexes that they utilize and build on so that by the end of the first year, for example, they can walk. While some aspects of behavioral development can be exciting to watch, initially you'll find that your newborn does very little besides sleep. Newborns start out as a sack of potatoes and end the year as wobbly little puppies.

> **TIP**
>
> Begin solid foods with easy-to-swallow purees. Avoid raw fruits or vegetables such as grapes, raw carrots, and raw apples, as they are choking hazards.

You might notice:	You can respond by:
As a newborn, he does a lot of sucking, swallowing, gagging, grabbing, and stepping; he likes to sleep; he gradually begins to hold his head up at a 45-degree angle. Poor ability to focus or discriminate colors, with eyes closed most of the time or, when open, crossed.	Letting him suck your finger. Carrying him around a lot in the beginning. Placing him on his back to sleep, to minimize the risk of SIDS. Respond to her cries quickly to build trust. Holding objects 8 to 12 inches away and moving them slowly to help him practice focusing. Celebrating when he does something like lift his head.
Around 3 months he is able to keep his hands open and can clap; while lying on his back he can roll from back to side or rock on his belly. He smiles more and is able to lock eyes with you; his hands go into his mouth; he has developed a death grip and grabs at hair, earrings, etc.	Mirroring him. When he smiles at you, smile back; when he claps, clap back. Getting down on his level as much as possible; letting him reach out to you and touch. Connecting with him by feeding him, whether it's bottles or, later, solid foods.
Around 6 months he can control pacifier use; he becomes adept at sitting up on his own; teething begins; he is showing signs of rolling over and may be able to push his torso off the floor; he can prop himself up on hands and knees; he is getting ready to crawl, maybe even pull himself up onto his feet. He prefers contrasting colors like black and white, is interested in faces. He can move his head and eyes fixed on a moving object. Depth perception is fully developed; he likes to watch objects disappear. The first signs of teeth begin around 6 months, and he'll have about eight teeth by his first birthday.	Intentionally giving him "tummy time" around 4 months. Have him lay on his stomach for a few minutes every day until he gets frustrated. This will help him build back and neck muscles and by 6 months he will be able to prop himself up. Holding your closed fist about 10 inches away and then slowly opening your fist, one finger at a time. Giving your baby teething toys or a clean, frozen wet washcloth. Brushing soon after you see the first tooth. Limiting pacifier use, since we now know it can cause overbite.

You might notice:	You can respond by:
Around 9 months he may be standing with support; he could be taking his first steps; he pulls things down; he's not aware of his own strength; he's able to help a little with dressing himself. He recognizes the familiar and unfamiliar.	Making sure he doesn't roll off couches, chairs, changing table, etc. Even if he usually stays put when you leave him in one position, there's no telling when he'll learn a new move. Baby proofing the home.
Around 12 months he is able to focus and adjust to far and near objects; his vision motivates him to get involved in the world. He may be walking on his own.	Being vigilant in watching him and supervising him—making sure he is not going near stairs, putting things in his mouth, or touching things he shouldn't be touching.

TIP

Newborns typically lose 5 percent to 10 percent of their birth weight in the first week of life. Full-term babies are usually back to birth weight within 2 weeks; preterm babies may take a week or longer.

TIP

Never leave your baby alone with a bottle, as she could possibly remove the nipple and choke on it.

MEASURING UP

Average Weight
• Birth: 5 to 10 pounds
• 6 months: 13 to 21 pounds
• 12 months: 17 to 28 pounds

Average Height
• Birth: 18 to 21 inches
• 6 months: 24 to 28 inches
• 12 months: 27 to 32 inches

Emotional and Psychological Development

The emotional development of a newborn through her first year may seem slow at first, but gradually she becomes more alive and active the older she gets. As she spends more time awake the more you will be able to get a sense of her emotional temperament. Small children seek that which is pleasurable. Usually what pleases a baby at this age is putting things in her mouth—Freud called this the "oral phase."

You might notice:	You can respond by:
During the first months, she may cry a lot. She makes certain sounds to get attention. At birth she likes to cuddle skin to skin (called "kangaroo care"), be wrapped in a swaddle or sling, and be held close while feeding.	Letting her cry for no more than a minute as a newborn; as she gets older the length of time can increase ever so slightly. Swaddling for the first 4 months. Showing her happy animated facial expressions. Using sounds that communicate your sympathy, compassion, and love; mirroring back to her what you see or hear. Paying attention to her type of cry. This helps her in the development of the self.
Stranger or separation anxiety sets in around 6 to 9 months. She can pick up on your moods.	Creating a happy home and being happy. Playing peekaboo, looking at books with pictures hidden behind flaps, rolling balls back and forth, stacking blocks and knocking them down.
She likes pulling things, animal sounds, repetitive games, and water.	Playing with toys that she can push and pull with a string, playing repetitive games, making animal sounds, and splashing in the water.

Deciphering Different Cries

It can be a challenge to decipher what your baby is crying about. Is she needing one of the BIG FIVE? Is she tired, hungry, uncomfortable, or just letting off some steam? How should you respond? (And, by the way, not every cry needs to be directly responded to.) You will likely find yourself confused, uncomfortable, and sometimes quite distressed about what your little one is trying to say when she cries. Here are some possibilities:

I need attention. You know the cry has to do with attention when you give her attention and the crying suddenly stops. By the way, there is nothing manipulative or wrong about a newborn needing attention—we all need attention.

I'm unhappy I've been separated. When your baby has formed attachments to people, places, and things and those things are taken away, crying and screaming can and will follow. She will get over it. Young children tend to have their feelings and then move on.

I'm in discomfort or pain. This cry may be quiet at first and then become loud, a clear communication that your child is experiencing a pain of some sort. It may be due to a rash on his bottom, teething, or a fall and bump on his head.

I'm tired. This cry tends to be less enthusiastic and is generally accompanied by yawns or the rubbing of eyes—dead giveaways.

Feed me. This is often a whiny cry and perhaps a little more difficult to discern. Again, you'll know she is crying from hunger if it stops once food has been offered (and accepted).

I might have colic. This is often indicated by inconsolable crying, usually in the evening and nighttime. The causes are not completely known but experts suspect that it is abdominal pain due to intestinal gas. This condition almost always goes away by the end of the third month. Here are some tips for coping with colic, which may seem, at times, intolerable:

- Swaddle, keeping your baby in a warm, womblike setting.
- Rock, move, and pace, lifting your baby up and down in a slow elevator-like fashion.
- Ask your pediatrician if there is anything you can give her.
- Take breaks for stress relief. If your partner is the primary caregiver, relieve her. If you are, ask for a breather.

Consider This

If you don't know what your child is feeling, use your own emotional barometer to figure it out. Many times what you are feeling is a byproduct of your child's emotions. It's what therapists call "induced feelings." So if you find yourself feeling intense anger, impatience, or irritability, there's a good possibility that your child is feeling the same thing.

Cognitive Skills

As you watch your baby become a person, particularly before he develops the ability to speak, you may find yourself wondering,

"What is he thinking?" It's a great thing to be curious about. Keep wondering this as he grows and—guess what?—someday she will be able to tell you. Cognitive skills develop slowly and cover things such as reasoning, problem solving, and thinking with intention. The brain grows more during the first year than at any other time, reaching approximately 60 percent of its adult size by the end of the first year.

You might notice:	You can respond by:
When objects are out of sight, they literally don't exist anymore (abstract thought comes at around 9 months). Around 3 months he is fascinated by the world; he begins to understand cause and effect; he is able to respond to names and familiar voices. Little intentional thinking.	Playing peekaboo or hiding objects and making them appear. Stimulating his thinking with age-appropriate toys and objects. Playing soft music.
Around 3 months he is fascinated by the world; he begins to understand cause and effect; he is able to respond to names and familiar voices.	Stimulating his thinking with age-appropriate toys, objects, books.
That there is major brain wiring going on—you can almost watch it happen—but there is very little intentional thinking.	Playing soft music for her.
Around 6 months there is evidence of more sophisticated cognitive wiring as he intentionally chooses to crawl and move his legs and arms.	Creating a mini obstacle course or hiding an object to see if he can find it. Make it really easy and watch his delight in solving these small-to-you but big-to-him problems. Be curious about what his little brain is thinking.
Around 9–12 months cognition informs behavior, so there is more intentional (as well as impulsive) activity with little to no sense of consequences.	Playing games to foster cognition, such as hiding an object with a napkin and letting him find it.

Language Skills

Your baby won't be able to speak clearly until she is about two and a half, although significant strides are made during her first year. Consider this time a primer for a lifetime of conversation.

You might notice:	You can respond by:
Around birth her main form of communication is crying; she is also grunting, squeaking, and cooing.	Talking to her as much as possible. Mimic her, name the feeling she seems to be expressing, tell her you understand and reassure her that all will be well. Gentle humming or singing can be comforting, if not for her then for you.
Around 3 months she recognizes familiar sounds and responds; she tries to speak; she's working on volume control; she begins to babble; she draws out single syllable words—*baaa, maaa, laaa, kaaa, paaa*—for no reason; she begins to laugh and giggle.	Pointing to objects and saying the words. For example, point to the sun and say, "sun."
Around 6 months she babbles more and is able to say her first words; she makes two-syllable sounds—*dada, mama*—without intention; she cries less and talks more; she begins using body language to communicate needs, such as by pointing fingers, reaching, and squirming.	Getting in the habit of talking her through what you are doing as you do it. For example, "It's time for nigh nigh," or "It's time for bath."
Around 9 months she expands her vocabulary almost daily; she continues to talk "baby talk" (it's very important to listen to it); she says *mama* and *dada* intentionally; she may be able to tell you when she has a wet or soiled diaper; she understands the word *no* but does not typically obey.	Repeating the long vowel sounds. There is no need to talk like a baby back to her. Speak in your normal tone. Again, mimicking her is a great way for her to know that you are paying attention.

You might notice:	You can respond by:
Around 12 months she can say some words but only you'll know what she means. She imitates your phone conversations, sometimes with the same inflection.	Talking, talking, and talking, even when you'd prefer silence. Continue to read to her.

Social Skills

You might not think of babies as having much in the way of social skills. Well, they don't, because social skills, particularly "appropriate" social skills take time to learn, such as not pinching daddy's nose or pulling grandma's hair. Clear limits around what is "nice" and what is "no, ouchy" are important to establish early, even though your child won't understand right away.

You might notice:	You can respond by:
At birth he has very basic needs and doesn't deliberately socialize. But generally he'll like to be held and touched, and may smile fleetingly.	Playing with him as much as possible.
Around 3 months he responds to tickling, funny sounds, or kisses on his belly (dads seem to have a great ability to get their babies to laugh, so take advantage of it); he's able to make gestures to signal when he wants to be picked up.	Getting down on his level. Gently tickle, blow gently in his face, blow gentle raspberries, and give him kisses on his belly.
Around 6 months he uses his body and voice to express himself; he's better able to mimic facial gestures.	Teaching him about what is "yes" and what is "no."
Around 9 months he responds to his own name and uses more intentional body gestures like arms up in the air to get picked up or falling to the ground when upset.	Interacting by playing the "so big" game with arms outstretched.
Around 12 months he is able to wave bye-bye; he points to things he wants, says *no* and shakes his head no.	Correcting aggressive touching (he won't know social boundaries), playing with floppy or bouncy items to spur laughter.

> **TIP**
>
> From a very early age babies will imitate what they see. This is spurred by mimic neurons. If you place your face about 8 to 12 inches away from your baby and stick your tongue out, he will likely do it too.

CONCERNS ABOUT DEVELOPMENT

Get used to being told what percentile your child is in with respect to weight, length, height, and even head circumference. Knowing these details can be reassuring to a parent. But at the same time, it can be hard not to worry if your little one is not "measuring up" or is "off the charts." Suffice it to say that each newborn grows at his or her unique pace. If you are concerned about how your child is growing and developing in any of the milestone areas, talk with your pediatrician. Most of the time any worry you might have can be easily be mitigated by information and or subtle shifts in routine. It is important to talk about these concerns before you and your family fall into habits that will be harder to break later on. Other times the worry is a little more serious and it may be the case that your baby is delayed in some way. Talking with your pediatrician and explaining your concerns in detail will help you figure out what to do next. Even if it's just a gut feeling but you have no concrete evidence for concern, err on the side of talking with your baby's doctor.

> **TIP**
>
> The "soft spots" on an infant's head are called fontanels. They allow the skull to grow. There are normally four fontanels, at the top, back, and sides of the head. They close over time (between one and nineteen months) and become solid bone.

The Brazelton Approach

T. Berry Brazelton is a professor of pediatrics emeritus at Harvard Medical School and author of more than forty books on child development. His theory is worth considering when you watch your child grow. The theory can be explained like this: "Children develop their skills in many different areas at the same time. When children show a sudden burst in one area of development, they often regress, or backslide, in another area. These bursts can disorganize children's feelings and actions and disrupt caregiving routines, such as feeding and sleeping. Just think of the budding toddler who has just learned to walk and now no longer wants to nap predictably or sit for a meal!" Brazelton believes this is a positive sign that development is moving forward, but parents and health-care providers might find themselves worried, or disagreeing with one another over what to do about it.

In some ways it is two steps forward, one step back. What I like about this approach is that it honors the part within humans that may be ambivalent about growing up. It also teaches parents that development is progressive *and* regressive. Sometime we need to fall back to move forward. Brazelton suggests that a parent can expect these touchpoints or regressions to occur at three weeks, six to eight weeks, four months, seven months, nine months, twelve months, fifteen months, eighteen months, and two years. For more information on the Brazelton approach toward child development, check out www.touchpoints.org.

Primary Needs in the First Year

As I've previously mentioned, the five primary needs of a newborn do not shift too dramatically over the course of the first year (or across the lifespan for that matter). As you take care of your baby, you can self-assess how well those needs are being met. No one achieves perfection, and remember: There may be times when the right thing is for your baby to satisfy her own need. For example, a newborn can self-soothe by sucking her thumb. Think of yourself and your partner as the primary satisfier of needs who observes and allows your baby as she grows in her ability to care for herself.

HOLDING

Why do newborns *need* to be held, and what is the father's role in the holding department? Newborns have been "held" for nine months in the womb. The need to be held is left over from the warm holding that the womb provided. This is why newborns respond so well to being swaddled. It provides a sense of security. The more you can provide womblike holding for your infant, the better, because it establishes a foundation of contentment and trust in your child.

Hold Me Now

Since newborns sleep a lot, you won't have to hold your baby too much. Still, time spent holding your child, even when she doesn't need it, will help you bond with her. (I'm of the belief that lots of holding does *not* encourage "spoiling" of babies.) You will both be getting to know each other through the practice of holding. Your baby will get to know you through her senses . . . smell, touch, sight, and hearing.

I recently met with a group of dads as a part of my research for this book and a common theme that came out was the awkwardness most new dads feel in comforting a crying baby. Many men worry that they'll either drop the baby or hold it too tightly, too. If your partner is in need of sleep or recovering from labor or if you simply want to hold your baby, you will need to learn what soothes her.

A father's hold may be distinctively different than a mother's. For instance, your strength may enable you to hold the baby in a variety of positions and for longer periods of time. Below are a few holds for you to experiment with. Whatever hold you choose, keep in mind that it is critical at this early age that you provide your baby with solid back, neck, and head support.

Different Ways to Hold

There are a number of holds you can experiment with, but an exhaustive study is beyond this book's scope. Try these out for size and see which one(s) best suit you and your baby.

The chest hold. I'll never forget watching our hospital pediatrician hold our baby. He seemed so comfortable and confident that he wasn't going to hurt the baby. As he examined the baby he held him firmly on the front of the chest and flipped him over to examine him, all the while supporting his head. It was so great to watch another man handle him with such care and confidence. The chest hold was something I adopted for transferring newborns from their front side to their back side.

The traditional hold. This hold is best for when you are in a seated position. It very much mirrors the hold a mom would use when breastfeeding and works particularly well when the baby is swaddled. The front of the baby is pressed against your belly by your arm or arms, which support his back. Be mindful of tension in your shoulders and try to drop them. Pay close attention to your breathing patterns—I recall holding my son in this position and experiencing some of the deepest breaths I've ever experienced. Your calm breathing can calm your baby.

The shoulder hold. The baby faces in toward you with his head on your shoulder. This can be an awkward hold for your shoulders when the baby is really tiny. It may become more comfortable while you're lying down. This is a particularly great hold for skin-to-skin contact, as the baby can inhale your particular body scent and will be able to recognize that scent in the future.

The football hold. This is one of my favorite holds and is best used between two and nine months of age. The newborn is facing out and secured to your one arm. His back is up against the right or left side of your midsection, depending on what's more comfortable. Your forearm will gradually slide under his arm and your hand is situated in his crotch. He's positioned almost like the football in the Heisman Trophy statue. This hold is usually best when the baby is swaddled and while you are standing or pacing. This hold continues to be a great one to utilize even after your baby has shed the swaddling blanket.

Swaddling

Don't leave the hospital without being taught how to swaddle your baby. This is one of the first skills or tricks a father can learn, and it will often come in handy over the next couple months. Try the burrito method:

1. Place a swaddling blanket down on a large flat surface.
2. Dog-ear one corner.
3. Place your baby on his back so that his head extends off the dog-eared corner.
4. Take the right side of the blanket and fold it across your baby's chest, including the arms, and tuck it under his left side.
5. Take the part of the blanket at your baby's feet and fold that up to the chest (fold it down if the blanket covers your baby's face).
6. Take the left side of the blanket and fold it across your baby's chest, tuck it snugly underneath your baby's body, and secure.
7. Hold your baby firmly.

Real Dad

"Someone once told me that I held my baby too much and that I would spoil him. So what?! If a baby depends on being held by me, I see this as a good psychological achievement."

—Walt, 25

Winning Strategies for Soothing a Crying Child

- Hold him.
- Rock him.
- Pace with him.
- If your child can express himself, listen to him. Sometimes children know exactly what they are feeling.
- Take nice long, deep breaths for yourself. Your baby may be tense, but you don't have to be. As you relax, your baby will relax too.

FEEDING

If your partner is breastfeeding, you may have occasional opportunities to feed your newborn with breastmilk in a bottle. But you can play a critical role in assisting your partner to breastfeed, whether it is by getting the baby from his crib and handing him to his mother for feeding, or, if (or when) the baby is taking formula feedings, you can make bottles and clean the supplies. You may even become the primary expert on these things in your household. Soon after my wife stopped breastfeeding, she was baffled by all the bottle-feeding options. Here I could be her competent helper.

> **TIP**
>
> Though you may be tempted to be jealous of your partner's bonding time during breastfeeding, remember that breastmilk is liquid gold and should be treated with great respect.

SLEEPING

Babies need to sleep in order to grow. Finding the right sleeping system and routine for your family and baby can be one of the first major challenges. It's potentially a very contentious issue between couples who are generally used to full nights of sleep. Couples will argue over how soon to pick up the baby, where the baby sleeps, and who should get the baby in the middle of the night. Don't wait to

develop your sleep plan together. Unless there is one of you who really wants to take responsibility (for instance, if one of you is staying home to take care of the infant), reinforce the idea of taking shifts before you go to bed. For example: You get the baby if he wakes up between 11 P.M. and 3 A.M., your partner gets him if he wakes between 3 A.M. and 7 A.M. Or alternate days.

If you notice your baby is sleepy, try getting into a cozy and comfortable holding position and very gently run the tip of your finger in between his eyes and over the bridge of his nose. This is a calming gesture, and you may notice that this helps your baby close his eyes.

Jean Kunhardt, psychotherapist, author of *A Mother's Circle*, and cofounder of Soho Parenting in New York City, has discovered that parents' work schedules and their baby's sleeping schedule often clash. In Jean's work with couples, dads report that they rush home in excitement to see, hold, and play with the baby. But the baby is about to go to sleep, and now the routine has been disrupted. Understanding their excitement, Jean advises dads to either be home in time to be a quiet and calm part of the bedtime ritual, or plan to arrive home after the baby is asleep.

To encourage your baby to sleep, consider the following:
• A fresh diaper, clean clothes, and full tummy can go a long way to support sleeping.
• Fill his awake time with activity, so he's adequately sleepy for naps and bedtime.
• Try putting your baby down to

sleep while he is drowsy but still awake.

- Develop a naptime or bedtime ritual, such as rocking or dimming the lights.
- Babies love routine. Track his naptimes to keep him on a consistent schedule.

More likely, you'll be the one who's sleep deprived, not the baby. For more information, consult the companion book *Great Expectations: Baby Sleep Guide* by Sandy Jones and Marcie Jones.

CLEANING

Babies need to be kept clean but that shouldn't be confused with needing daily baths. For the first couple of months babies need only a weekly bath. And a bath for a newborn is really not much of a soaker; it's more like a sponge bath, and soap isn't even necessary for the first few weeks. However, there are a couple safety matters worth mentioning: (1) Test the water temperature with your wrist so that it's not too hot for baby skin, and (2) As you wash your baby, make sure you have a good hold on him, as he might be slippery when wet. (See chapter 6 for bathing gear suggestions, such as infant tubs and the like.)

Diaper Changes

If you are not using cloth diapers, then I would recommend diapers with more Velcro-like—as opposed to adhesive—closures. Adhesive may stick to and hurt your baby's skin.

During the first few weeks your baby will poop a black tarlike material called meconium.

After that, his bowel movements will resemble a mustardlike substance, which has a smell that only a parent can delight in. This is a sign that your baby is digesting his meals.

With the diaper opened wide and the adhesives or tapes facing up, place baby's bottom in the middle of the diaper. Bring the front of the diaper up between your baby's legs and onto his belly. Bring tapes or closures around and fasten snugly.

As you diaper your boy, point his penis down so that he doesn't urinate up and out of the diaper. For girls, wipe down and away from the vaginal area.

Umbilical Cord Care

Your newborn will be discharged from the hospital with a plastic clamp on the inch-long umbilical cord stub. The stub should fall off on its own within the first week or two. Apply rubbing alcohol to the base of the cord three times per day. This will help the area stay clean and will assist the cord in falling off. Never pull the cord off, and watch so that it doesn't rub too much against the diaper. If you suspect an infection, or if the cord has not fallen off within a month, talk to your pediatrician.

Circumcision Care

Circumcisions usually heal within ten days, and the care involved is fairly straightforward. First, keep the area clean with a gentle soap and water. Then you'll want to use some petroleum jelly on the penis until it is healed. Some pediatricians recommend a gauze covering, too—others do not. Finally, do not be alarmed if your newborn's circumcised penis is red, oozing some yellowish fluid, or has a tiny bit of spotty bleeding—these are all normal. But you'll want to contact your pediatrician if there is excessive bleeding, if your baby seems to have trouble urinating, or if he has a fever, swelling, and/or crusty sores.

GETTING MEDICAL CARE

Nothing seems to give new parents the jitters (and rightly so) as the thought of their baby needing medical care. A proactive approach can go a long way in reducing your concern, so I advise parents in my practice to do as many of the following things as possible before baby is born.

Pick a Pediatrician

It's essential that you trust your baby's doctor. When selecting a pediatrician, find out about her philosophy, whether it's a holistic (broad, in consideration of the whole body) or a medical model, and how she feels about medication, vaccinations, and other interventions. There is a wide range of approaches. Assess what feels right to you and your partner. Get referrals from friends you trust, as well as recommendations from your family doctor, hospital, and midwife or obstetrician. Most doctors will take a few minutes of their time for a prenatal interview

with new parents, but that is all. Pay attention to how the doctor fields your questions. Does the doctor have experience caring for special-needs (such as premature) infants? Are there any readily available special services within the practice, such as lactation consulting? Do you feel you can ask the so-called stupid questions? On your first visit, pay close attention to how the doctor is with your baby, how he handles and holds him.

Take an Infant CPR Class

Learning infant CPR (cardio-pulmonary resuscitation) is highly recommended, especially since the baby will be putting things in her mouth from about the age of six months to three years. Classes are offered through community centers, hospitals, and local chapters of the American Red Cross or American Heart Association, and they don't require a lot of time. In this case, no book is a substitute for the hands-on learning of a class—be sure the instructor is certified. Also, keep in mind that there are separate CPR courses for when your baby is a year or older.

Buy a First Aid Kit

Consider buying a first aid kit for the home and for each car you own. First aid kits are handily preassembled, but you can make your own, too. See www.redcross.org for a list of items the American Red Cross recommends for every first aid kit. Be sure to check on items in the kit that may be too old and need replacing, and replenish it as items are used.

Observe Your Baby

Your observation and touch are important ways to discern if your baby is sick. If he's pale, seems lethargic, or has lost his usual verve, pay attention to that. Feel his forehead and other parts of his body to see if he's warm or hot and adjust his clothing and blanketing to make sure he is not overheated. Babies tend to run slightly higher temperatures than adults, typically around 99°F to 100°F. Some bacterial infections cause fevers to go up to 102°F and some viruses can cause a spike up to 105°F.

Buy a good infant thermometer (usually for the ear) and keep a log of how well he's eating, how frequently you're changing diapers, his temperature, and any other observations. When in doubt, call your pediatrician.

CHALLENGES OF NEW FATHERHOOD

The first year of fatherhood is likely to be one of the most rewarding times of your life. It can also be a great roller-coaster ride, with feelings of elation and pride and love one moment, followed by frustration, feelings of incompetence, fear, and even loathing the next moment. It is important for men to at least acknowledge and perhaps give voice to these feelings and challenges and to seek the support and help they need to overcoming them.

Fear of Hurting the Baby

For some men, the skills required to fulfill their baby's needs are instinctual. Many others are baffled for to how to care for a newborn. Many dads describe a pervasive fear that they may hurt their tiny baby and can't imagine how to hold a baby. They may be paralyzed by fears of dropping the baby, or of SIDS, or worry that they could injure, traumatize, or even kill their infant. You are not alone if you are feeling protective or fearful about how you will manage it all or if you're having difficulty making the necessary adjustments.

Real Dad

"At the end of my daughter's 9-month checkup, I showed the doctor a small splinter in her ankle. The doctor said the splinter would come out on its own and that forcing it could cause more trauma than it was worth. Sure enough, it did come out on its own, and I learned that fixing things is not always necessary."

—Timothy, 34

It doesn't make you a bad dad, just a human one.

As we all know, life at this stage is fragile and needs to be cared for with great tenderness. Because newborns are so fragile there are certain precautions one should take to protect even the healthiest of babies. Remember, too, that you and your partner are also in a fragile place at this stage, both emotionally and practically speaking. Tenderness should be extended to the both of you as well.

> **TIP**
>
> To prevent SIDS (sudden infant death syndrome), put your baby to sleep on his back instead of his stomach and keep pillows, quilts, and stuffed toys out of his crib. To find out more about SIDS from the American Academy of Pediatrics, visit www.aap.org.

Postpartum Depression

Postpartum depression (PPD) does not discriminate; both moms and dads experience it. It is more common for new moms to feel sad and tearful after the birth of their baby. In fact, it occurs in roughly 10 percent of postpartum women. The fluctuation in hormone levels alone seems to justify the condition, but I think the emotional and practical demands associated with giving birth and motherhood also add

to it. PPD is characterized by a severe depression that usually sets in within the first few months of motherhood. It can be very serious if proper treatment is not sought. It can cause a rupture in the relationship between mother and baby, and can also place huge strains on you and your marriage. In worst-case scenarios, the new mom becomes incapable of caring for her baby and may benefit from medication and or hospitalization. For the new dad this can be difficult and may require additional help from family, friends, and hired help to assist in caring for the baby. Many new dads who witness their wives in the throes of postpartum depression often feel like they're in nothing but survival mode. There are thousands of courageous men, ones you often don't hear about, struggling mightily through this unwanted affliction.

But PPD can afflict dads as well. One of my patients, Jim, had a very hard time making the transition after his first baby was born. During the first few months Jim and his wife decided that he would be the primary caregiver for their baby because, between their two careers, Jim's was the one that was more flexible and less profitable. As a freelance writer, he could more easily resume his work after they adjusted to the first couple of months. The first few weeks were great—he loved spending time with his baby. But at the same time he noticed a growing resentment that the baby was interrupting his sleep and that his work was indefinitely being put on hold.

It was a confusing time for Jim. He felt cornered and increasingly depressed and anxious. And then one day he reported a symptom that is often associated with PPD in new moms: the scary thought of throwing his baby out the window. Jim assured me that these were just thoughts and that he would never act on them, but he knew he needed some help to deal with all the changes in his life.

Jim is not alone. According to a recent study by James Paulson of Eastern Virginia Medical School, fathers of nine-month-olds are about twice as likely as other men their age to show symptoms of major depression. Certainly this impacts the father and mother but this research also indicates that it affects children too—they tend to know slightly fewer words by age two. *USA Today* reported about Paulson's study, "Depression in mothers is known to hamper children's academic performance and mental health. But the study on fathers . . . [suggests] that fathers' depression in early childhood affects children [too]."

With fathers taking a more active role in childrearing, they have to balance parenthood and career. A lot of new dads are opting to be their baby's primary caregiver. It is critically important for Jim and others in his situation to talk through their feelings and come to a determination of what they need most. Things for Jim got harder before they got better, but they did get better with the help of therapy and medication. This is one of the many aspects of fatherhood, and parenthood for that matter, that rarely gets acknowledged.

Wondering, Wandering, and Infidelity

For some new dads, having a baby undoubtedly brings them and their wives closer. Their sex life is heightened, their emotional intimacy is enhanced, and they feel their connection has grown deeper as a result. It is also true that many new dads feel a growing distance or wedge between themselves and their wives. Some feel they are grossly undersexed and may find themselves wondering what it would be like to be with other women, or they may begin to question their love for their partner.

With a baby in the picture, it is hard for them to bail on the marriage. Yet many men feel they can't bring it up with their partners for fear of igniting World War III. They feel stuck. Some men do more than just wonder; some actually wander and act on their curiosity. It is very common for new dads to either wonder about or wander away from their marriage. I'm reminded of the truism that "an unmet need does not go away." For many men, sex is a need that doesn't get met during the first year, so it's important to identify a marital problem and find some ways to cope.

For many new dads, whether it's wondering or wandering, here are four common reasons for feeling discontented:

1. I've been demoted. A man may feel secondary now that the baby has arrived and his partner has a new first love or top priority.

2. I'm not attracted to her anymore. A man may feel his partner has lost her good looks or that her

body has become flabby or her breasts are no longer "his."
3. I'm not getting any sex. A couple's sex life may decrease significantly during the baby's first year for multiple reasons, such as being too tired, or not interested, lack of time, and so on.
4. I'm still ambivalent. Perhaps a man went into his marriage and even into fatherhood with ambivalence that didn't get resolved.

Scott Haltzman, M.D., author of *The Secrets of Happily Married Men*, suggests a fifth reason: "They no longer see their wife as a sexual object, she is now *mother* and, for some men, seeing their wife as mother reminds them too much of their own mother." This, of course, often happens on an unconscious level and men need to become conscious of the feeling so that it can be dealt with.

Here are four possible coping strategies for the discontented dad:
1. Recruit an "accountability partner." Share your concerns with someone you trust.
2. Out yourself. The act of keeping a secret gives it great power.
3. Get plenty of physical exercise. It is one of the best ways to get out some of your sexual or other frustrations.
4. Masturbate more often. When your libido doesn't match hers, this is a slightly more direct way to take care of your needs. Sometimes it is a necessary coping strategy.

The First Birthday

Congratulations—you made it through the first year! As you read through this chapter, you were inducted into the world of your growing one-year-old. You learned ways to support your partner and your baby's growth, how to respond and care for him, and a few of the potential challenges to the first-year of fatherhood.

The first birthday is a true milestone worth celebrating. The firstborn child usually gets the "full treatment" birthday party. As a father of three I admit that each successive child got a slightly less flamboyant celebration. Let's get one thing clear: The first birthday celebration is more for the parents than it is for the child. That's okay;

making it through the first year is a great reason to celebrate. Here are some ways to make it memorable without feeling the need to go over the top:
• Capture moments through pictures or video.
• Ask attendees to write their names or make a drawing on a big sheet of paper as a record of the event. Keep it with the baby's other keepsakes.
• Save the newspaper from that day.
• Write your child a note about this day and how it makes you feel. Refrain from lofty notes about how you want him to go to Harvard Law and how high your aspirations are for him. Capture

things he did, who was there, and the vibe of the day.

• Invite grandparents. Keep it simple.

By now you might be feeling like an expert in how to meet your baby's developmental needs. This will be the ongoing challenge. The next chapter will focus on balancing his needs with yours and your partner's—not an easy task, but certainly one worth taking up.

Real Dad

"My son turned one and when I saw the birthday guest list, I realized he knew more people than I did!"

—Uri, 42

REFLECTION QUESTIONS

1. What routines or rituals are helping you care for your baby? Where does your family need help in making the necessary adjustments? For example: If your partner is breastfeeding, how is it going? Does she need a lactation consultant?

2. What skills do you need to develop? For example, soothing, diapering, etc.?

3. What's been the best part of being a dad so far, and what's been the most challenging?

4. How have you changed? What shifts in your behavior, thinking, or feeling have you noticed?

Striking a Balance: Family, Work, and Self

Trying to Do It All

With the rise of dual-income households, shared parenting or co-parenting, and third-party caregivers (relatives, babysitters, or nannies) it can be a real challenge to balance it all. Sometimes it will feel like all the world is conspiring against you. The confluence of needs and demands forces a new dad to make tough decisions between work and family and, for many dads, work wins out and family time suffers.

Family time is not an easy thing for a new dad to sacrifice. In my work with new dads I am regularly struck by how much they long to be home with their kids. Their often unmet desire to be home does not get talked about too much but it is prevalent, real, and profound. The dad who can't find much wiggle room in his schedule can find ways to be present even in his absence. (I will explain this more a little later in the chapter.) For most dads the very real experience of being tired, stretched thin, consumed by myriad responsibilities—to work, other deadlines, family, friends, bottom lines, e-mails, missing socks, a partner you hardly see anymore—is commonly associated with the feeling that you are barely surviving and letting everyone down.

Four things to remember: (1) You can only do your best at fathering, working, maintaining a marriage, and taking care of yourself, and it's all really hard work; (2) Priorities can be shifted, and creative solutions can be found and reevaluated; (3) This too shall pass and nothing stays the same; and (4) Help and support is out there, so if you need help, get it!

With so many demands placed on you, life can seem overwhelming and lead to heightened, stress, anxiety, and depression. I've got some ideas for what you can do to reduce the strain, like *setting priorities, establishing a division of labor,* and *getting a better understanding of your fatherly instincts.*

WHAT GETS AFFECTED?

In a word: everything. The apple cart has been upset. Even though your baby may be small his impact has had a dramatic shift on the dynamics of time, your memories/psyche, sense of purpose, sleep, relationship with your partner, and competing needs, just to name few. Fortunately and unfortunately this will have a trickle-down effect on your family, co-workers, and so on.

Your Time

Your sense of time will shift from something that appeared to be in your control to something that is largely dictated by the needs and demands of your baby, partner, and/or work, thus leaving you in a state anticipation or future focused. Alternatively, having a newborn can force you to live in the moment. You may find yourself—and I really encourage you to do this—observing your baby's every movement, noticing the rise and fall of his chest as he sleeps or pondering her little hands and tiny feet. There is nothing like a newborn baby to slow down time and make us realize how precious and fragile life is.

During the pregnancy the focus was on the future and all that came with preparing for and anticipating your baby's arrival. Now that the baby is here you might find yourself shifting into the present and, in particular, into what some parents call "survival mode." If having a baby is anything like having a dinner party, then the nine months of gestation was all about the preparation and planning. Once the guest of honor arrives, however, you have to switch gears to what is happening right now. And "right now" is going to last for, oh, at least eighteen to twenty-two years.

It's going to be a long dinner party and it will take a while before you hear any thank-yous for the meal, but it's well worth the effort. The point is that time is no longer just your own. This shift in how you spend your time will come as a welcome surprise for some and a total disruption for others. Pay attention to how you feel about it.

A typical week has anywhere from 105 to 115 waking hours. If you are working 80 hours per week that's 70 to 75 percent of your awake time, leaving you with 25 to 35 hours left to spend on yourself, your partner, and your baby, not to mention your friends and any surprises that may come up during the week. One recent report suggests that fathers spend, on average, 11 hours per week with their children. Everyone's time demands are different, but here are a few things to consider as you assess how to spend your time.

- Audit your time. Over the course of a month, log how much time "awake time" you spend at work, with your partner and/or family, with your friends, and by yourself. At the very least it will answer the age old question of "where does the time go?"

• Change your priorities. Note where you are lacking hours spent and make some changes as needed. (Need a hand with that? See more on page 80.)

Your Childhood Memories and Reflections

These are what I call psychic shifts. New thoughts and old memories come up about your own childhood. This will shift the way you think and feel about your father and inform what kind of father you want to be. Having a baby has a profound ability to force you into remembering moments that have been buried. Often times the goal in therapy, as Freud once put it, is to make the unconscious conscious, and this can become the work for the new dad who is experiencing increased irritability, acting differently, or flooded with old memories.

It is not always easy to figure out what we are not aware of. I believe most men are unaware of their emotions, whether it be anxiety, sadness, overprotectiveness, disengagement, or irritability. There are always at least two reasons for these reactions, the emotional past and the practical present. Unresolved or unprocessed emotions from the past can get resurrected and the practical demands of the present can contribute to your behavior. When the two combine it can cause quite a stir in the new dad and force him or his partner to wonder why he is having such strong reactions. For example, Luke, a patient of mine, kept wondering why he was

reacting so irritably after his baby was born. He was convinced that his reaction went deeper than just the practical demands of the present (that is, little sleep), and this sense guided us into deeper territory, helping him uncover an earlier life experience he was carrying around. When Jim was a year old he had an older brother, age three, who had died accidentally. Consequently, Jim and his parents didn't sleep well for years. Now, the combination of not sleeping well and having a year-old child—the same age he was when his older brother had died—seemed to inform his strong reaction.

Another common psychic shift is to put yourself in your father's shoes and ask questions like: How did my dad manage? Where was he? How involved was he? Who supported him? How did he support the family? The point here is that this newfound experience as a father can lead you to a deeper curiosity and investigation of who your father was. This, in turn, can lead to a greater appreciation and intimacy—or detachment and estrangement, depending on the nature of your relationship with your father. I'm regularly struck by how powerful it is to become a father—it really impacts us in the present and provides an opportunity to resolve stuff from the past.

Your Sense of Purpose

Many dads report experiencing a shift in how they perceive their purpose in life. For example, my patient Zack once said that he was no longer living just for himself. Since the birth of his newborn boy he was living for something much bigger. This "bigger" sense of purpose can make you feel connected to the past and the future. In John Badalament's PBS documentary *All Men Are Sons*, Terry Real, author and family therapist, says that dads are the "bridge" between your father and your sons.

I believe there is a shift in purpose because you've been on both sides of the creation process. It's a powerful thing, remarkable how such a tiny baby can make you feel powerful. I can recall times while holding my firstborn that my breathing was deeper than I had ever experienced. I like to think that this tiny little baby was allowing me to access something powerful and purposeful.

Your Sleep

One of the first questions you'll get from friends, family, and even strangers is, "So are you getting any sleep?" I've been tempted to reply, "Why, are you willing to help out with the midnight feeding?"

In most cases your partner will have already had plenty of experience with this compromised sleep thing. During the pregnancy, particularly in the last few weeks, she's probably had interrupted sleep due to discomfort, acid reflux, or some other reason. The whole sleep thing is a hot topic. Because our behavior is profoundly affected by how rested we are, nighttime feeding is one of the first matters you should tackle. Depending on your situation, it may mean you need to help out with nighttime feedings, or it

may mean that your partner will nurse the baby at night to keep her milk supply strong, allowing you those glorious extra minutes of slumber. Whatever situation you choose, most experts will tell you that a baby should be able to sleep through the night by about four months. This is something to mark on your calendar. If this doesn't happen for you, consult *Great Expectations: Baby Sleep Guide* by Sandy Jones and Marcie Jones.

Your Relationship with Your Partner

With a baby in your midst, you can count on changes in your relationship with your partner. This may largely be a function of different parenting styles, a difference in what you think is right for your child, or the fact that children change you and therefore change the relationship. When my son was born I was surprised at how important it was for me to sort and put away his clothes. The attention and care I exerted was above and beyond what I would've expected, yet I felt compelled to do it. My wife reacted unfavorably to this compulsive behavior. For her it meant that I was encroaching on a job that should have been hers. We were both finding our way as new parents and we were forced to confront new questions such as how to treat each other as we parented this baby. The key takeaway is to be conscious and open about any tensions that arise and commit to talking them through. (See chapter 9.)

Your Competing Needs

Welcome to the incredible challenge of juggling competing needs. There is no job in the world that will excite you and humble you more than being a father. Lesson number one: Realize now that because you will be confronted by competing needs, you will end up neglecting some and satisfying others. If both you and your partner work away from the home, then the challenge to tend to every need is made all the more difficult. Expect to have sleepless nights and to disappoint others.

A good friend of mine said to me in an accusing voice, as his son was about to turn one year old, "You never told me how hard it would be or how tired I would be." Ooops, had I neglected to mention that? My kids were older, and how soon we parents (want to) forget. My friend was working full-time as an executive assistant while simultaneously caring for his son during the day. When his wife came home at five thirty from her job, he went off to his art studio (his real passion) or finished up the work he hadn't been able to do during the day. When he returned home at approximately 1 A.M., he'd find his nine-month-old son still awake and raring to go. Countless attempts to get him to sleep failed. Nursing him, pacing with him, and all the usual tricks didn't work. They eventually had to find a system that worked for them, which they did quite by accident when they bought the baby an organic cotton mini blanket that became his security object. Turns out, babies between six and ten months are ripe for bonding with a transitional object, when they're mobile enough not to smother on small stuffed animals or lightweight mini blankets and are learning to self-soothe.

The challenge often becomes: How do I handle it when I can't fulfill either my own or others' needs? Can I forgive myself? Do I chastise myself for not being able to do more? Make no mistake about it, you will not do everything perfectly and you will disappoint others. You will have moments when you are stretched thin and left wondering if you are letting everyone down, including yourself, and doing more harm than good. All this is normal; just remember this is a new experience for you, your partner, and, of course, your baby, which makes all of you somewhat vulnerable and fragile. So keep in mind that you are not expected to be perfect. It is difficult for everyone to deal with competing needs.

When all these things—time, memories, sense of purpose, sleep, relationship with partner, and competing needs—are affected it can cause a considerable amount of stress and anxiety. Your challenge? Finding the fun in fathering. Each new dad needs to do his best, forgive himself for being human, and figure out his limits. The end result may be that it becomes important to accept that this is how it is for now and reexamine your expectations and priorities as your situation changes. And in the process, you'll find a lot of forgiveness among your friends and family, particularly among those who know the demands parenthood.

ADJUSTING EXPECTATIONS AND SETTING PRIORITIES

I can imagine that many dads will read this and say, "How do you expect me to balance an eighty-hour workweek and be a positive presence in the lives of both my child and my wife, not to mention find some 'me' time? Show me the time and energy!" The point is, you can't. One of the hardest things to do is to realize you can't do all that you used to do. While the necessity of working and paying the bills is inescapable, it will be important to constantly readjust your expectations and reevaluate your priorities after the baby comes home. Getting clear about what's important and what you value is mission critical. In my practice I often hear new dads talk about how little time there is for themselves, so I will start with that.

Self-care or "Me Time" Primer

Parenting requires you to sacrifice so much of your own needs that it can be easy to forget you have them. Or perhaps you weren't so good at self-care even before the baby arrived. Well, now you have a most compelling reason to get good at taking care of yourself . . . a baby who needs you to be around!

In my practice, one dad in particular, along with his wife, discovered that neither of them were going to get any "me time" unless they scheduled it. So now they both have "me time" at different points throughout the week. This helps nourish and rejuvenate you. I spend a whole chapter on this topic (see chapter 8).

Consider these suggestions for taking care of you:

• Take five minutes out of your day to just listen to yourself breathing.
• Take one hour a week and play a sport, do yoga, meditate, whatever.
• Get the physical examination you've been putting off.
• Drink six glasses of water per day.
• Close your office door and take fifteen minutes to just shut your eyes or even take a "power nap" at work.
• Walk around the block.
• Go to a movie by yourself.

Work

Before your baby arrived, perhaps you were accustomed to working long hours to provide for your family. Your presence at home is also vital, and it's probably where you'd prefer to be. The guilt many men feel about not being home is noteworthy, because there seems to be very little leeway. If you're feeling that way, know that your longing is valid. Listen to that feeling and see if you can figure out a creative way to spend more time at home. Check out the ThirdPath Institute at www.thirdpath.org, an organization designed to help moms and dads maximize their time with family.

While You're Away

- Carry a picture of your baby and partner with you.
- Give your partner as much notice of travel plans as possible—when you are leaving and when you will return.
- Tell your partner how you feel about leaving even if it's negative, such as "I'll miss you" or "I wish I wasn't leaving."
- Let her and the baby have their feelings and reactions to your being away.
- Write a note for each day that you will be gone and leave them for your partner to find.
- Buy a computer with a webcam that allows you to see your partner and baby (and vice versa) even if you are on the road.
- Arrange regular times to call and check in.

When Your Partner Returns to Work

If your partner is going to return to work, make sure you mark the day and do something for her. She may feel excited about not having to deal with all the challenges a baby poses, but she will not relish not being the one to care for and bond with her own baby during the day. My wife, who had been a business owner and hard worker, said as she walked out the door that that there was something inherently wrong about having to go to work. Her instincts were to stay home. It became clear to me at that moment how much loss and sacrifice working mothers feel when they have to return to work.

Partner

Your relationship with your partner is important and needs tending to. How will you care for your relationship with this new baby in town? Will you greet each other first before the baby? Will you keep a regular date night? Will you keep the baby in his own bassinet or crib? Consider these questions and check in with each other about how you are adjusting to life with your new baby. Every couple will do things differently but the goal is the same—to find time to cherish each other, process the experience, and prevent resentments from growing.

Real Dad

"It was an adjustment when my partner told me that Sundays were reserved for family time. I had been used to just doing my own thing."

—Connor, 26

Resuming Intimacy

- As soon as you can, find a babysitter you are comfortable with, and take some time away from the baby. It does not have to be long.
- Be clear with your partner about your schedule so she knows what to expect.
- Don't expect sex for at least two months following the birth of your baby, or longer. The first step is to get clearance from her doctor, the next step is to get clearance from her. She may not want to have sex. Consider new ways to be intimate by talking with each other, marveling over your baby, sharing feelings, and giving and receiving massages.
- When you do resume sex, go slowly, take your time, and be attentive.
- Upon coming home from work or a trip away, greet each other first before the baby; this is an intentional way of making the marriage the priority.
- Check in with each other regularly and share any resentments that are starting to develop.
(See also chapter 9.)

Baby

Carving out time for the baby will have to be a priority for now, whether it's feeding, changing diapers, giving baths, or going for walks. The time you take to meet your baby's basic needs may, in ways, benefit you even more than it does the baby. In my rush to get out the door, I often forgot to say good-bye to the baby, and our babysitter, Sue, would call out to me, "Don't forget Mary!" So I'd rush back and give Mary a kiss on the forehead and breathe in her sweet baby smell. I was so glad and thankful that Sue got me to slow down and acknowledge her. In Mary's early months this pause benefited me more than Mary when I brought her more into my consciousness. But as Mary got older, it was for both of us; it helped us both connect.

Connecting with Your Baby

- Give the baby a kiss at the beginning and end of the day—and certainly in between.
- Grab some time just holding your baby.
- Take a nap with your baby.
- Go for a walk or to the park.
- Remember that positively involved fathers have a significantly positive influence on their children.

Extended Family and Friends

As we all know, extended family and friends can be a blessing and a pain in the butt. You and your family are in an intense period of adjustment and trying to establish "your" way of doing things. Perhaps your partner is breastfeeding but uncomfortable doing so in front of others, or maybe your mom wants to stop by and she always has something intrusive to say. Depending on your relationship and your partner's relationship with friends and family, "your" way of doing things can be interrupted if you are not intentional about working it through with your partner. Soon after the birth it's a good idea to discuss how she wants you to help out with visits from family and friends. Get clear about what is best for her, the baby, and you in terms of who comes and when. You can play a boundary-setting role just as you did in the delivery room.

- In a gentle and loving way, remind your family that you want their help but that it is also important for you to figure stuff out on your own. The logic is that you are trying to establish your own routines and rhythms.
- Depending on your family dynamic, try to equalize time spent with your respective families, especially around holidays.

Division of Labor: Job Responsibilities

The work of caring for baby and household will be more manageable when you and your partner share the responsibilities. Sounds like a no-brainer, right? What often happens is we do exactly what our parents did—or we do the exact opposite. Instead of working solely off of *that* map, consider splitting the tasks based on your respective interests, abilities, and time constraints. For example, if you haven't done laundry since college, then it may not make sense to do your baby's. (On the other hand, if it is a chore of contention, it might make sense to learn how to launder the baby's clothes.) It's also a good idea to revisit your pre-baby chore list and see if new assignments need to be made. For example, even though your partner cooked the meals prior to the baby, it may not be realistic for her to keep that up. You might need to take that job over, or take turns. If you're used to doing light housecleaning and it is no longer realistic to keep that up, you might consider hiring someone for that job.

One of my patients shared that he thought his wife resented him for the first four months of their baby's life because she was always the one to get up at night and feed the baby. His guilt reached a boiling point and he finally asked his wife if she was indeed resentful. He was surprised to find out that she was not feeling that way at all. In fact, not only did she not expect him to get up and help with this task, she was feeling some guilt and concern that she and the baby were not quieter during their middle-of-the-night feeds. Many misunderstandings and fights can be avoided if you talk with each other about who is doing what.

Here is a sample list of job responsibilities—add to this list as you see fit. Anything that needs to be done to make your household run is up for grabs, whether it's taking out the trash or paying the mortgage. You may also want to distinguish whether or not the job is (1) shared, (2) predominantly yours, (3) predominantly hers, or (4) belongs to a third party (i.e., another family member, babysitter, day-care staff, or another helper of some sort).

- Nighttime baby feedings
- Diaper changes
- Baby bathing
- Grocery and baby-supplies shopping
- Laundry
- Doctor visits
- Housecleaning
- Cooking

Consider This

A recent study from the University of Wisconsin's National Survey of Families and Households shows that wives (working or not), regardless of social class, do about twice as much housework (cooking, cleaning, yard work, and home repairs) as their husbands. When it comes to child care (attending to the physical needs of the child, dressing a child, cooking for a child, feeding and cleaning a child), women do about five times as much.

FATHERING DUTIES AND FATHERING INSTINCTS

The word *instincts* is more commonly used when referring to mothering. In our culture it's widely believed that women have "motherly instincts." Generally this means that mothers nurture and comfort well. But fathers have instincts as well, though they may not be tapped and exercised as often.

What are a father's instincts?

It has been said that a parent's instinct are to love, protect, nurture, teach, and eventually let go. Most experts agree that the instinct to protect is particularly well developed in most fathers. I have seen this in my practice and felt it myself as a dad. It's not so surprising when you consider more "primitive" cultures, in which men were or are largely warriors and hunters, and women were or are the societal glue and food gatherers. Though these may seem like stereotypes, there is *some* basis—that is, millennia—for how we slide seemingly effortlessly into these roles. We can still be the integrated males (and females) that we are and still appreciate where we've come from.

The fatherly instincts that tend to get activated first are to love, protect, and nurture. These instincts may not yet be fully refined or they may have atrophied, and it may feel awkward at first. You might not trust your own instincts, but keep practicing and try not to get discouraged or let anyone else discourage you. Many new dads report a profound, almost primitive instinct to protect. Don't be surprised if you fear dropping or breaking your tiny newborn. That fear is part of the protective instinct.

You may feel the need to revisit or relearn the nurturing instinct. In our culture, we often see a de-emphasis of the nurturing instinct in boys from a very early age. Girls are still commonly given dolls to care for while boys are given trucks to bang up. Boys, generally speaking of course, are conditioned to compete and fight, not to nurture or express tender feelings. Therefore, many men are at a disadvantage when it comes time to nurture their own babies.

Here's a scenario to describe what I mean: It's early morning on a weekend and the new dad is on duty while his partner lies in bed, savoring an extra few minutes or hours of sleep. The newborn has been fed and slept well during the night, but now, while lying in a portable bassinet, she begins to fuss and cry. The father picks up his baby and places his clean pinky finger in her mouth for sucking and soothing purposes. In doing so, he accidentally cuts the roof of her mouth with his fingernail and the baby bursts into tears. Mom comes running out of the bedroom to see what happened and dad feels horrible for making the baby cry even harder. Mom swipes the baby out of dad's arms and gives her some breastmilk. Baby immediately feels better, stops crying, and falls asleep while Dad is left feeling badly. After repeated incidents like this one, Dad comes to believe that his instincts to soothe and nurture are faulty somehow, so he stops trying. The unspoken agreement between Mom and Dad becomes that she comforts and he provides.

Though the details can vary, this is a common enough scenario in the lives of new fathers and it can lead them to detach from their wives and/or children. I feel passionate about this subject and want to encourage you to not give up on nurturing, comforting, and soothing your baby. All children need to experience a father who can be tender yet firm, awkward perhaps, but persistent in making himself available to his child and being present. In our culture, we often tend to "pick a side" and dig our heels in. We suffer from dualistic thinking. Things are "either or" not "both and." A state is politically either red or blue, a worker supports either union or management, a person is either good or bad, and a mom is soft and nurturing while a dad is hard and strict. Instead, I encourage you to strive to offer your child an experience of an integrated man who embodies myriad qualities, not just the stereotypical ones.

It is very common for both dads and moms to think that they are inept at caring for their babies. But when dads invariably do something wrong—and we all do at some point or another—the result can be that they get squeezed out of the child-care matrix with the thought, "Oh, that's the mother's job." While your partner may spend more time with the baby and has her own soothing powers, it's also true that you have the capacity to soothe and nurture and be with your infant in significant ways.

So if you aren't quite sure in the beginning how to make your child feel better, how to hold her, or even how to play with her, that does not mean there is something wrong with your instincts. It just means that, like all of us, you have some things that you do well and others that you need to work on or learn.

What fathering instincts are you finding yourself gravitating toward? Some examples include protecting, loving, teaching, providing, playing, and nurturing.

Ask your partner if she notices a particular instinct of yours that you are strong in. Conversely, an instinct you are weak in? Think of it a bit like a job evaluation, except better. In a typical job evaluation, the first five minutes are spent lauding your performance, but the remaining twenty-five are dedicated to outlining the many and varied ways in which you screwed up.

Since we are in charge of this particular evaluation, concentrate on the positive—without being blind to the negative. What aspects of fathering are you good at? What fathering instincts do you think you need to work on? What makes you feel successful as a father, and what have you caught yourself doing that is not helpful?

DO YOUR BEST

Your tiny baby has made big demands on you, both practically and emotionally. It's amazing how such a small body can bring about such enormous changes.

No matter how hard you try, there will be times when balance is impossible. You may need to be absent because of work, or you may have to take a day off of work when your child is sick. Sometimes there just isn't enough time in the day for everything. You leave a sink full of dirty dishes or you aren't able to stop your baby from crying right away; it's not the end of the world. All dads have been there

before. Simply be aware of it and realize that it has an impact on your baby, your partner, and you. Then ask yourself whether you can do anything about it. Remember, you may not be able to change the reality of the situation but you can change your reaction to it. For instance, you can talk about how much you miss your partner and the baby when you're working long hours. Knowing when things are out of balance is half the battle, but then insight or reflection without follow-up may not be particularly helpful, either.

REFLECTION QUESTIONS

1. Consider creating a weekly ritual or routine with your baby, like going to the playground on Saturday mornings. What does this ritual mean to you?
2. Observe yourself in this ritual activity. Are you engaged? How can you improve upon it?
3. How do you respond when people depend on you?
4. If you had to list your priorities, in what order would you put them?
5. What have you noticed about your focus or attention? Where does your attention go? What are you most tuned in to?
6. Identify one doable thing you can do this week to restore balance in your life.

6

Getting Gear

Stuff, Stuff, and More Stuff

Newborns are little, their clothes are little, their needs are little (that is, basic), so why is there such a big pile of baby gear? What's it for?

Perhaps by now all the baby shower gifts have been unwrapped and put in their rightful places. Maybe you've begun assembling some of the furniture and learned that you can't follow even a basic assembly schematic. And all this gear makes you wonder what is essential and what you can do without.

So how do you tell what's needed and what's a waste of money and space? Some gear can be handy, but personally, I believe that you can do without about 90 percent of it. When it comes to gear, I'm a minimalist. The most important piece of equipment is YOU!

This chapter includes my picks for must-have gear for new dads and what they may want to make

life a little more playful and fun. The primary focus is on gear that will enhance your ability to connect with your growing baby and toddler. For example, the soft front carriers that harness over your shoulders and position your baby to face you get a thumbs-up.

Read on for my opinions on what you need (and, perhaps more important, what you don't need) shopping resources, and helpful safety tips as you navigate the first three years with your child. I've broken it up into five categories:

1. Clothing and accessories
2. Feeding and soothing supplies
3. Furniture and accessories
4. Carriers and transporters
5. Toys

For each category, I've provided gear recommendations by age group (birth to 6 months, 6 to 12 months, and so on).

WHAT YOU DON'T NEED

Every year new gizmos and gadgets appear on the market. Manufacturers try to convince you that your baby *really needs* these products, and that you will be laughed out of playgroup at the least or at the most, somehow, depriving your child of latest and greatest.

Each parent has to decide for himself which products are worth buying. In my opinion, you probably don't need most of the stuff that's out there, but here is my Top 5 list of products you don't need:

1. Wipes warmer. This keeps the wipes warm so that your precious baby is not startled by a cold wipe on his buttocks. *Not necessary!*
2. Diaper Genie. This device twists the diapers into what looks like a sausage link to contain the smell. Save the money. If you're using disposable diapers, use a nursery trashcan that can be lined with a plastic grocery sack.
3. A dozen different teethers. One or two will do. They tend to be short lived, get lost, or aren't used frequently enough to warrant stocking up on them.
4. The "smart" music baby products. The music is not going to make your baby any smarter than he already is or will be. If your baby likes classical music, there are a multitude of traditional and online classical radio stations.
5. Three different strollers. Two at the most—one for when he's a newborn and the second for

when he turns six months, which should last until he's about three years old.

WHAT YOU DO NEED

As you'll see below, there are plenty of things your baby really does need, enough to satisfy most dads' yen for "retail therapy." Are you buckled in? Here we go . . .

Clothing and Accessories

It is easy to go overboard on clothes because manufacturers make baby clothes that are *so* cute and you, a parent want your kid to look even cuter. You could probably get away with not spending a dime on clothes because friends and family will not only lavish you with new outfits, but they'll also offer their used ones. I recommend gratefully accepting hand-me-downs and buying from secondhand clothing stores (also called consignment shops), thrift stores, and even yard sales. You can also check out www.eBay.com and www.craigslist.com for Internet bargains.

The qualities to look for in clothing are durability, ease of getting it on and off, price, softness and comfort, and style. Try to avoid clothes that are stiff or scratchy and that have items on the clothes that can be choking hazards, like decorative buttons.

Babies grow fast and you will be regularly upgrading to new clothes. Your baby will grow out of clothing within months. This concept never really sank in until I watched it happen with my own kids. I suggest you not buy a stitch of clothing until you've gone through what you've already received from baby showers and hand-me-downs, then buy what you still need.

Sizes are usually based on age: preemie, birth to three months (newborn), six to nine months, nine to twelve months, twelve months, eighteen months, twenty-four months, 2T (two-year-old toddler), and 3T (three-year-old toddler). **Birth to 6 months.** A newborn very basic clothing needs. Here are some items you'll want to have on hand.

Bathing tub. For the newborn, it's a good idea to get an infant tub. This helps confine your slippery baby and has handy little compartments for soap and shampoo. Check your local Target store for options that range from $18 to $35.

Burp cloths. Buy a ten-pack of these gems—they're usually white cotton cloths that will absorb spills and spit-ups and protect your clothes from getting stained. Primary use is over the shoulder when burping your baby after a feeding. Highest usage is during the first six months, which is when babies spit up the most.

Daytime outfits. These are often called jumpers. It's a full-body outfit (minus the feet) that has snaps from neck to ankle. You probably need at least six, since your newborn will go through multiple changes. They will last at least four months.

Diapers. Everyone has their favorite brand—such as Huggies or Pampers. I recommend against diapers that have sticky adhesive. It sticks to the baby's skin and to parts of the diaper that you don't

want it to. Diaper sizes increase according to the baby's weight and generally go like this: newborn, 1, 2, 3, 4. There is some debate as to whether cloth diapers are cheaper, particularly if you use a cleaning service. It is true that cloth is more environmentally friendly. Most children will be out of diapers by age three or four. Buy in bulk if you can. Check out www.diapers.com for options.

Diaper bag. When you are out of the house, it's important to have a well-stocked diaper bag. It should include a couple of diapers, a changing pad (something to lay your baby on), wipes, and at least one change of clothes. Check out www.dadgear.com for some fashion-conscious dad-friendly (skulls and flames, anyone?) diaper bags. (For more on what to bring on an outing, see "Outings: What You Need" on page 102.)

Footwear. Socks and booties will suffice for now. There are also Zutano brand fleece booties (see resources at the end of the chapter) that work great but are a splurge. Babies do not need walking shoes until they are about ten to fourteen months. Shoes are not recommended because newborn feet are malleable and should not be restricted. (Tiny shoes are adorable and often show up as baby shower gifts. If you don't have the heart to return them, hang them in the nursery as a decorative accessory.) Six pairs of socks and two pairs of booties are enough for now.

Headwear. Headware is needed to maintain body temperature. Make sure it's snug but not tight fitting. After the first several weeks you can ditch the newborn caps and buy brimmed hats for summer babies and warm knit hats for winter babies, both with elastic or Velcro chin straps.

Onesies. These all-cotton undershirts snap between the crotch, and I think they're a great everyday garment. They can be worn alone in the summer or as a first layer of warmth and protection in winter. Buy some long-sleeve Onesies for the winter too but avoid turtlenecks at this age. By the time your child is two you probably can do without the Onesie. You'll need at least six to start with.

Sleeping outfits. Generally these come with attached feet, which is great because you don't have to worry about socks falling off and chilly toes. I do not recommend the "sack" for newborns because their feet tend to poke through. The sleeping sack has an opening at the bottom and cinches closed with a drawstring. (In general, for this age group avoid loose-fitting clothes and drawstrings.) All sleepwear should say that it is flame resistant on the label.

Snowsuit. These are great in freezing temperatures, with or without snow. They keep your newborn warm, head to toe. My daughter was born in October and she practically lived in one of these suits (when outside, of course) during the winter months. Make sure this is not too big and that it has a zipper from neck to ankle for diaper access. It should also have a hood, arms, and legs, like a whole-body suit. Ideally it will be wind and water resistant.

Swaddling blankets and swaddle wraps. Swaddling blankets (also known as receiving blankets) are a key soothing tool in the first few months. You probably swiped a few by the time you left the hospital. These blankets are what you can wrap your baby in using the burrito method. (See page 66 in chapter 4 for instructions.) The swaddle wrap is slightly different from the blanket in that it has a Velcro closure. It slips over your baby and safely protects and keeps him warm while still allowing his legs to kick and stretch.

Wipes. I recommend buying the kind that pull out like tissues and are thick and durable. As long as your baby is in diapers, you'll also need wipes for your own sticky fingers. When you buy in bulk you usually get a travel case and a dispenser for the home.

6 to 12 months. Things are starting to change with your baby, and before you know it she'll be crawling, cruising, and walking. Here is the essential gear for your growing infant.

Dresses. It will be tempting and absolutely okay to put your little girl in dresses, but just remember that they interfere with crawling. My wife and I have very funny video footage of one of our babies trying to crawl in a dress. That doesn't mean she can't wear them; it's just something to consider when you want to encourage her new crawling skills.

Footwear. As your baby begins to crawl, cruise, and walk, her socks should have those little rubber grippers on the bottom to prevent slipping. I'm a big fan of the suede-soled booties made by L.L. Bean (check out www.llbean.com). Just make sure the elastic is not too tight around your baby's ankles. If you are going to buy shoes at this age make sure they have a flexible sole and no forced arch.

Pants and shirts. During this period your baby will be able to wear pants and shirts. Make sure the pants have snaps for easy access for diaper changes. Make sure the shirts also snap at the crotch to prevent the shirts from riding up. Blue jeans are particularly cute on babies this age. You'll need about four to six pairs of pants and eight to ten shirts. Check out Baby Gap (www.gap.com) and Children's Place (www.childrensplace.com) stores for affordable options.

Sleep sack. When your newborn outgrows her swaddle blanket, buying a sleep sack (a wearable blanket) for the cooler fall and winter months makes good sense. If your newborn has been kicking off the swaddling blanket, consider it time. It keeps your baby warm without overheating and allows for spontaneous leg and arm movements. All you need is one. Check out www.halosleep.com for the SleepSack.

12 to 24 months. The infant world as you knew it sure does change after that all-important first birthday into toddlerhood. Consider these few pieces of essential clothing and accessories.

Footwear. Usually you'll buy your baby's first pair of shoes between ten and fourteen months. When you do buy them, get the ones with flexible soles. Babies grow out of their shoes very quickly, but you want to be sure that the shoes are well designed with no forced

arch supports. Check out www.striderite.com and www. ibizakidz.com/Footwear.htm for well-made shoes at varying prices.

Outerwear. Winter and summer hats that tie under the chin are best. The summer hat should have a protective brim to prevent sun exposure. Winter gear is important, and sometimes you can get away with buying a size up and getting more than one season's wear out of it.

Real Dad

"I was surprised at how annoyed I became about snapping my toddler's clothes together after a diaper change. Snaps are great for quick access to diapers, but they can be a nuisance when your child cries, squirms, and wriggles around. Getting his clothes back on seems much like calf wrestling."

—Tim, 34

24 to 36 months. Now that your child is firmly entrenched in toddlerhood, she graduates to some new gear that's representative of her new toileting skills and less baby-ish fashions. Nothing thrills a tot more than retail evidence that she is nearly "all growed up."

"Mini-Me" clothes. Who knew that dressing your kid in clothes that you might wear would be so much fun? Call it narcissistic and self-centered but dressing your kid in like-styled clothes is kind of fun, helps the bonding process, and may even be helpful in identifying him if he pulls a Houdini in the grocery store while your back is turned.

Potty training pants. Try to use these, popularly known by the brand name Pull-Ups (www.pull-ups.com), as your child transitions from diapers to going without. The advantage to Pull-Ups is that you can pull them down quickly and pull them up just as quick. One concern about potty trainers, if used too frequently, is that children don't experience the consequences of peeing in their pants or bed, which can be a teachable moment as long as it doesn't happen every night and is not done in a shaming way. Eventually your almost-three-year-old will pay attention to the bodily sensation of having to pee. Your child should graduate from night-time use of Pull-Ups around age five.

Sunglasses. You can probably do without them and your toddler will probably either take them off repeatedly or lose them, but they do look pretty cute. If you do get them don't spend too much money because they will likely get lost or be broken pretty soon after buying them. The life expectancy of a pair of sunglasses is so low, in fact, that you probably won't have to worry whether they've got UV blocker or not.

> **TIP**
>
> A good way to score points (not that anyone is keeping score—it just made for a good pun) and show your partner that you are "in the game" is to take charge of the laundry. One dad friend of mine does it every Saturday night and even considers it his "me time." You do not need to buy special baby laundry detergent; it's a waste of money and takes up space. The only reason to switch from what you are already using is if your baby's skin or nose becomes irritated, in which case you might want to go with a fragrance-free detergent.

Feeding and Soothing Supplies

Anything that has to do with food and babies is guaranteed to result in a mess at some point. What's your comfort level? Some parents want to do everything they can to avoid messes while others shrug it off or even embrace it as part of parenthood.

Early on, bottle or breastfeeding is not very messy, but as you introduce finger foods and independent feeding, it gets messier by the month. You can contain mealtime messes with a couple strategies: Limit the amount of time devoted to meals—figure on twenty to thirty minutes—after that they become restless and tend to throw and play with food. I suggest you stage the event in the same place (i.e., in a parent's arms, in the high chair, or at the table) with minimal distractions. The goal is to give your child an opportunity to *feel* what it's like to be satisfied by food and therefore to know when to stop, which requires that he listen to his body, not the TV. Nutritionists tell us that the ideal eating environment is calm, relaxed, and free from pressure and or bribing. I wouldn't be surprised if much of our nations obesity problem is caused by poor eating habits. In that vein, I also do not recommend allowing your toddler to eat on the go (in the car, or while running to the subway). There's a popular television commercial for a breakfast product that has the whole family eating in the car. It's a sad statement on our culture that we can't find the time to slow down and eat. Let's face it, our society is too hurried, so teaching your kids that there is a time and a place to rest and nourish is an important thing. As your child gets older, eating can (and should!) be something you all do as a family, and when it happens it's a wonderful reconnecting and bonding experience. Expect feeding to be frustrating at times for you and for your little one. Keep your eyes peeled for signs that your baby has had enough to eat. She may not say, "Dada, I'm full." Instead, she may throw her food to the floor.

With respect to soothing, the goal is to help your growing baby learn ways to cope with frustration, loneliness, anxiety, and so on. The ultimate objective is to allow your child to become a separate, self-reliant person who uses healthy soothing mechanisms. As you soothe your child, you might also want to think of how you soothe yourself. For instance, how do you comfort yourself when you can't sleep? The point here is to pay attention to your methods of coping. Do they parallel your child's? If they do, and they are not healthy, take it in stride and keep working on finding healthier ways to soothe. If they don't and you find yourself being more comforting toward your baby than you are toward yourself, take note and recommit yourself to modeling effective coping strategies. Many men in my practice can be incredibly critical toward themselves and likewise have a low frustration tolerance for their baby.

Babies already possess many of the necessary soothing skills. They're born with reflexes that can help them self-soothe. All three of our babies attempted to suck their thumbs (the reflex is called "rooting") within hours after they were born. I was amazed to discover that, if taught, a baby can refine her skills to self-soothe. Case in point: When my daughter was four months old, her babysitter taught her how to hold her own bottle. Talk about self-reliance.

Every parent will nourish and soothe their kids differently. Here's what you need as you find your way. **Birth to 6 months.** There are a number of tools and tricks you can break out to help in the effort to nourish and soothe you newborn. Here are a few suggestions.

Bottles. Again, there is an overabundance of choices. Keep it simple, be flexible, and experiment. After that, stick with it and try to be consistent.

Breastmilk. Has a double benefit: It nourishes while it soothes. The act of sucking calms babies. For this reason, take good care of your wife's breastmilk. Breastmilk can be stored in the refrigerator for four to seven days or in the freezer for three to six months (write the date on the bottle or bag and don't store it in the door). Warm or thaw bottles in warm water; do not boil or microwave. Serve it warm.

It is hard to tell how much your baby eats while breastfeeding, as she will continue until satisfied. Feeding a baby with a bottle allows you to measure the amount taken in. Your newborn will probably take two to three ounces every three to four hours for the first few weeks, for a daily total of sixteen to eighteen ounces.

Burp cloths. Mentioned earlier, these white cotton cloths protect shoulders from spit-ups.

Drooling bibs. These are helpful up through the sixth month and help keep shirts dry. I recommend the ones that fit over the head like a T-shirt—this prevents them from pulling them off, at least for a few more months.

Nipples. Every baby and parent has a preference, and there are many choices. To avoid losing your cool while standing in your local drugstore looking for just the right nipple, learn what your baby and partner have decided upon.

> **TIP**
>
> *Consumer Reports* states that silicone nipples are preferred because they're nonallergic and less likely to harbor bacteria. Before stocking up make sure your baby takes to the nipple you've offered her, then replenish your stock every three to four months. Boil new nipples, then wash with soap and water. Start with a slow-flowing nipple early on, followed by medium or fast flow after three months of age, all depending on your baby's preference.

Pacifiers. They can be helpful although certainly not necessary, and ultimately your baby may be the one who decides. It may take multiple tries before your baby takes to a pacifier, but if she does and it seems to soothe her, buy several and put them in places where you'll most need them, such as the car, crib, or stroller. My kids fell asleep with theirs in their mouths but then we took them out soon after. The downside is that extended use (anything past the fourteenth month) can shift the internal structure of the mouth and cause an overbite. The American Academy of Pediatrics recommends that breastfed babies be at least a month old before being introduced to the pacifier so that they take to the breast. Pacifier use in the first year may reduce the risk of SIDS (sudden infant death syndrome), and pacifiers are recommended over thumb sucking.

Use a pacifier clip, which attaches to your child's clothing to prevent the pacifier from getting lost or dirty. Make sure the clip cord is not long enough to go around your baby's neck, since it is a choking hazard.

Soothing products. Check out Slumber Sounds (www.slumbersounds.com), which offers a number of options to help your fussy baby sleep better. My wife and I have consistently used a sound machine (aka a white noise machine) with good results. They also offer a variety of baby massage products, teething soothers, music, and DVDs.

Swaddling blankets. Swaddling blankets aren't just a baby accessory (see page 90). They're a source of soothing and can be great during the first several weeks because they recreate the feeling of being held in the womb.

6 to 12 months. The following aids will help you adjust to your growing baby. If you are conscious of messiness it might be wise to have a damp paper towel with you as you feed your little guy.

Feeding bibs. As your baby starts to eat from a high chair you will need feeding bibs to protect his clothes, and maybe even a protective mat for under the high chair. I recommend bibs that you can wash with a sponge (to minimize laundering) and that have Velcro or a tie in the back (to minimize a battle of wills between you and baby). See if you can find a bib that has a pocket that catches food. Very cool.

Formula. By this age your baby will typically be consuming 6 to 8 ounces every four to five hours of either breastmilk or formula. Even if your partner is still breastfeeding, it's very possible that you will be using formula to supplement her breastmilk by this stage. The two major brands are Enfamil and Similac. Never refrigerate, microwave, or freeze formula; make it as you need it. Try to buy in bulk at warehouse stores such as Sam's Club or Costco, as it's generally up to 16 percent less than at supermarkets, according to the U.S. Department of Agriculture.

TIP

Go easy on water. In the first year, too much water can be dangerous for your baby because the kidneys cannot excrete it fast enough, which can cause serious complications. Your baby will get enough water through breastmilk or formula, so it's not necessary to give her any extra. Avoid juices—they tend to have no nutritional value.

High chair. Buying a good high chair is important. We purchased a used Peg Pérego (www.pegperego.com) high chair that lasted through three kids and seven years. Look for a wheeled high chair with a covered cushion that can be wiped down with a sponge and offers one-handed tray removal. There are also reclining chairs for when baby is having a bottle. Buy it when your baby is about four to six months or eating jar food and it should last until your little guy is about three and ready for a booster seat.

12 to 24 months. Your toddler will need the following devices to make his feeding times more fun (especially for you). You will be teaching him how to eat with utensils, and as is always the case with something new, expect a mess.

Bibs. Babies are typically at the height of messiness at this age. Food is worn on their clothes, embeds in their hair, and lands just about anywhere, even in some unlikely places. You may need to buy some new feeding bibs to fit a larger child.

> **TIP**
>
> Toddlers often insist on feeding themselves, so get in the habit of cutting up all foods so they don't choke. Some kid-friendly foods: Cheerios, raisins, strawberries, sliced bananas.

Bottles. Try to wean your baby off of being fed by a bottle by around twelve months. Prolonged bottle feeding (after fourteen months) can cause your baby to consume too much milk and not enough food. It can also lead to tooth decay.

Sippy cups. Introduce the sippy cup around ten months as you begin the process of weaning off the bottle. Buy two or three.

Utensils. Most kid utensils are made out of a rubberlike substance that prevents sliding and breaking. They come in fun colors and shapes. Check out Ikea (www.ikea. com) for inexpensive tableware.

24 to 36 months. Your developing toddler will be exerting his will during this stage of development and may be showing off his ability to throw, hide, and play with food.

Bibs. In general, toddlers at this age are less likely to be wearing last night's dinner in their hair, but you'll still need some toddler bibs to protect all those cute clothes from staining or the floor from crusting up with macaroni and cheese.

Booster seat. This replaces the big thick telephone book our parents used to put us on. Three main reasons why a booster is helpful: (1) it saves on space, (2) it's helpful while traveling, and (3) it introduces your toddler to the dinner table and sitting with grown-ups. Make sure the booster fits securely onto the chair it's harnessed to, or made of nonslip material. See One Step Ahead (www.onestepahead.com) for options.

Furniture and Accessories

Since baby and toddler furniture tends to be expensive with a short life span, seek out secondhand or accept hand-me-downs. If space is tight you'll want to find items that close up easily and compactly. Whether you're buying new or accepting seconds, check to see if your products meet the standards of the ASTM (American Society for Testing and Materials; www.astm.org) and/or the JPMA (Juvenile Products Manufacturers Association; www.jpma.org).

Birth to 6 months. It seems like the smaller they are the more furniture you'll need. Some of the gear is short lived and some will last you at least the next three years.

Co-sleeper. These are relatively new products, so new that the Consumer Product Safety Commission (www.cpsc.gov) hasn't yet established safety standards. They attach to your bed and allow your partner quick access for breastfeeding and bonding. If you are considering a co-sleeper, keep in mind the "risk" factor resulting from a lack of safety standards and also remember that you will be giving up some of your private time with your partner.

Bassinet. It's not critical to have one—the baby can sleep in the crib—but a bassinet allows for portability and keeps the baby close to you and your partner as you move about. If you buy one, it will usually last for the first six months, until your baby outgrows it.

Baby monitor. The less expensive ones tend to exude a lot of static and interference. Pay more and you usually get better quality. One time my son's monitor picked up a phone call by a college student ordering pizza. Monitors can be used as long as he is in a crib, usually two years or more, and are handy when you're traveling.

Bouncy seat or swing. Your baby is in sight but you can still load the dishwasher or watch the game with your hands free. You probably don't need both a bouncy seat and a swing, especially if space and money are a concern.

Changing table. Look for models that are high enough for a dad, so that you are not bending over too much during diaper changes. Consider creating your own if you are handy and looking to save money. We converted an old dry-bar cabinet by painting it and replacing the knobs to make it more kid friendly. I bought a cat bed mattress pad and cut it down to size. Remember to never leave your baby unattended on the changing table. Check out www.ikea.com for some options.

Crib. *Consumer Reports* suggests you buy a crib made after 2000 because older models may not meet the voluntary safety standards for slat attachments so that your baby's head doesn't get stuck between the slats. Also, make sure it is JPMA-certified (Juvenile Products Manufacturers Association; www.jpma.org) or certified to meet the ASTM (American Society for Testing and Materials; www.astm.org) voluntary standards (ASTM F-1169 and ASTM F-966). Avoid the drop side, which is a nice feature in theory but one that often compromises the strength of the crib. Never buy a used mattress, as it may not fit your crib and may be unsanitary.

Don't hesitate to ask for help assembling the crib. I called on my father and it was a nice bonding experience for us, particularly since we are both incompetent when it comes to assembling anything. Prices range from $100 to $600. Stop using the crib when your toddler is able to climb out, usually between ages two and three.

Glider. The glider has replaced the rocking chair, probably because it doesn't pinch toes and fingers, and it is useful to have for feeding, soothing, and story time. You'll get the most use out of a glider when the kids are younger, but it can be kept and used as long as you want it. Check that it has arm pads.

Portable crib. Also known as a Pack 'n Play or a play yard. These are useful when you are traveling but can be used at home as well. They last for approximately two years and should be retired when your child is able to climb out.

6 to 12 months. The main thing to consider is increasing mobility. You'll want to support his growth and autonomy while also keeping him safe.

Baby jumper. This is a great apparatus to place your child in while you make your partner dinner or take care of some other chore. It clasps onto the frame of a doorway and hangs down. Your baby will sit in a legless seat and jump up and down for a good long while. Babies usually grow out of these by around their first year. One brand name is the Evenflo Johnny Jump-Up (www.evenflo.com) doorway jumper.

Safety gear. As your baby crawls and cruises around he will be curious about what those outlets are, and he'll want to open every cabinet and stick his hand in the toilet, while closing his hand on the door. Pick up some safety gear at your local drugstore or buy online at Baby Guard (www.babyguard.com) or www.safety1st.com.

Walker or exerciser. The swivel seat rotates 360 degrees, giving your baby access to all sorts of things to flip, push, squeak, make disappear, and track with his increasingly sophisticated vision. It's perfect for when your baby is able to support his own back and will last until he is able to walk, usually only a few months. Check out the Evenflo Exersaucer at www.evenflo.com.

12 to 24 months. Toddlerhood means exploration, which heightens the need for safety gear.

Safety gates. As your toddler negotiates the world on foot it's important to protect him from dangerous places, such as fireplaces, kitchens, or stairs. Check out Baby Guard at www.babyguard.com for safety products.

Twenty-four to thirty-six months. The only major piece of furniture to consider is new sleeping quarters.

Bed. The closer you get to the third birthday, the more you should consider a bed. Whether you get a junior bed or a twin, it is important to get a railing of some sort so your toddler doesn't fall out. The bed is a big milestone and you can expect that when you do make that leap, your toddler will come and visit you in the middle of the night. It's going to take constant redirecting if you want her to stay in that bed. Check out www.toddlerbeds.com for options.

Carriers and Transporters

When buying a carrier, one of the most important considerations is comfort for both you and your baby. For example, if it's a backpack, does it give you good back support? Likewise, with a stroller, does it adjust to different heights? The second most important consideration is durability—will it last for possible future babies? And finally, is it something you can afford? Some strollers cost as much as $700.

Birth to 6 months. Your baby will weigh anywhere between 5 to 21 pounds during the first 6 months. This will dictate the carrying device that's best suited for her and you. Pay close attention to safety standards on the products you buy.

Convertible car seat. We carried each of our three kids home from the hospital in one of these. They are secured by a car seat belt and then you can detach it from the base and carry it around or place on top of a stroller specially designed for your baby's car seat. While in the car the baby is facing the rear and should be in the middle of the back seat. A car seat is good for the first year or so, or until your baby is about twenty pounds. Read instructions carefully on how to install the seat and secure your child safely.

Sling. This is womblike cloth that drapes over your shoulders for carrying your newborn. As they are usually worn by moms, you may receive a few raised eyebrows if you choose to don one. They work best for ages three to five months, sometimes older.

Stroller. Newborns need to be in a stroller that mostly reclines. The car seat serves this function, which is why it's a good option to get a car seat that secures itself onto a stroller.

6 to 12 months. One of the main considerations with this age group is comfort for you, the carrier.

Backpacks. I am a big fan of the Kelty backpack (www.kelty.com). This was one of the coolest and most functional baby items we owned, though your baby does need strong back muscles since there is no built-in back support. It stands upright your baby can stay in the pack while you ride the subway, bus, or train. One downside: It's not great in cramped quarters.

Soft carriers. This is a front-carrying pack. I really enjoyed the Baby Bjorn, which afforded me the opportunity to bond with my baby. This carrier is best used when she has developed some back strength, around five to seven months, but people use it with newborns as well. Have her face outward and grab the attention of every passer-by. Get one that supports your lower back. They last about five to nine months. Check out www.babybjorn.com.

Stroller. Up until now the baby has probably been strolled around in her car seat that doubles as a stroller. Usually by the eighth month you can have the baby in a more upright position. There are so many different brands of strollers now and the range of technologies and styles is unbelievable. Some of the wheels have treads better than those on the tires on my car. This is one area where you can definitely go overboard and spend more than you need. If money is tight, try your best to get a quality hand-me-down. You can get good ones that have only been used for a short period. Longevity depends on when you want your kids to start walking around more, but you'll likely use it until your toddler is about three, give or take a few months.

12 to 18 months. The theme with this age group is *upgrade*. Your little guy is riding in style (and safety) and needs some styling shades to go with his new ride.

Car seat. Your baby is now officially a toddler and is facing forward in the car so you can see him in the rearview mirror. He'll need a forward-facing car seat when he's between twenty and forty pounds. Read instructions carefully on how to install the seat and secure your toddler safely.

Stroller. If you need to upgrade, I recommend the brand BOB (www.bobgear.com). Note that the tires actually have air in them, so they have to be checked and maintained. They maneuver quite well in bad weather.

24 to 36 months. Your sure-footed toddler is ready for her own ride. She may even be ready to start peddling. It may not be the quickest way to get around but boy does it give them a sense of pride to maneuver themselves around.

Wagon. When your kids are old enough to sit without popping up every five seconds, you'll need a wagon to wheel them around in. It's a win-win. Check out Red Wagons (www.redwagons.com).

Toys

Kids don't need a whole lot of toys early on, and actually, more often than not, the things they like playing with best are not the store-bought toys but the pots and pans under the counter or a large box. Every toy manufacturer indicates the age the toy is best suited for on the packaging, so let this be your guide. Do not give a child under the age of three a toy with small objects since they tend to put everything in their mouths. Small pieces pose a choking hazard.

When buying a new toy, consider whether it will help you engage versus detach, erring (of course) on the side of engagement. The following recommendations will help you determine what's best for your child during each stage of development.

Birth to 6 months. The primary developmental task in the first few months is to exercise fine and gross motor skills. Give your baby toys that help him reach, grab, see, and stimulate all five senses. For example, a baby gym is a soft square mat that has an apparatus that arches over your baby's body. The arching device has dangling objects that your baby can see and reach for. It folds up nicely for convenient storage.

6 to 12 months. The key consideration with this age group is promoting their growing mobility. As they crawl and develop higher functioning skills you'll be amazed at how fast they grow. From propping himself up to rolling over, to crawling to walking—it all happens in this period.

Stacking toys. As he gets closer to twelve months, he will really enjoy putting things into or on top of other things.

Teething toys. Everything goes in the mouth at this age so it's important to give your child clean and safe things.

Toys with sounds. Right around twelve months your tot may get fascinated with noisy toys. Whether it's a dog that barks or a phone that rings toys with sounds can be a big hit.

12 to 24 months. The key task at this age with respect to toys is supporting their mobility and growing independence.

Cell phone. I realize this may be too much, but it is very cute to watch your toddler imitate you or your partner talking on the phone. If you don't want to spend the money on a toy cell phone, which I can understand, they will use other things like remote controls and bananas to talk into.

Durable photo album. These are great because they get to see the most important people in their life in a photo album made especially for them.

Pedaling toys. Check out Back to Basics Toys (www.backtobasicstoys.com) for a selection of these and other great toys.

Walking toys. Toddlers love toys that they pull or drag as they walk along. When my daughter was sixteen months old her favorite toy was her "dowey" (doggy), whom she took for a walk almost every day.

24 to 36 months. This age group is starting to be a little more intentional with its actions and more adept at using its fingers to manipulate objects. Building games, such as soft blocks, can be introduced too, but be aware they tend to like destroying (which is fun in and of itself) more than creating.

Baseball and bat. I had my two-year-old boy and girl hitting with oversized, lightweight bats and balls while they were still in diapers. They make these in traditional plastic or a cushioned variety; start with a cushioned one at first. When they connect, the crowd goes wild.

Bicycle. A number of companies make bikes for children under three. What's unique about these bikes is they don't have pedals; instead, the toddler propels himself and stops with his feet. He needs to be old enough to be able to steer and balance. These will train him nicely to ride a "real" bike. Check out Ride On Toys for Kids (www.rideontoysforkids.com).

Creative game ideas. You don't need to buy a toy or boxed game—a magazine subscription or two will provide creative ideas for countless hours of fun.Check out Disney's Wonder Time Web site (www.wondertime.go.com) and Family Fun magazine and Web site (www.familyfun.go.com). And after you're done getting ideas give the magazine to your child and watch him shred—kids love to shred at this age.

Games. Age-appropriate puzzles are great to break out as they promote fine motor skills like putting objects inside other objects and placing pieces into other pieces.

Play-Doh. Play-Doh is great for him to play with as it allows him to squeeze, hammer, and pound without doing damage. Supervise closely so they don't ingest. Check out www.hasbro.com/playdoh/en_US/.

The Five Os: Don't Buy More Than You Need

- Overwhelming—the stuff you accumulate can be too much.
- Overcrowded—it can take up a lot of space.
- Obsolete—the stuff you buy will only last a short period, since children grow fast.
- Out-of-pocket expense—it can be a waste of money.
- Off focus—focus on time spent with your child, not things bought.

Why Dads Love Gear

Before you became a dad, you might have cursed a department store or shopping mall, but now suddenly you're skimming circulars for the best baby-gear sales. Here's why:
- Dads feel good when they provide their kids with necessary and fun things.
- Dads love gadgets, wheeled vehicles, and the like, as they're a tangible way to connect with a child.

OUTINGS: WHAT YOU NEED

The Daddy Checklist

Many new dads wonder but are afraid to ask what they need to go on an outing with their baby. The list below may feel like too many things to remember, but keep in mind that babies are in a state of complete dependence. Use this checklist to prepare for a successful outing:

___ Diapers (one per hour you'll be gone)
___ Travel pack of wipes, for you and baby
___ Diaper rash cream
___ One or two burping cloths
___ Baby outfit
___ If sunny, baby sunblock (generally SPF 50 after six months of age—check with your pediatrician) and a sun hat
___ A bottle of breastmilk, milk, or formula (with the nipple in a plastic resealable bag)
___ At least one comfort object (toy, teething object, rattle, stuffed animal)
___ If appropriate, a container of baby food and baby spoon; container of snacks (cereal or crackers)
___ Bib
___ Extra pacifier (in plastic resealable bag)
___ Cell phone for emergencies
___ Changing pad (many diaper bags come with one)
___ Several large plastic bags, for tossing dirty diapers or storing soiled clothes
___ Water and a snack for you

Family Excursions Checklist

Babies can be pretty flexible and sleep most anywhere (sometimes better in the car than at home in the crib). Here are a few additional things to pack when packing up for a family outing:

___ Portable crib
___ Soft carrier or backpack
___ Emergancy contacts list
___ Additional food, snacks, drinks
___ Weather-appropriate clothes
___ Toiletries (bubble bath, diaper rash ointment)
___ Additional soothing supplies (pacifier, stuffed animal)
___ Tub toys

Gear versus You

The issue of baby gear does not come up too often in my practice as a therapist and I certainly don't consider myself an expert in market trends or consumer shopping. But I have watched many fathers (myself included) get caught up in the desire to buy more stuff than they or their kids need. Next time you are in a baby superstore notice within yourself what I call "the scan of envy and doubt." This is when you start looking around at what the other parents are buying and in subtle ways begin asking yourself if you should be getting that as well. Then you start doubting if you are a good parent because you chose not to get the mobile that plays six different variations of Beethoven's Ninth Symphony.

It's all tempting. A friend of mine calls baby gear "candy for parents," since it's so hard to resist. This is particularly true because all parents want their kids to have the best and want to believe that they are parenting the right way. If another parent has the best new stroller with all the bells and whistles it makes you wonder if you need to get the same thing. We're all guilty at some point in our lives of trying to keep up with the Joneses. If you feel you might succumb to buying more than what you really need, try to remember this: The thing your baby needs most is your care and your love.

Resources

Consider some of the following for shopping and saving on baby gear.

Babies "R" Us (www.babiesrus. com): Toys, clothes, gear, and essentials.

Baby Gap (www.babygap.com): Mostly clothing.

Bambino Mountain (www. bambinomountain.com): Zutano products, clothing.

Biz Rate (www.bizrate.com): Online deals.

BJ's (www.bjs.com): Toys, clothes, gear, and essentials. Membership required.

Buy Buy Baby (www. buybuybaby.com): Toys, clothes, gear, and essentials.

The Children's Place (www. childrensplace.com): Clothing, accessories.

Consumer Reports (www. consumerreports.org): Product information.

Costco (www.costco.com): Toys, clothes, gear, and essentials. Membership required.

Coupon Cabin (www.couponcabin.com): Online coupons for major stores.

Diapers (www.diapers.com): Multiple brands of diapers and much more.

Hasbro (www.hasbro.com/playdoh/en_US/): Play-Doh is great for toddlers.

IKEA (www.ikea.com): Baby care, toys, furniture, eating products.

Kmart (www.kmart.com.com): Toys, clothes, and essentials.

Melissa and Doug (www.melissaanddoug.com): Great wooden and soft toys.

NexTag (www.nextag.com): Online comparisons for best deals.

One Step Ahead (www.onestepahead.com): Baby and toddler shop.

Pull-Ups (www.pull-ups.com): Potty training diapers.

Sam's Club (www.samsclub.com): Toys, clothes, gear, and essentials. Membership required.

Shopping (www4.shopping.com): Online comparisons for best deals.

Target (www.target.com): Most everything, from clothes to furniture to toys.

Zutano (www.zutano.com): Great cotton baby clothes.

REFLECTION QUESTIONS

1. How much of the baby's "stuff" do you think you could do without?
2. When you're considering buying a toy or other baby gear, by what criteria do you judge it to rationalize its purchase?
3. So far, what gear has been really helpful for you?
4. So far, what gear has been really helpful to your partner?
5. If you could invent a new line of baby gear just for dads, what would it be?

Coming Up for Air: 12 to 24 Months

> *For in the baby lies the future of the world. Mother must hold the baby close so that the baby knows it is his world. Father must take him to the highest hill so that he can see what his world is like.*
>
> —Mayan Indian Proverb

Right around the time that your child turns one you will notice that her world is getting bigger. You may be taking her to more places, perhaps the highest hill or a bigger playground. Or perhaps she's going out into the world without you or your partner (with another adult supervisor, of course). This is when and where she will encounter more peers her own age, perhaps bigger kids, larger jungle gyms, louder sounds, and a world bigger than what she's been used to. She is no longer in the literal womb, nor the womb of home. This is all normal and part of the growing process.

Fathers are particularly good at helping their children expand the scope of their world. Your partner has likely been the more significant person in the baby's life up until now, but you as the father can step in as the child gets older and become a gigantic figure who provides adventure, exploration, and play. Dads tend to love this stage of development as it allows them to interact with their toddlers in active ways.

Just as your child is expanding her world, you may want to consider expanding yours as well. You've probably adjusted somewhat to life as a father and realized that much of your focus has been on your partner and child. Now may be a good time to connect with old or new friends, consider renewing your gym membership, and resuming or starting an activity. The following chapters describe why it is important for everyone in your nuclear family to continually expand the scope of your zone—perhaps even your comfort zone.

Transitioning from Infancy to Toddlerhood

Thinking, Walking, and Talking

The developmental milestones, abilities, and limitations of a twelve- to twenty-four-month-old are unique. Knowing this information can help you maximize the fun you have with your little guy or girl. Not knowing this information can lead to confusion, anxiety, and sometimes unnecessary frustration. For example, if you tell your twenty-month-old that he won't be going to the park and he has a meltdown, you may become frustrated and wonder why your kid is overreacting. But if you know that developmentally twenty-month-olds have a poor ability to tolerate disappointment, then you might respond differently.

"NORMAL" DEVELOPMENT

When encountering other children your child's age, you may feel compelled to ask, "How old is your child?" followed by a discussion of the children's accomplishments or challenges. This is very common, even among strangers, and speaks, in part, to our need to have a sense of how our kid is measuring up.

Of course, what's normal for one child may not be for another. Pay attention to the part of you that feels like there might be something amiss with your child. Be careful how you judge your own child and use the word *normal*. It is meant to describe a wide range of developmental characteristics because children develop at different rates. Many parents' minds go into overdrive, wondering if their child will ever talk, or if he will fall behind in school. Will he be unable to make friends? Will people think he's stupid?

I work with parents dealing with these sorts of issues all the time and I usually start by trying to calm their worries. The anxiety and fear has a way of spurring parents to make irrational and impulsive decisions. Besides, it's often the case that there is nothing wrong with their child at all and he ends up speaking soon enough or ends up with an abundance of friends. All kids have their own schedule. If you discover that your child is developmentally delayed or "not normal" in some way, it's best if both you and your partner work with your pediatrician to find a solution. In some cases you may be referred to a developmental psychologist for an evaluation. This can be one of the many parent challenges, but many parents of special-needs children have paved the way for you.

FIVE DEVELOPMENTAL MILESTONES

Once again I will take you through the five developmental milestones and discuss how each applies to children in this age group.

Gross motor skills: the use of large muscle groups to stand, sit, balance, walk, change positions, and run.

Fine motor skills: the use of smaller muscle groups, i.e., hands and fingers, to pick things up, draw, write, dress, and so on.

Language skills: verbal and nonverbal communication as well as understanding what others say.

Cognitive skills: learning, comprehension, problem solving, reasoning, and remembering skills.

Social skills: interacting with others, picking up on social cues and body language, and having relationships with others where there is cooperation and responding to the feelings of others.

In the following sections, I divide the milestones and skills under the following headings: Physical and Behavioral Development (which includes gross and fine motor skills), Emotional and Psychological Development, Cognitive Skills, Language Skills, and Social Skills.

Physical and Behavioral Development

During this stage, your child will get ready to take off and discover a newfound sense of autonomy and independence. His walking skills improve greatly, as does his ability to run away from you. He'll open doors, climb stairs, and hone his fine motor skills by holding and coloring with crayons, unwrapping presents, picking up finger foods, and turning pages in a book. Children at this age have more and more control over how they maneuver their bodies. Energy levels are high so they will need you to rein them in through redirection and reminders of what is okay and what is not okay.

You might notice:	You can respond by:
Children become more mobile and try to master things like walking, climbing up stairs, coming down stairs, using utensils, pulling open drawers, eating things off the floor, putting hands in the garbage or toilet, and maneuvering their bodies to get around a tight space. All this will be done somewhat awkwardly.	Keeping a close eye on her. Try not to let your child out of your sight for too long. The more she's able to get around and get into things, the more closely you'll need to monitor her. Spot her. Be there when she falls.
Walking into things, bonking his head, and tripping is commonplace because he hasn't learned how to master his own body, although this improves a lot as he gets closer to his twenty-fourth month. He'll put things in his mouth. And he'll probably continue to do this until around age three.	Offering alternatives and redirecting him. Steer him away from dangerous or inappropriate acts. For example, instead of letting him put a stick in his mouth, you can take the stick away and give him a teething toy instead.
He relies on you to hold hands or carry him around. He might appear shy or scared in certain situations.	Holding his hand, letting him depend on you, especially when out and about. This kind of reliance doesn't last long, so soak it up, particularly as he gets closer to two.
She points at things she wants, often accompanied by a whine or groan.	Putting words to the things she's pointing at. Praise her for pointing—it's totally appropriate at this age.
He makes a mess, seems to love chaos and disorder	Remaining calm, giving age-appropriate games and toys that don't require mopping or vacuums. Bring in a cleaning crew, show him how to clean things up—make up a song about cleaning up.

You might notice:	You can respond by:
She drools a lot, which in cold weather causes chapping or a rash around the mouth and chin. Coughing or diarrhea may accompany the chapping due to swallowing excess saliva.	Applying Vaseline or another moisturizer around the mouth. Rubbing your finger around the gum line to verify if and where a tooth is coming in. You will feel a slight swollen mound.
He gnaws on random things like shoes or books. His gums are inflamed, which can cause a fever, discomfort, and crying. He may grab his ears or the side of his face when this happens.	Giving something to chew on. A cool frozen teething ring (run water over it before giving it to your child), ice (make sure the pieces are small), or a frozen wash cloth for no longer than 10 minutes can help ease the pain. Massaging his gums with your finger, using a homeopathic soothing gel. Giving medicine. Infant Tylenol or Motrin will help if the pain is bad or if a fever persists. Consult with a pediatrician for dosages under the age of two. Taking your baby to his first dentist appointment. This is recommended before the age of two. Try to find a kid-friendly one.
He wants to sleep in your bed.	Talking with your partner about what you want to do. Read the children's book *If You Give a Mouse a Cookie*, remembering you give up some of your own personal "couple" time when you allow co-sleeping.
She naps during the day for about two to four hours total. She is sleeping through the night. She can and generally does sleep about twelve to fourteen hours of sleep per night.	Having a party! Just keep the noise down.

You might notice:	You can respond by:
He's not sleeping through the night. He experiences interrupted sleep, waking up in the middle of the night and crying hysterically. The problem persists.	Waiting before you go in to get her. Sometimes giving her five minutes to calm herself down works just fine. If that doesn't work, assess what the issue is, remembering the Five Big Needs. Commit to a routine. Take shifts and create a schedule. Consider a sleep consultant.
She seems tired and close to sleep but is easily startled.	Remembering the sleep button. Your child's sleep button is right between her eyes. Stroke it very lightly and gently with the tip of your finger only when she is almost ready to fall asleep but resisting.
He resists going to bed—seems wound up or wired or blatantly refuses to go to bed.	Making an announcement that it is bed time. Don't play with him right before bed. Either be a part of the calm bedtime ritual or don't disrupt it. Avoid long drawn-out "good night"s.
She eats nothing but sweets or carbohydrates. She is a really finicky eater.	Avoiding artificial sweets and drinks with high-fructose corn syrup in favor of water and milk. Feed your child at regular times, without being too rigid, in response to his need or desire for food.
She's not eating her food and often throws it overboard.	Giving her smaller portions of food. Children this age can get overwhelmed by a tray full of food.
He leaves a big mess on the floor when he eats, throwing food and dropping it over the tray of his high chair.	Supervising him more closely. This promotes responsible and independent eating behavior. For instance, if he puts too much food in his mouth or if he throws food, you can correct that behavior.

Discipline

For a full discussion of discipline, see chapter 12. But when disciplining your toddler, keep in mind:
- **Less is more.** The fewer words you use the better. You may find yourself using the word *no* a lot. You may need to repeat yourself a number of times before your child understands.
- **Beware the mischief makers.** This age group loves to open drawers, pull things off bookshelves, pick up food off the floor. This is all "normal." Try not to get mad, but redirect and offer safe alternatives. Monitor the tone and level of irritability attached to your redirection.
- **No time-outs yet.** Kids this age are too young to understand, benefit from or comply with time-outs.
- **Mean what you say and say what you mean.** If you say *no* to something, then mean it and be consistent. You will probably need to follow up with a demonstration, knowing that she'll misbehave again. You are laying a foundation that communicates to them that you are a man of your word, and that you will follow through. It is a trust-building opportunity.

Emotional and Psychological Development

Children have large doses of feelings, and fathers have large doses of logic or reason. This can make for an interesting combination. The growth curve being what it is, you will undoubtedly watch your child get frustrated. She is learning a lot that both excites and frustrates her at the same time. Watching your twelve- to twenty-four-month-old grow emotionally is full of ups and downs. She'll want you one second and not the next, be laughing one moment and having a meltdown the next. Children this age are full of emotion, which often gets expressed through crying and screaming or laughter and giggles. It can be helpful to remember that their emotions will come and go like the wind. If you expect a level-headed, even-keeled child you will probably be disappointed.

> **TIP**
>
> When disciplining, use the collective we. For instance: "We don't throw food or utensils" or, "We don't put our hands in the toilet."

> **TIP**
>
> To discipline is to teach. You'll know you crossed the line into punishment when you feel angry all the time, you're constantly taking things away from your child, and or there is no discernable lesson in your words.

You might notice:	You can respond by:
Your child gets so excited and or frustrated, she seems like she just wants to burst. She may hit, bite, or swat in overexcitement.	Naming it. As your child begins to acquire words (usually closer to age two), help her name the feeling that you suspect she is experiencing, such as sadness, anger, happiness, or fear. It is a great life skill to be able to name what you feel.
He gets so distraught he breaks down and cries and screams. Children at this age have a low tolerance for frustration.	Reflecting it. Become your child's mirror. In a sincere way reflect back to her what you see and hear. For example, if she has a angry face, you can say, "Oh, I see you're upset."
She is unable to express in words what she feels. She may get so frustrated (moan, groan, and whine) as a result.	Validating it. In your own way, affirm the feeling, take it seriously, and try not to minimize or make fun of it. By validating the feeling, you are not condoning the behavior that goes with it. For example, you might say, "You can be mad but you cannot kick." Validate the feeling, not the behavior.
He is unable to monitor or regulate his feelings. Children at this age are not in control of their feelings and will not learn how to do this for a long time to come.	Holding or containing it. When he is feeling sad, for example, hold and soothe your child. You want him to feel free to express anything.
She gets very excited when she sees someone she knows—or when she accomplishes tasks, such as pushing, pulling, or walking.	Getting excited too. Crouch down and speak to your child on her level as much as possible.
He has meltdowns when he is separated from people or objects. He pushes you away one moment and wants to be held the next. He picks up on your moods.	Allowing him his meltdowns, as long as he's not hurting himself or others. Don't take it personally if he rejects you. Be mindful that he is always watching you.

Saying Good-bye

You have a lot to teach your toddler about how to say good-bye. He may completely fall apart when you or your partner have to leave. A couple of things to remember:

- Even though he's young, prepare him by saying something like, "Daddy has to go to work now."
- When it's time to leave, try not to make a habit of dodging out while he's not looking. Let him have the feelings, and reassure him that you are coming back and that you love him. By doing this over and over he learns to trust you and realizes that you can (and he can) endure those tough feelings.
- After the separation it usually takes him a few minutes to calm down. It sometimes feels like he will cry forever.

Cognitive Skills

Your child's brain undergoes a rapid increase in neuron connections during the first three years of his life. More specifically, your twelve- to twenty-four-month-old will begin to: find hidden objects; plan and solve simple problems with intention; identify an object in one place and realize he's seen it in another place; sort objects based on different categories (soft, hard, quiet, loud). While complex words, tasks, and behaviors will still be beyond his grasp, you will witness him having more and more "breakthroughs" all the time. For instance, he might see a boat in a book and then point to his wallpaper, which has a boat on it. Your response to his realization reinforces the cognitive connections he is making. Their cognitive development works in close tandem with behavior, emotion, and the response he gets from you. These cognitive patterns and connections get made with a lot of repetition. It's a wonderful thing to watch your child make connections for the first time. You can practically see the brain synapses at work. Things start getting good in a whole new way.

You might notice:	You can respond by:
She will imitate you. This can be adorable and is a very important way for them to learn how to behave and act in the world.	Being aware that she will do this and being a model of behavior. Be mindful of how you act and what you say. Consider it an honor that someone wants to imitate you.

You might notice:	You can respond by:
He is just starting to be able to think through what would happened if . . . Cause and effect is not quite understood by children this age.	Keeping it simple. Avoid long explanations for why he should or should not do something. For example, as your baby pours soapy bath water in his mouth, you calmly say "no" and make a face that communicates yucky. If need be, you direct the cup away from his mouth and show him where she can pour the water instead or if she persists you take the cup away and say: "No bath water in mouth."
She can obey simple, one-step directions. For example, "Take this ball to your mother!"	Engaging her brain. Once you notice your child is able to follow simple directions, such as, "Take this ball to Mommy," help her expand by suggesting new tasks, like "Now bring the ball to me." Remember to tell her and show her—by clapping—how proud you are of her when she gets it right!
He crawls or walks after objects he wants. It's because of his new cognitive skills that he is able to crawl or walk toward a desired object or conversely avoid objects that he doesn't like.	Helping him make safe choices. Initially you make the choices for him and gradually you present him with good options to choose from. For example, you might allow him to climb up into a chair and spot him as he stands on the chair or direct him to sit down—both safe choices. This will work more effectively the closer he gets to the two-year mark.
She is able to use trial and error to solve simple problems, like putting a round peg through a round hole.	Reinforce the positive connections. Whenever you see a positive cognitive connection, praise her for it by saying something like "Good thinking!"

TIP

Toddlers learn by repetition. Whether it's reading the same book or pointing *every* time you see a fire truck or rolling the ball back and forth and back and forth. It is through these repetitive actions that learning happens.

Language Skills

The most intensive period for language development occurs in the first three years. Children this age are in the very early stages of the talking business. Around twelve months they might be uttering, "Baba, Mama, Dada," and understand more than they can say. By twenty-four months they will be able to say twenty to fifty intelligible words and make a three-word sentence. They say a lot less than they understand.

You might notice:	You can respond by:
Your child imitates the sounds of language before she has mastered any actual words. Experts call it babble or baby talk. It is cute, especially when she talks into a phone and imitates you.	Talking back to her. Even if you can't understand her, act as if she's making complete sense. By doing this you reinforce the effort, not so much the outcome or accuracy. Give her simple directives early on, followed by more complex ones as she gets closer to 2 years.
He speaks his first words. Children will generally utter their first simple words around the twelve-month mark, although there is wide variation in when this happens, some as early as ten months and some as late as three years.	Encouraging him to talk to others. Let him hang around children who are older and can talk well.
He knows your name. He recognizes whose name belongs to whom. He is also learning the power words have in moving and getting reactions from grown-ups, siblings, and others around him.	Talking in your normal tone with him. There is no need to talk like a baby to him.
She's shy or seems to be willfully not talking.	Backing off. If she's not ready, don't put pressure on her to speak.

You might notice:	You can respond by:
He speaks more. By about eighteen months your child will use approximately five to twenty words and understand simple directives. In fact, she can understand a lot more than she is able to say.	Reading books out loud. Have her point to different characters or objects in the book as you say the words.

TIP

The first few words babies speak are almost always the words that are easiest to say and also identify their favorite people or objects. *Dada*, *Mama*, *doggie*, *cup*, *shoe*, and *spoon* are some of the most common.

Social Skills

As your child spends more time on the playground or in activity groups, you will witness a wide range of social temperaments, everything from real gregariousness to timidity, from possessiveness of objects to a true philanthropic spirit. You may also see more disturbing behavior, like your child getting pushed by more aggressive kids or doing the pushing himself. It's all part of your child's attempt to understand his place in the world.

You might notice:	You can respond by:
Your darling daughter, who used to be a fabulous sharer, is now stingy with her toys. It is common for children, once they have learned the concept of "MINE!" to need (a lot of) reminders about how to share.	Paying close attention. Sometimes sharing can be really hard—give her time to get used to the idea.
He cuddles up to familiar family members—e.g., Mom—and rejects other family members—e.g., you.	Allowing for him to reject you at times and picking your battles. His rejection of you may be hard to accept but it is normal.

You might notice:	You can respond by:
She puts her face in your face or bites your nose. Children this age have little sense of appropriate social boundaries and again are not fully aware of consequences.	Teaching socially acceptable norms. For example, we don't pick our nose or put our hands down our pants in public. Praise her when she puts something into practice, i.e., sharing or covering her mouth when she coughs. Emphasize *we*. When you teach, protect his fragile sense of self by saying things like, "*We* don't bite." Avoid shaming him and overusing the word *you*—as in "*You* shouldn't do that!"
He shies away from strangers at times and other times is real gregarious. Or he may hide in your arms or in between your legs.	Trying not to label him. Try to accept his behavior for what it is without making inferences that he is your "shy guy." Separation anxiety and stranger anxiety is part of becoming his own person.

Real Dad

"I brush my toddler's teeth with a finger brush and special toddler toothpaste that has no fluoride and is safe to swallow. She loves doing it with me."

—Marcus, 29

MEASURING UP

Average Weight
• 12 months: 17 to 28 pounds
• 18 months: 20 to 32 pounds
• 24 months: 23 to 33 pounds

Average Height
• 12 months: 27 to 32 inches
• 18 months: 28 to 35 inches
• 24 months: 32 to 36 inches

WHEN TO BE CONCERNED ABOUT DEVELOPMENT

You may have noticed that your child is not developing quite like his peers. This may or may not be a sign of something to worry about. As I said before, the range of what's normal is really quite large. If you are concerned, first call your pediatrician and get confirmation on whether or not something really is amiss. I encourage you to fight through the feeling or thought that says "don't ask" and go ahead and ask, even if it ends up being nothing.

Below is a list of additional resources you might want to consult for childhood development information or suspect your child's development is delayed in a particular area.

Emotional development: *Between Parent and Child* by Haim Ginott

Language development: *The Late Talker* by Marilyn C. Agin, Lisa F. Geng, and Malcolm J. Nicholl

Developmental milestones: *The Baby Book* by William Sears and Martha Sears; *Me, Myself and I* by Kyle Pruett; *Touchpoints* by T. Berry Brazelton

Safety Precautions: Toddlerproofing

This stage of development requires you as father to supervise your child like a hawk, but you can do so without being overprotective or an alarmist. Now is the time to develop the antennae you never had. No matter how childproofed your home is, your toddler *will* get into stuff she is not supposed to, so she should not be out of your sight for too long. She's at risk of falling, putting things in her mouth, falling down stairs, and getting stuck in awkward places. Thousands of children are rushed to the hospital or die every year as a result of preventable accidents.

Use your common sense and know that this is the age of great exploration, often of areas that shouldn't be explored. Be aware but calm. Here are just a few safety considerations:

- Install a cover over every exposed electrical outlet.
- Use baby gates around stairs and to sequester your tot in specific locations.
- Keep small objects out of reach, to prevent choking.
- Install safety latches on cabinets and drawers, especially ones holding cleaning products.
- Install a latch on your toilet.

- Never leave your child in the bathtub or bathroom unsupervised, even for a few seconds.
- Put child guards on all windows.
- Use rounded bumper guards on table corners.
- Watch out for fingers around doors. (Consider doorstops and door holders.)
- Keep long cords and strings (such as pull strings on mini blinds) out of reach.
- Get rid of all balloons.
- Check batteries in fire and carbon monoxide alarms.
- Get or renew your CPR certification.
- Prevent burns by keeping your child out of the kitchen; turn pot handles toward the back of the stove and do not hold your child while cooking.
- Post this number near the phone: American Association of Poison Control Centers hotline: (800) 222-1222.

MEDICAL CONCERNS AND EMERGENCIES

As your child becomes more masterful at navigating the world, he will fall and hurt himself. If you encounter any of the common injuries below, expect blood-curdling screams, many tears, and a look of fright or terror on your child's face. This can be alarming for you, but your job is to stay calm and self-assured. If you have the honor and the fright of being there, you can solidify your place in their psyche as protector, caretaker, and soother.

> **TIP**
>
> Keep the phone number of your baby's pediatrician on you at all times or programmed into your cell phone.

Common Injuries for 12- to 24-month-olds

When encountering medical problems that you don't know how to handle, or if you are scared or uncertain yourself (which is totally normal), always play it safe and call 911 or take your baby to the hospital. There is no shame in being conservative when it comes to safety.

Bites. Other children, family pets, stray animals, or insects are the most common culprits. Clean wounds if skin is broken and get medical treatment as needed. For dog bites make sure the dog is not rabid (showing very aggressive behavior and possibly frothing at the mouth), or seek medical assistance immediately.

Cuts and abrasions. Make sure all dirt has been cleaned out of a wound, and apply antibacterial ointment with Band-Aids. Your kids will grow to love Band-Aids and may even view them as rewards. There are lots of fun styles available now.

Head injury. If your child is unconscious, call 911 immediately. For less severe blows to the head, monitor for dizziness, nausea, vomiting, or disorientation. If ever in doubt, call 911 or go to the nearest emergency room.

Mild burns. Pour cool water over the burned area as soon as possible and for about ten or fifteen minutes. Avoid ice. Gently wrap in gauze or lint-free cloth with a dressing, and speak to your pediatrician about administering a pain reliever.

Splinters. Do not force removal of a splinter. If it doesn't come out on its own, call your pediatrician.

Sunburn. Always use SPF 30 or above, but don't use SPF on children younger than six months. Apply aloe vera lotion and/or cool compresses of water and baking soda on sunburns. Have your child drink lots of water.

Tick bites. Remove the tick with tweezers by grabbing as close as possible to the skin. Pull slowly and firmly. Don't try to use a singed tip of a match. This could result in a burn or force the tick to burrow deeper.

> **TIP**
>
> Do not administer cough medicine to a child under 3 without explicit doctor approval. Children can suffer convulsions, rapid heart rate, and loss of consciousness with some cough medicines.

Family Emergency Plan

It's not too soon to plan for an emergency, and you can do so in a way that minimizes your child's fears. Check out the Web sites www.ready.gov and www.sesamestreet.org/ready for age-appropriate ways to prepare for the unexpected. Some basic things to consider when creating an emergency family plan:

Phone numbers. Compile all phone numbers on one card, which each adult (including the day care or other caregivers) can carry in a wallet or purse.

First aid kit. Have one in the home and car. Make sure it's well stocked and that you store it in a designated place.

Meet-up place. Designate a place to meet your partner, baby, and child-care provider in an emergency.

Supplies. Stock up on water and peanut butter or some other form of protein in the event you're stuck at home during an emergency.

ID kits. Prepare an emergency kit for each child in your family. In a resealable plastic bag labeled IN CASE OF EMERGENCY, include the following information: full name, address, telephone number, sex, date of birth, height, weight, blood type, name and number of pediatrician, a photocopy of the front and back of the insurance card, a recent picture and laminated lists of relatives to contact and medications and allergies. Place the bags with your other emergency supplies (such as a fire extinguisher).

Toddlerhood Reviewed: Your Growing Child

This chapter reviewed the developmental milestones of a twelve- to twenty-four-month-old and explained what you might see and how you might want to respond to best support your child's growth. I summarized the physical, emotional, cognitive, language, and social cues for age-appropriate behaviors. The next chapter will focus on how you can take the best care of you so that you can take the best care of your child.

REFLECTION QUESTIONS

1. Assuming that there is a degree of mess associated with having a one-year-old, how do you typically react to the mess? With frustration, anger, tolerance, or acceptance?

2. What does your reaction depend on? Your stress level? The amount of sleep you got?

3. When your child resists something you see as important, how do you typically respond? Is

it really the end of the world if he doesn't eat his vegetables, and is it a battle worth fighting to get him into bed at the same time? Is it even worth thinking of it as a battle? You are on the same team.

4. How do you typically deal with emergencies? What do you need to do to better prepare for the unexpected?

Taking Care of Yourself

What Is Self-care?

During every preflight safety announcement, the flight attendant says, "In case of an emergency, oxygen masks will fall from above. Please administer the mask to yourself first and then to your child." The implied message is that you have to take care of yourself first before you can help your child. This is true for every day, not just during emergencies.

How do you care for yourself? What oxygenates you as a man? I meet with men all the time who are depleted and have little to give themselves, let alone to their families. Being a father is draining. Being a working man, husband, son, brother, uncle, and friend leaves little time for you. It's tough to be successful at any of these if you're not finding ways to refresh yourself.

The first year of your baby's life is often full of wonderful moments; there is no doubt about that. It is also probably one of the most challenging years you will ever experience. By challenging I don't necessarily mean bad—there is usually a silver lining, something to be learned or something to be healed. Because there are so many new adjustments in the first year it can take some time to come up for air and even consider your needs. Up until this point you and your partner have correctly been focused on caring for your child. Continue to do so since she is in a dependent state, but you also need to take care of your own needs. Last year at this time you might have been on the elliptical machine at the gym or out on a date with your partner. Or maybe you were playing four or five hours of golf per week or were part of a motorcycling group. Things have changed.

It is not rocket science—self-neglect will have a detrimental effect on you, your marriage, and your child. Now is a good time to shift your focus once again and bring *you* back into the picture. You may not be able to do whatever you want whenever you want, but you can find new ways to satisfy your needs. This chapter will focus on four different forms of "oxygen" that I call outlets, which are particularly important for men to attend to. They are: social, creative, recreational, and spiritual.

Why Dads Don't Tend to Themselves

There are two main things dads say to rationalize against self-care:
1. I'm too busy. I have no time.
2. I can't do something for myself. If I'm not at work, then I should be home.

WHAT IS THE POINT OF HAVING OUTLETS?

There are four main reasons why men need these outlets. Not all of them may resonate for you but they are all worth considering when doing a self-assessment.

Fight Isolation

The antidote to most challenges is to know that you are not alone. Perhaps you're dealing with an infant who is not sleeping through the night, and therefore you and your partner aren't either. Those can be long, painful nights. You and your partner are at odds about how to deal with it. You are not alone. More than 25 percent of all infants and toddlers have sleep disturbances. Perhaps you long to be home with your baby and partner but work requires you to stay late and you rarely get to see your baby while he's awake. You are not alone. Of the working dads in my practice, the majority of them work at least sixty hours per week. Perhaps you are an at-home dad who hasn't had a meaningful adult conversation in days. You are not alone. In the last four years there has been a 60 percent increase in stay-at-home dads. Check out the Rebel Dad blog (www.rebeldad. com) for an online community that supports at-home dads and media coverage of competent at-home dads.

I was conducting a workshop recently at a preschool where twenty-two dads showed up. I asked them to introduce themselves and briefly say why they came and what they hoped to get out of the workshop. As introductions were made, there was a lot of head nodding and chuckles indicating that they all knew what the other was talking about. We got about halfway around the room when one dad said he had already gotten something out of the workshop in that he realized he was not the only one. New dads need to know they are not alone.

Develop Resources

A network of practical information gets shared when dads give themselves the opportunity to talk with one other and with mothers. This can happen anywhere—at the playground, in the elevator, or anywhere you come in contact with other parents. Things you can learn from your fellow parents:

- Ways to keep your marriage fresh and alive
- Places to take your partner on a date
- What to expect from the preschool application process
- Ways of dealing with the nanny or other child-care options
- The best places to go with the family for an outing
- Work advice or career networking

One cautionary note about trying to keep up with the Joneses: It's amazing how competitive parenting can be, but it stems out of lack of confidence, so make sure you're not parenting out of a need to keep up with your neighbor. One way to prevent this is to ask yourself two questions: (1) Am I taking into consideration my child's best interest? (2) Does this fit what we want for our family?

Find Fuel and Inspiration

Let's face it, it can be a chore to get up and take care of the many needs associated with fatherhood. There may be times when you want to give up, stay in bed, or retreat into the cave. What will fuel you? What will inspire you? What will bring you out? Your love for your child is probably your greatest inspiration, but you may also need other outlets

to refuel you. For instance, one dad I know rides his bike regularly, another creates artwork, and another has a weekly breakfast with a friend. You do not have to be in crisis to need refueling. In fact, if you take the time to refuel yourself regularly, you may avoid getting to the crisis stage. No matter what you are going through, having a friend that you can be honest with or an activity that keeps you grounded is fuel and inspiration.

Gain Insight

"Wow, I never thought of that," I often hear when dads get together. Because fathering is so personal and colored by so much of your own opinions, experiences, and beliefs, it can be difficult to see the forest for the trees. For example, I was conducting a group session when one dad realized that he lost his temper much like his own father. It wasn't until he talked about it for a few moments and reflected on the shock and fear his own child had shown that he knew he needed to stop the cycle of rage. By gaining insight and making connections between past and present, you are afforded the opportunity to make changes in the future.

BUILDING SOCIAL OUTLETS

The nature of fathering often confines your social parameters to work and home. If you are an at-home dad, then your outlets may be even smaller. This is one of the most notable changes for the new dad. In a very practical way your freedom has been compromised, and for some men this can be a major life shift. But when you become a father you actually join a "secret" brotherhood of men. The brotherhood is secret because it can be hard to find and access. You may have noticed that men have more difficulty than women in reaching out to one other. But when they do connect—and more and more men are—wonderful things happen.

In my work as a psychotherapist and my life as a father I have observed in others and experienced within myself the tendency not to reach out. Men tend to father in isolation. Women have a long history of mothering in community, and we dads can learn something huge from this. Instead, men keep their experience of fathering to themselves—they tend not to share particularly negative thoughts, feelings, and behaviors. We have been taught not to show weakness, although more and more men are overcoming this, as evidenced by online support networks for fathers, more books on the subject, and actual products and services for fathers. There is something about fatherhood that makes men feel like they should already have it all figured out. Perhaps it's the vestiges of the *Father Knows Best* attitude: He must do the best, be the best, and even think the best.

The groups I run for dads in New York City are confidential and therefore safe places for men to fight isolation, obtain information, get fuel and inspiration, as well as gain insight. In the process

they learn that talking about their feelings is not as dangerous as it may have been on the childhood playground. This takes courage, energy, and a willingness to do something uncomfortable. It is often said that all men want to do is talk about sports scores, the Dow industrial, or what kind of car they drive. While this might be the most comfortable subjects for some men and true to a degree, I am continually impressed by how, if given the opportunity, dads want and need a place to talk about their emotional lives and be a part of a community. So while men might not engage in an emotional way naturally, when there is intention and safety it becomes more possible. It is through this process that I believe they have a greater capacity to care for themselves, their wives, and their children.

Tips for Being a Social Dad

Try the following ideas for increasing your socialization.

- Begin a conversation with another dad or mom who has a child the same age as yours. Ask him or her the Three Big Questions: "What is your child's name? How old is she? Is she sleeping through the night?" Or try something more spontaneous like, "Have you ever noticed how they . . ."
- Connect online through Web sites and blogs like Dad-O-Matic (www.dadomatic.com) for opinions, reviews, advice, and news for dads.
- Participate in preschool programs or other activities for your

baby where you can meet other parents.

- Look into programs at your local church/synagogue, YMCA, or counseling center where you may be able to connect with other dads.
- Give support to a fellow dad. Mothers do these things all the time for one another, so why can't dads do the same?

The Benefits of Dad Therapy

- You have a place to talk about your life—the good, bad, and ugly. So many times I hear men say, "There is no other place in my life where I can talk about this stuff."
- Your emotions get understood, validated, and normalized. When you keep your emotions to yourself it is easy to feel like you are weird or abnormal.
- You become better at expressing emotions rather than acting on emotion. The language of emotion is a hard thing to grasp, especially since men have often been taught to suppress theirs.
- You become more emotionally present to your child and a good model for emotional health.

BUILDING CREATIVE OUTLETS

Many dads in my practice don't have enough creative outlets. Prior to having a child they felt more engaged in a creative process, whether it was through photography or music, tinkering in their garage restoring old cars, or some other creative form. New dads in particular can feel like they don't have the freedom to be creative because of the obligation to be home with their family, not to mention the pressure and anxiety associated with being a provider. Many new dads feel caught up in the routine of providing and caring for their kids and say to themselves, "Is this how the rest of my life is going to be?!" With nothing new and nothing inspiring, there is little creativity in their lives and they describe themselves as feeling almost deadened. For the guy who has a need to be creative (and most men do, whether they know it or not) this routine can be particularly excruciating. "Same old same old," is the phrase they utter. Pay attention to it and do something about it, because it can get old quickly.

Tips for Being a Creative Dad

Try the following ideas for increasing your creativity.

- Maybe you used to play an instrument or have always wanted to learn one. Music is a great thing to share with your baby.
- Take an art class or, on a smaller scale, carry a sketch pad with you wherever you go to use for writing or drawing. Draw a picture of your baby or of your dream home. Write about some of the experiences you have together.
- Creative outlets can be small, simple things as well. Create a

silly song to sing as you change your baby's diaper—you can even steal the melody from your favorite tune. When my son was blowing out major poops I created what almost sounded like a doo-wop song: "Almost up the back . . . almost up the back . . . good God almighty it was almost up the back." Your baby—and you—will love it.

- Find a spot in your home that is yours and no one else's. Go there every day for ten minutes.
- Schedule one hour per week

Real Dad

"I leave for work at 7 A.M., and come home at 6 P.M. to relieve my wife, who is about to pull her hair out. I have a few hours to be with the kids, get them fed and bathed before they go to sleep. By then, I'm beat. All I can do is eat some leftovers, watch a little TV, and then fall asleep . . . to start it all again tomorrow. I often wonder, How much longer will this routine last?"

—Warren, 27

---

to write, paint, draw, build, fantasize, or play.

- Write a story about your baby and make it into a book just for her. Or write a letter to her that she can read when she gets older.
- Think about all the hobbies you've engaged in during your life. Which ones might you want to revive now?

BUILDING PHYSICAL OUTLETS

Taking care of your body, eating well, getting enough sleep, and exercising—all these things can easily fall by the wayside or feel like just one more thing to do, especially during the first year. The days of five-hour golf outings, ski weekends with buddies, or even a couple hours at the gym may be long gone. It's hard to find the time and energy, not to mention the disposable income, to do such things. Or maybe you haven't seen your doctor in a while and you skipped your last dental check-up. It may be a hard fact to accept but you are at a different point in your life. New needs and priorities have come to the fore. Renewing your gym membership may not be in the cards right now, but there are small things you can do to feel better and healthier.

Tips for Getting Physical

- Walk around the block with your baby every Saturday morning. Pick a destination and go for it.
- Make one recreational goal for a six-month period. For example: I

will play tennis on Fridays for one hour, or I will start taking kung fu classes.

- Find a regular practice of mindful breathing. When your breath is short, your temper is likely to get short. Breathe in deeply till you can feel your lungs expand. This practice brings energy to your body, and it is calming at the same time.
- Begin your day with ten push-ups.
- Take a catnap whenever you're feeling tired.
- Eat fruit every day. Drink six glasses of water a day.
- Be accountable to a friend about whatever goal you've set.
- Check out the Men's Health Network (www.menshealthnetwork.org), an informational and educational site that recognizes men's health as a specific social concern.

BUILDING SPIRITUAL OUTLETS

By spiritual I mean anything that connects you to a greater purpose or sense of being. For some dads this might mean their god or perhaps it's their role as father or perhaps their role as provider and husband. As a dad, you're no longer living just for yourself. The majority of dads in my practice wonder how they will ever slow down long enough to just *be*. They are always running, doing, meeting, and strategizing and have little time to be still. The too-busy lives we live are not conducive to cultivating the spiritual.

At the same time, there is something about having a baby that slows you down long enough to be curious about your spiritual roots. This might force you to wonder how you will spiritually raise your child. In addition to thinking about your child's spiritual well-being and what sort of values and traditions you want him or her to grow up with, this can be a fruitful time to wonder as an adult what your religious upbringing meant to you. To explore questions of faith, read the book *Parenting as a Spiritual Journey* by Rabbi Nancy Fuchs-Kreimer.

Spiritual Questions That Often Come Up for New Dads

- As a man, how can I cultivate my own spiritual life?
- Where can I get spiritually fed?
- How do I start the practice of meditation?
- Do I want to return to (or remain in) a place to worship?
- Do I believe in what I was taught as a child?
- How can I serve others?
- As a dad, what do I want to teach my own child?
- Do I want my child to be raised with the same beliefs I was raised with?
- How do I want to shape or inform my child's spiritual upbringing?
- Do we baptize? And if so, when?
- Do we want to have a Bris (circumcision)?

The "Me Time" Challenge

This chapter focused on bringing you back into the picture and suggested ways in which you can take care of yourself—a healthier you often means a healthier relationship with your partner and child. By tending to social, creative, recreational, and spiritual outlets you actually train yourself to tend to those same aspects in your child. This is important training and modeling.

REFLECTION QUESTIONS

1. Which outlet do you feel is lacking the most in your life: social, creative, physical, or spiritual?
2. How might connecting with other dads and sharing your experiences serve you?
3. Name something you have always been interested in learning or doing but never did. Where could you register for a class?
3. Try to think of three reasons why you might resist a social, creative, physical, or spiritual outlet?

Nurturing Your Marriage

Focusing on Your Relationship

I strongly believe that one of the best things you can give your child is a healthy marriage. This chapter will explore the challenges of maintaining and building upon a healthy marriage after you and your partner become parents. How the two of you navigated, survived, or flourished in the first year as parents and as a couple will inform how the next twelve months goes. You, just like every other couple, undoubtedly had your challenges so now is a good time to be intentional about focusing on how you did and how you are going to get through the second year even stronger than before.

A healthy marriage is important as you care for your child, each other, and yourself. I have counseled many couples who have watched their marital relationships disintegrate right before their eyes. They come in dazed and confused

and in pain and wondering, What happened? When did things go wrong? It's no surprise that for many of them having a baby put a strain on the marriage. What generally happens is your energies get directed toward your child, leaving your relationship on the back burner. Second, the new baby can bring up emotions from your past. And finally, there is the practical stress of another mouth to feed, another set of needs to take care of, not to mention the fact that you're probably not getting enough rest or relaxation. Simply put, the first year of being parents is hard.

It requires intentionality to bring the relationship back into focus. One of the first things to suffer in a marriage as a result of having children is communication. The main topic of communication over the past year has probably been the baby, as it should have been.

But what gets lost is the kind of communication that focuses on the couple. In order to strengthen your marriage I strongly recommend you to take time away from your baby so that you can check in with each other. A couple in a healthy marriage knows when time with each other is lacking and makes a concerted effort to put the marriage first. Dr. Michael E. Lamb, one of the premier researchers in the United States on fatherhood, said in a 2004 interview, "One of the best established findings in developmental psychology is how harmful marital conflict is to children."

BECOMING A PARENT CHANGES THE MARRIAGE

Becoming a parent changes the marriage in positive and negative ways. Here are some of the ways in which parents report their marriage has changed:
- We don't talk as much.
- We haven't gone out on a date.
- We have little time for each other.
- He is more anxious, angry, and irritable.
- I (the husband) am softer, a mush ball, and able to cry.
- She is a wonderful mother; she's tender and sweet.
- She doesn't care about me as much.
- He is more protective and anxious.
- I (the husband or partner) am more aware and perhaps more forgiving of my own father or mother.
- She or he is hyperfocused on the baby.

BEING INTENTIONAL ABOUT KEEPING YOUR MARRIAGE HEALTHY

It's been said that when you have a child it's like having your heart removed and watching it move about the world. It's no wonder then that it can be hard to carve out time for the marriage. Who in their right mind would want to leave their heart behind? It's not your child's fault, but she or he can be a wedge that separates you as a couple. It will take effort to remain connected. Here are some ideas on how to keep the marriage a priority.

Love Your Partner

Don't be afraid to kiss and hug in front of your child. This is particularly important to model as a man, since many men (another huge sweeping generalization) do not like to show their affection. When children see expressions of love then they too become comfortable expressing it themselves.

Greet Each Other First

When you or your partner comes home from work, try to greet each other first. It can be so natural and easy to make a beeline for the baby or toddler and completely bypass each other. There will be times when this is hard to do, but try to make a point of acknowledging each other.

Keep Short Accounts

Resentments and anger can build when communication is put on hold. The old biblical saying "Let not the sun go down on your anger" (Ephesians 4:26) is a good one. If you want to avoid accumulating resentments and anger then find a way to say what you are feeling and thinking. Use "I" statements and do not expect your partner to change for you. The goal is to let your partner in on how you are being affected by some aspect of the relationship.

Make a Sacred Date Night

Every couple has a different timetable as to when they feel comfortable going out on a date and leaving the baby with a caregiver. I know one couple that had their first date, post-child, when the baby was no longer a baby—at age six! Other couples begin a regular date night weeks after the baby is born. It is important to make time for fun, romance, and intimacy, and going out on a date is just one way to do that. Don't be surprised if it feels weird or different. Dates are different now that you're leaving your "heart" at home. And don't be surprised if all you do is talk about the baby or feel a strong need to call the sitter. No need to go far or do anything fancy. The purpose is to have some time together. Go fancy if you want but try to avoid putting pressure on yourselves.

Consider Couples Therapy

It is a myth that you have to be in crisis to be in therapy. Choosing to go to couples therapy can mean you've noticed a change in how you communicate and/or how you experience each other. As new parents you have both taken on new identities and you are undoubtedly processing stuff about your own childhoods. Couples therapy offers the opportunity to communicate with minimal distraction.

Don't Forget Mother's Day

The first Mother's Day seems to be important to a woman. I mistakenly figured it was a Hallmark holiday and didn't think it meant much to my wife. Your partner, just like mine, went through great lengths to bring this baby into the world. You don't have to do anything grand (then again, some partners like grand), but you can acknowledge the day, get her a card, and sing her praises. If it's desirable, take her out to dinner. Do something that she would appreciate.

Schedule Household Talks

Life has a new pace and new demands but there are still basic things about managing your lives and home that need to be talked about. Who is going to do what? Who is paying the bills? Is there enough money to cover the expenses? Communicate about money-related issues once per month, covering topics such as changes in either or both incomes, any big expenses coming up, and anything that needs buying, and finally reviewing the budget and making changes if necessary. It can happen over lunch or on the weekend when the baby is asleep. It usually requires some form of preparation.

Schedule Regular Check-ins

I recommend regular check-ins. These tend to happen more spontaneously and are a great way to stay connected. Whether it's communicating your love or mundane practical information, they are important to maintain. With so many ways to communicate, find what's best for you and your partner. Whether it's through text messages, phone calls, or e-mails, make it happen.

Avoid Keeping a Private Score

As in life, parenting isn't fair. One of you may have gotten up with the baby the last three times; the other one may have done the dishes the last several times. The key word in this tip is *private*. Since you probably will keep a tab in a general sense, the goal is not to keep it private, because then you run the risk of resentment, anger build-up, and using it as a line-by-line degradation during an argument.

CO-PARENTING

To parent a child with your spouse can be one of the greatest joys in all of life. It is one of those shared experiences that has no comparison. To know that you co-created this baby in love and brought a new life into this world is remarkable. If your marriage has been generally trouble-free, it can be surprising when you encounter your first major conflict around how to raise your baby.

It's important to remember that this baby is a physical (full of your DNA) and psychic (emotional and psychological) extension of both of you and at the same time totally separate from you. This combination of *like me and not like me* or *of me* and *not of me* is one of the things that makes co-parenting a real challenge.

What typically happens is something like this: One of you sees qualities of yourself in your baby—both good and bad ones—and think, "Oh (or oh no!), she's just like me." For example, you may have a temper and have been known to get angry pretty quickly. Your two-year-old has a fiery temper as well. Your partner makes a comment that suggests your baby is and will be just like you. The challenge for your partner in that moment (and likewise for you if the situation is reversed) is to see you as separate from your child. Traits do get passed on, there is no doubt about that, but at this early age it does nobody any good to merge negative traits.

It is important that you and your partner agree not to use your respective knowledge of each other's pasts against the other. The classic example is telling your partner, "You're becoming your mother" or, "You are just like your dad." This is below-the-belt fighting and can be really destructive.

> **TIP**
>
> It's okay if you and your partner parent differently, just as you probably load the dishwasher differently.

Co-parenting Questions to Ask Each Other

- How do you feel about how your mother parented you? How your father parented you?
- What aspects of your parents do you think you share?
- I think you are like your mother or father in this way. . . . Do you agree?

COMMON DIFFERENCES IN CO-PARENTING

There are any number of areas where you and your partner might disagree as parents. Below are some common areas of disagreement that might arise between the two of you.

Reaction to Crying

Your partner may feel that the baby should not cry by herself. Perhaps you feel that a little crying is okay. Whatever your specific beliefs are about crying, remember that conflict over the issue is likely to have an impact on your marriage. You don't necessarily have to have the same approach, but you need to learn how to accept and ultimately embrace your spouse's way, even though it may not be your way.

Holiday and Birthday Traditions

Traditions have a lot of meaning for people and they get ingrained in us during childhood. We carry these traditions and, whether we like it or not, we perpetuate them, sometimes without even knowing it. It's important to talk with each other about it and become more conscious of which traditions you want to continue and which ones you want to create together as new ones.

Different Gender Expectations

You may have different opinions about how boys should be raised or how girls should be raised. This may reveal itself in subtle ways or screamingly obvious ways. For example, you may be a harder disciplinarian on your boy than your partner is. The key is to talk about it and understand the differences.

Approach to Differences

Before you go overhauling yourselves, it's important to remember that your differences may actually be beneficial. Children benefit from different approaches, as long as the underlying philosophy is the same. For example, if they come to experience you as more playful and your partner as more comforting, this shows them that different needs can be met by different parents. The goal is not to be carbon copies of each other but, at the very least, to be curious about how your differences are having a positive or negative impact on your child. It is vital that you not undermine the other parent because her ways are different than yours. For example, you want to avoid saying things like, "Mommy is being mean; you don't have to listen to mommy."

To make the challenges of co-parenting a bit less challenging, I suggest you try the following:

Get to know each other's stories. Having children offers you an opportunity to deepen your understanding of each other's personal histories, which is critical. The more you get to know your spouse's life story, the less likely you will judge and criticize how she parents. For example, when a patient of mine learned that his wife's uncle had been sexually inappropriate with her as a little girl, he found himself much more understanding of why his wife seemed overly concerned about keeping the baby's "private parts" private. One of the best places to get to know a partner's story is while on a road trip, after the kids have fallen asleep, when there are few distractions.

Earn her trust. One patient of mine explained it to me this way: "How am I going to get my partner to trust me around the baby? She's always looking over my shoulder. She's always telling me what to do. 'You are being too rough with him! That's not what he likes!' I wish she would back off and just let me parent my kid." Many dads whom I see in my practice complain that their wives don't trust them to be alone with the baby. In its worst form the mom will literally not leave the father and baby alone together. In a slightly better, but still mistrustful, way the mom will regularly make comments about how the father ineffectually cares for the baby. There are times, I'm sure, when these comments are warranted and times when it says more about the mom and the couple's different parenting styles than anything else. No doubt there are some clueless dads out there and no doubt there are dads who just parent differently. The goal here is to get to the bottom of the issue without degrading the other. This is where seeing a couple's counselor might be particularly helpful.

Speak up and stand up. One of the artful aspects of parenting is knowing when to intervene and be involved and when to step back. There are times when it is important to step in and take charge, but I often see dads on the sidelines and not taking an active role in parenting their children. One of the things that will help you intervene is knowing how important your involvement is. There is increasing evidence that suggests that the relationship with the father may have an especially long-term impact on the child's ability to have meaningful relationships.

Be quiet and sit down. Just as there will be times for you to get involved there will also be times for you to be quiet. Again, it's a part of the artful dance. Often for new dads, it's best to let your partner take the lead when you have lost your cool and become frustrated by your child's behavior. One the great things about co-parenting is that when one of you is incapable for whatever reason, the other can often cover. Ideally this goes both ways.

Listen well. As adults, it is often assumed that we have developed the skill of listening. I find this assumption incredibly lacking since listening rarely gets taught adequately in daily living. I find, as a therapist who works with couples, it is often this skill that needs to be worked on the most. And when this skill is mastered improvement is experienced in the relationship. A common impediment to good listening is the need to get your point across first—or focusing only on your next opportunity to speak. Learning to listen empathically and actively can go a long way in keeping your marriage healthy.

Empathic listening means listening for the feeling behind the words and coming to understand and accept whatever that feeling is. Here is an example: A partner complains that her husband never calls when he is away on business even though she asks him all the time to call and check in. The empathic listener will hear this complaint and respond with: "It sounds like you are frustrated that I don't call and that I haven't responded to this request." As you empathically listen you want to make sure you don't assume that you know what the talker is feeling. Instead, communicate what you think she is feeling based on what she's told you by using phrases like "it sounds like" or "if I'm hearing correctly" or "as I listen I think I'm hearing . . ." And then allow your partner to correct you if that's not what she meant.

All these possibilities may sound weird and very much *not* like you, but they are proven strategies for effective communication. If these suggestions don't fit your style, find words that do. The point is to communicate your desire to understand your partner's feelings.

Active listening involves listening through nonverbal cues such as eye contact and body posture. These nonverbal expressions show that you are with her. Oftentimes we are forced listen while we are in bed about to fall asleep or as we multitask. While this works in some cases, it can prevent you from listening accurately. So put the cell phone down, turn off the TV, and have a conversation the old-fashioned way—one-on-one, giving each other your full attention, with as few distractions as possible.

Consider This

If you look up the word *husband* in the dictionary, it will likely say something like: to manage esp. with prudent economy. Sam Keen, the author of books on masculinity, writes in *Fire in the Belly,* "to husband is to practice the art of stewardship, to oversee, to make judicious use of things and to conserve for the future. The husbandman is a man who has made a decision to be in place, to make commitments, to forge bonds, to put down roots, to translate the feeling of empathy and compassion into an action of caring."

The Cost of an Unhealthy Marriage

For many men, the threat or even the possibility of divorce can force them to slow down and reflect on what is really important, and give them a much-needed pause in the action of life. There is no doubt that separation and divorce can bring about a lot of heartbreak for all involved. The toll it takes on children is significant. The impact on the parents can be devastating depending on how they treat each other and the custodial arrangement. I have worked with many couples who have separated and I cannot think of one father who likes the time away from his child. The ambiguity of the paternal role can become even sharper after a divorce. Many fathers already feel marginalized and undermined, and now, with only partial visitations, your role in your child's life is even harder to establish. We all know that not all divorces end in maternal custody but most do. And regardless of how the custodial arrangement works out, it is bound to have a significant impact on the lives of everyone involved.

Here are a few facts about marital conflict and divorce:

- The U.S. Census Bureau tells us that more than one million children per year are affected by divorce.
- Twenty million children in the United States live with only one parent and about seven million are under the age of six.
- A study by John Gottman of the Gottman Institute reports that men who are in unsatisfying marriages are more likely to withdraw from their wives and children, thus depriving their children of the positive impact an engaged dad can have.
- Children as young as eleven months can pick up on the mood of their father and will not seek their father out for help in distressing situations (separation anxiety) if they sense their father is unhappy.

A STRONG MARRIAGE

Raising a child is one thing. Staying married while you raise a child is another. This chapter highlighted some specific things you can do to keep your marriage alive and well. Of the many things mentioned in this chapter, the one that I want to emphasize here is the importance of learning each other's stories. This has a way of minimizing judgments and offering up the possibility of acceptance and forgiveness when your spouse does something you completely do not understand.

REFLECTION QUESTIONS

1. Prior to having a child, what kind of fun dates did you have with your partner? Consider recreating a fun date night.
2. What are you and your partner not talking about that needs to be discussed? Are there any resentments? (It's probably

best not to have this particular conversation during your first fun date night.)

3. Since becoming a parent, have you noticed any new behaviors in your partner or in yourself that you love?

4. Try to come up with at least three ways you want to be like your father and three ways that you do not want to be like your father. Do the same for your mother.

5. Think of things you can do to be a better listener.

Full Engagement:
24 to 36 Months

IV

> *"Toddlers, unlike infants, can come looking for you, demand your attention and make your day with their unconditional love and affection. They can also drive you nuts with their oppositional tendencies, stubbornness and 'in your face' communication style and attitude."*
>
> —Kyle Pruett, author of *Fatherneed*

The third year of your child's life will be marked by an increase in physical autonomy, emotional volatility, and cognitive growth. It will also pose a wonderful opportunity for you to engage with your child in three distinct ways: through play, through discipline, and by modeling emotional expressiveness.

In this section I will devote a chapter to the developmental milestones and each of these three aspects of fathering and provide helpful advice on how best to engage with your two-year-old. Your growing toddler will begin to mimic behavior in more overt ways, which makes it even more important for you to be conscious of what you say and how you behave.

The main idea that we will explore in this section is paternal engagement, which means taking an active interest in helping your child deal with himself (his internal world) and the world around him (the external world). Internally, this could mean helping your child put his feelings into words and express frustration in a way that adults can understand. Externally, this could mean helping him to learn the limits and realities of the external world, such as that fire is hot. These are tough lessons, but your active engagement through play, discipline, and modeling emotional expressiveness will make the lessons easier to learn.

Raising a Toddler

The Not-So-Terrible Twos

The period between twenty-four and thirty-six months is often called the "terrible twos." While I get it, it does require a lot of work, they can get into everything that you don't want them to get into, it can also be thought of as a period of intense training in becoming a person. In fact, I would like suggest that this is actually a period of great wonder and exploration and, yes, rebellion. Your two-year-old is working on the developmental task of forming his identity, his sense of self. To do this he will need to separate from and reject you. He will proclaim, "Me do!" or demand "NO!" or exclaim "I hate you!" This is him being two and it will be your job not to retaliate. The thing we want to avoid is acting like two-year-olds ourselves.

I heard a recent story where a father didn't talk with his son for two days because his three-year-old son screamed at him and said, "I hate you!" While it can certainly be challenging, frustrating, and even infuriating the goal has to be to not retaliate or behave like a two- or three-year-old yourself. You have to stay the adult. By staying the adult you can help shape your child's behavior by being firm, tender, and understanding without acting out of revenge. And, as usual, you will need to protect him from his own ignorance of the ways of the world. It really is the first time in your child's development where the two of you can have a back and forth, whether it be through conversation or nonverbal play. You may, however, need to be somewhat flexible with what is comfortable for you. For instance, when my middle daughter was close to three, my schedule allowed me to spend Thursday mornings with her. We would regularly have breakfast at a diner and then return home and do a project or activity. One activity that she really loved was to put nail polish on my fingernails. I was not a big fan of the idea for several reasons: Despite my progressive thinking about what it means to be a man, it made me slightly uncomfortable. Plus, I had clients to see in the afternoon, and I was sure she would make an absolute mess. The whole thing just left me wondering where my old GI Joe was, but this was precious time and I wanted to connect with her. I figured out a way to minimize the mess and maximize the fun, which helped me put aside some of my anxieties and just be with her. She would do my nails (and the surrounding area) and I would paint hers. It was a blast! I'll never forget it. My daughter is now six and we occasionally reflect back on those Thursday morning manicures with fondness and affection.

So do the twos have to be so terrible? They don't have to be if you are willing to join in, lighten up, get down and dirty, and experience them as the *magical twos*. Engaging your child on his level without behaving like a child will help you understand what's going on for him developmentally. This chapter will explain in detail the milestones of a growing two-year-old and what you as father can do to support that growth.

Aggressive Children and Parenting

Dr. John Gottman of the University of Washington has studied four-year-olds and discovered that aggressive behavior in children can be decreased if parents learn how to do what he calls "emotional coaching." It goes like this:
- Validate the emotion your child is demonstrating: "I see and understand that you are mad, upset, or frustrated."
- Help your child verbalize the feeling behind his behavior: "What were you feeling when . . . ?"
- Help your child come up with solutions or alternatives, such as, "The next time you get mad I want you to come to me and we'll work it out."

DEVELOPMENTAL MILESTONES

The development markers that psychologists and pediatricians generally use when assessing your child at this age are the same ones they used in the first year: gross motor skills, fine motor skills, language ability, cognitive ability, and social skills. (See chapter 7 for a full explanation of each of these areas.) As before, I have added emotional milestones to the list.

Physical and Behavioral Development

From a physical and behavioral standpoint, this period of growth is about mastery, autonomy, and separating from you, which can be very exciting, challenging, and scary. It is during this stage that your child's newly discovered abilities will allow for fun new activities, like potty training and riding a tricycle. Your job is to watch, praise, spot, and redirect his behavior into healthy alternatives when he runs into trouble.

You might notice:	You can respond by:
He has trouble controlling his impulses. His desire to do is greater than his capacity to not do, meaning he has not developed the capacity for self-restraint and can be quite impulsive. He is, however, much less impulsive than he was at 12 months.	Reinforcing what is *yes*, *no*, or *maybe* behavior. Consider posting home rules up on the wall to make things clear, like no spitting, hitting, kicking, biting, or pushing, but yes to laughing, playing, dancing, sharing, etc. Since he can't read you'll have to point out the words and even add pictures if you want. You might want to consider these rules as guidelines for what warrants time-outs (see chapter 12 for more on time-outs).
She wants to do everything herself.	Stepping in when she can't do something herself. Be patient with the process. Repetition is key to helping your child understand what she can and cannot do.
She likes to climb out of her crib and wander away from you.	Supporting her need to explore, climb, and do for herself. Give her little jobs, like turning off lights or greeting people when they come home. Keep your expectations low. Protect her from her own curiosity. Even though she has a sense of consequences, kids can still do risky things at this age.

You might notice:	You can respond by:
He is accident prone, leading to lots of bumps, bruises, and tears.	Soothing and comforting those bruises. Try not to minimize it if he's obviously in pain. If he says *ouch* respond in kind with your own *ouch*. Crying stops faster when you mirror and validate their pain.
She makes valiant attempts at getting attention, acting very silly with a slapstick sense of humor minus the laughs.	Laughing when you can. Sometimes she'll bring the house down. Other times the humor is just not that funny—what's important is that she tries.
He likes to test out his own physical abilities, for example, by jumping on one foot, then the other, then both.	Watching him closely so he comes to see how capable yet limited he is. For example, remind him that he can't really fly. Reinforce the idea of pretend play.
He is capable new tricks: running, throwing a ball overhand, and a very funny rendition of a somersault.	Reminding him when not to run or hold his hand while running together. Kids at this age tend to trip a lot and can seriously hurt their teeth, chin, and hands. Praising specific behavior when he succeeds and masters a new task.
She likes to move furniture or boxes around.	Creating a safe place in your home for her to play, create, and make a mess.
She likes to color and not stay within the lines.	Giving her a desk or play table for drawing and coloring. Encourage her experimentations with color and creativity. Don't worry about staying in the lines—focus on effort, not results.
He puts things in his mouth, nose, ears, any orifice.	Keeping a close eye on him. You're beginning to understand why so many labels say "keep out of reach of children."

You might notice:	You can respond by:
She destroys towers at 24 months and creates towers at 36 months.	Destroying and creating with her, and trying not to react negatively to her destructive tendency.
He gravitates toward "boy" things, i.e., trucks, diggers, sports, or loud music.	Reinforcing this while also allowing him to experiment with "girl" things too. Where there is safe curiosity there is learning. Do not shame him for playing with girls' things.
She gravitates toward "girl" things, i.e., dolls, make up, playing dress-up, cooking.	Reinforcing this while at the same time allowing her to experiment with "boy" things too. Where there is safe curiosity there is learning. Do not shame her for playing with boys' things.
He doesn't eat as much as he used to.	Not panicking. Observe; don't force food. He may go through spurts when he eats a lot.
She doesn't eat enough fruits or vegetables. She has become a very picky eater.	Giving her vegetables first, either pureed or chopped up small. (Some benefits of vegetables are cumulative over a lifetime and you won't be able to control her choices forever.) If all else fails, use a dipping sauce like salad dressing for interest and additional flavor. Present other options after fruits and veggies.
He doesn't take to breastmilk or formula anymore.	Switching to a low-fat milk or nonfat milk by the time he is two. He doesn't need the fat for development any longer. He should be getting 2 to 3 cups (16 to 24 ounces) per day.
He wakes in the middle of the night, visits you in your bed, and insists on sleeping with you.	Bringing him back to his bed, over and over again, unless you and your partner have agreed otherwise.

You might notice:	You can respond by:
Your child has a full set of primary teeth (twenty). She likes to have her teeth brushed, especially when you make it fun.	Brushing her teeth at least twice daily. This is as much for her gums as for her teeth. Teach her how to get the top, bottom, insides, and outsides of her teeth, but don't expect her to brush her own teeth properly. Take her to the dentist sometime during this year.
He has an interest in sitting on the potty chair, or you've noticed all his peers are starting to use a potty chair. He may occasionally grab at his crotch.	Knowing the reality—this is not a quick and easy exercise; it takes roughly three to six months, with accidents still occurring, particularly at night. Give him your undivided attention while he sits on the toilet. Break out a book—no harm in making it comfortable. Create your own "code" for referring to poop and pee. Have fun with it. Encourage pottying before you leave the house but pack supplies in case of accidents. Teach him how to wipe. (Girls should wipe from front to back.)

Potty Time

It's hard not to brag about how soon your tot mastered potty training, but every child develops at his own rate and forcing the issue on your little one is usually frustrating and fruitless.

In assessing whether your child is ready to begin potty training, ask yourself the following:
- Is he curious about the toilet or potty chair?
- Has he expressed a desire to try it out?
- Is he able to tell you in actions or words that he has to go or has already gone to the bathroom?
- Can he get his pants on and off on his own?
- If the answer to any of these questions is no, you may want to wait a bit. But don't worry: He will graduate from diapers.

To this end my wife and I used the "Proud of You" song, a Mr. Rogers classic. I never thought I'd be singing a Fred Rogers song to my kids but when I saw the delight on my daughter's face it was absolutely worth it. (To hear Fred Rogers himself sing it, check out www.pbskids.org/rogers/songlist/song12.html.)

TIP

Using words to praise pottying success may be a more natural way to create a bond between you and your child, as opposed to rewarding with external objects such as stickers or candy.

Emotional Development

The emotional development or temperament of a twenty-four- to thirty-six-month-old is characterized by a full range of both positive and negative emotions. This is your child's way of interacting with and responding to the world around him. To put it in perspective, there is no other period in human development where the expression of both total excitement and complete despair occurs so spontaneously or changes so rapidly from one extreme to the other. The proverbial "cap" has not yet been put on your child's emotions. Pay close attention to how you treat your child's emotional expressiveness and see if your responses have to do with his or her gender. He has not been taught to contain his feelings and he has little to no shame. He walks around naked because it feels good, he eats ice cream and makes a complete mess, he pulls his mother to the toys he wants to play with and says, "Get on floor, Mommy" in a dictatorial manner. It is a precious yet demanding time. With their growing autonomy toddlers often feel like royalty, yet when they come up against the limits of the world they can easily feel like pawns. They are emotionally fragile and at the same time emotionally resilient.

You might notice:	You can respond by:
Your child getting frustrated easily as she tries to master certain tasks, like putting on shoes or climbing a jungle gym.	Supporting her big feelings. Validate the frustration and help her through it by either doing the task for her or, better yet, showing her that she can do it with your support.
His emotions change quickly— happy one minute, sad or mad the next. Fortunately he seems to recover pretty quickly.	Helping him name whatever it is that he is feeling, starting with *sad, mad, glad* or *scared*.
She bites other kids. (Children do this for a variety of reasons: It may have something to do with being overexcited, overwhelmed, angry, or envious.)	Firmly telling her that we do not bite, removing her abruptly from the scene, and helping her apologize. Keep expectations low.

You might notice:	You can respond by:
He has no empathy or compassion for other kids when they get hurt or get a boo-boo.	Not panicking. Empathy is a skill that develops over time. Model empathy by caring for others, such as your partner.
She nearly always needs to come out on top, win, or otherwise be victorious, even if it means not following the rules of the game.	Allowing her to win at games, wrestle you down to the ground, and show her super-human strength. Kids this age are generally not able to abide by rules of games.

TIP

Tantrums in public places are annoying for parents. Remember that toddlers can't regulate and manage big feelings. Focus on remaining calm, keeping your child safe, and sparing other people as much as possible.

Cognitive Skills

During the second year, cognitive development really takes off as she might be in the beginning of preschool. It is quite fun to watch her make the cognitive connections between ideas, people, and places. You will be in awe of how her mind works. Her ability to remember things is quite remarkable. This is important (and ironic) because you might find your memory starting to fade. It can be adorable to watch her try to count using her fingers. She exercises her imaginations and likes to play pretend more at this age.

You might notice:	You can respond by:
She begins to see a direct connection between people, places, and things. She's also beginning to realize that her behavior has an impact on things and others.	Reinforcing the cognitive idea that her behavior has an impact on others and that there are natural consequences to that behavior.
He knows that things exist even in their absence. This is the beginning of abstract thought and object permanence.	Playing hide-and-seek games. Give him jobs to do—simple two- or three-step requests, like "Please go into to the bedroom and turn off the light."

You might notice:	You can respond by:
She likes to use her imagination and play games of pretend. She may even have an imaginary friend or may dub you the king.	Introducing or going along with her imaginative play. Remind her, when you step out of the imaginative play, that you are now back to being Daddy.
He has a short attention span.	Not expecting him to sustain his attention for long periods of time.
She is able to discern parts of a whole.	Asking her to guess what you are drawing before you complete it.

Language Skills

Almost fluent, she understands a lot more than she can say. During this period your toddler starts out with about a fifty-word vocabulary and by the end has a three-hundred-word vocabulary—yet she will understand about nine hundred words. She will mimic you and parrot what you say, which can be both adorable and surprising.

Your ability to communicate with her will increase all the time as she understand more words and more concepts. She should be able to answer who and where questions. She will start to pick up on grammar rules but will often use them incorrectly, saying things like: "I runned home" or "he hitted me." Child care will also become a little easier as language develops.

You might notice:	You can respond by:
She makes verbal demands.	Teaching her polite ways to make a request. Encouraging verbal manners like "May I please?" or "Thank you" or "You're welcome."
He likes to say NO . . . a lot.	Encouraging him to say, "No thank you." Reflect on how often *you* say *no* to him.
One-word sentences become two-, three-, and four-word sentences. Her speech is clearer and strangers understand some of what she says.	Watching and praising! Reinforcing verbal accomplishments. For example, "I like how you used your words when you asked for the spoon, instead of grabbing it from me."

You might notice:	You can respond by:
She asks or demands that you read her a book.	Reading to her as much as possible. This is a great bedtime routine that helps with language development.
She makes a lot of mistakes as she talks.	Pointing to objects and characters in a book and reinforcing her understanding of these objects. Refrain from correcting her pronunciation of words or her use of tense. She will grow out of it and you don't want to put a damper on her enthusiasm for learning.
Other people talk to him using "baby talk."	Talking to him in your normal voice.
She loves reciting the alphabet and singing the ABC song.	Singing along with her or just observing her.

Social Skills

The social skills of a two-year-old really progress during this stage of development. Children at this age are introduced to a world beyond themselves, through preschool, playdates, and an overall expanding world. As she comes into contact with more and more people, you will see her in a whole different light. She may be really outgoing or really shy or perhaps she gets silly and inappropriate. However your child comes out on the social spectrum, it's important for you to work toward seeing her clearly, as connected to yet separate from you.

TIP

Objects have great meaning for toddlers and sharing can be very difficult. A few pointers: (1) Don't expect immediate sharing; (2) Give him a period of time to come around; (3) Explain why we share. Say something like: "We share so that your friend will share with you"; and (4) If you feel strongly about it and she continues not to share, explain the consequence. For example: "We will leave the park if you can't share."

You might notice:	You can respond by:
Her social temperament is either shy and reserved or gregarious and outgoing.	Loving her regardless of her temperament. Give her opportunities to develop other aspects of herself. Don't shame her for her social temperament, such as by saying, "What are *you* doing?" or "*You* always do that."
He acts differently in school than he does at home. (For example, he shares well at home but not so well with the other kids at school.)	Remembering this is normal for kids to act differently in different settings.
She shows signs of empathy—the capacity to feel for another person, animal, or doll.	Practicing empathy on dolls, toy animals, or other children. Ask her what she thinks the doll, animal, or friend is feeling.
He likes to mimic you.	Modeling the behavior you want to see.

TIP

Pacifier overuse can cause damage to the mouth, delay proper speech, and undermine self-soothing. Quitting cold turkey is the way to go.

WHEN TO BE CONCERNED ABOUT DEVELOPMENT

If your child is not meeting the milestones as mentioned above, do not panic or think that your child is faulty or going to be the laughingstock of the play yard or school. It may mean nothing or it may mean he needs some help. The first thing you should do is

MEASURING UP

Average Weight
• 24 months: 22 to 33 pounds
• 30 months: 24 to 36 pounds
• 36 months: 27 to 38 pounds

Average Height
• 24 months: 31 to 37 inches
• 30 months: 33 to 38 inches
• 36 months: 34 to 40 inches

consult with your pediatrician to see if there is good reason for concern.

Family Events and Regressive Behavior

There are times when a significant family event impedes on your child's development. Pay attention to these family events. For example, a two-and-a-half-year-old who has been very close to going to the potty by himself and seems ready to graduate from diapers does an about-face. What happened? Suppose that, just as he is on the cusp of this milestone, his mother gives birth to another child. The two-and-a-half-year-old isn't getting as much attention as he used to. Maybe he just needs some time to adjust to the change. If a major event happens in your family, you'll want to pay attention to how it affects your child. In many cases, the impediment is temporary; in other cases it's more permanent. Some examples of major life events are:

• Moving.
• Death in the family.
• Addition(s) to the family, such as a child or a live-in grandparent.
• Parental conflict, separation, or divorce.

You can help your child work through the life event by:

• Being aware and curious about what is going on within the family that might be having an impact on your child.
• Lowering your expectations that she will learn and grow as if nothing is going on.
• Being an ear to listen, a person to play with.
• Not retaliating to his aggression or negative behavior.
• Trying your best to understand.

BOOT CAMP FOR "BEING A PERSON"

This chapter focused on the not-so-terrible twos and was designed to help you see it as a time of wonder despite its frustrations. The primary challenge for you is to be patient with your child as she grows and matures—this is all training to be a person. It can be tempting to get ahead of yourself and think your toddler is older and smarter than she actually is. Be as engaged as possible. This period is loaded with the possibility of fun.

REFLECTION QUESTIONS

1. Do you have a memory dating back to when you were two or three years old?
2. If you don't have a toddler memory, see if you can research and find out what was going on in your family at this age. Where was your father? Your mother? This information may help you understand your child but also your own behavior.
3. What have been some significant family events in your own story?
4. How do you know when your toddler is just being a toddler and when you need to step in and correct her behavior?

Understanding the Importance of Father Play

Playtime: More Than Having Fun

Your partner is away for the weekend visiting a sick family member and you are on duty. You're flying solo and it's your job to take care of this child of yours. You're a father, not a babysitter. What are you going to do? How are you going to fill the time? You can't watch TV or play video or computer games all weekend. This chapter will provide you with specific ways you can play with your baby from one month to three years as well as explain the specific benefits and necessities of father play.

"Very often the effort men put into activities that seem completely useless turns out to be extremely important in ways no one could foresee," wrote Italo Calvino, an Italian journalist. "Play has always been the mainspring of culture." When it comes to children, play is almost as important as food. Psychiatrist, medical doctor, and president of the National Institute for Play Stuart Brown says that play is part of the "developmental sequencing of becoming a human primate. If you look at what produces learning, memory, and well-being, play is as fundamental as any other aspect of life, including sleep and dreams."

Play helps establish a foundation of trust between you and your child. It's the beginning of a shared life and a great way to get to know your baby. The cost of not playing with your baby or toddler may seem insignificant now, but the years do fly by. As he's ready to leave for college, you and your child could end up looking at each other with a blank stare, wanting to feel the loss inherit in the moment but instead feeling a lack that is all too familiar. You both exchange the obligatory comments—"I'll miss you," "I love you," and "I'll write"—yet the heart is empty, the eyes are dry, and deep inside you'll both feel more comfortable once it's all over.

It may seem like I am getting ahead of myself. Your child may have just mastered walking and I'm talking about her going off to college. Still, this is the time when your bond with your child gets built. The physical and emotional absence that pervades many father-child relationships is at the core of what this book is attempting to reverse. As Shakespeare wrote in *The Merchant of Venice*, "It is a wise father that knows his own child." Play is one very important way to get to know your child and a way for both of you to experience each other's physical and emotional presence.

The developmental psychologist Bruno Bettelheim adds that "many children who do not have much chance to play and who are infrequently played with suffer severe intellectual arrest and setbacks." Most of the literature on infant and child development will tell you that play is where fathers have the greatest impact, and yet playing with an infant or toddler does not always come easily. There are impediments to play that I've noticed in my practice and personal life. Below are a few common ones. What are yours?

COMMON IMPEDIMENTS TO PLAY

- Too busy, no time—blurred lines between work life and home life
- A concern, often voiced by the

mother, that dad will get the child too hyped up before bedtime
- The notion that play is useless
- Too much technology—computer, e-mail, cell phone, and TV
- Lack of confidence; a feeling of "I don't know what to do"

BENEFITS OF FATHER PLAY

There are many good reasons why father play is unique and beneficial and why it needs to be a priority. Following are some of the biggest and best ones.

Body Awareness

Father play tends to be more physical. Whether it's tickling, blowing raspberries on bellies, or tossing a ball around, dads tend to get more physical than moms. What the baby learns through this sort of play is a sense of what she is capable of and not capable of, what feels good and what doesn't feel good. In essence the child learns how to take risks and what her body can do. The father, in turn, becomes a human jungle gym and enforcer of external limits. For example, a two-year-old girl wants to fly around, and daddy shows her how to do it but also shows her the limits.

Mutual Bonding

Through play both father and child get seen, known, and felt. This leads to a strong bond and a foundation for a solid relationship between you and your child. Many of the dads I meet report that by the time their son or daughter becomes a teenager, they do not know how to get through to him or her. I suspect that what they really mean is: "I do not know my own child. I do not know what excites him, what upsets her, nor do I even know who he's really spending time with." The same is often said by teens and preteens about their dads: "I don't know my father. I don't know what he really thinks or feels. He just goes along with what Mom says." Many teens report that they are curious about their dad's relationship with his own father.

Studies show that children need to know their father, as it helps in identity formation. Early infant play enhances the bond between father and baby and lays the foundation for a lifetime a mutual intimacy.

Building Memories

As an engaged, playful dad, you develop memories through play and will remember things that your child will not. As your child grows up she will be creating a life narrative. It might start with her birth story, becoming a compilation of moments laced together that make up a whole story. Oftentimes the narrative will have gaps in it, particularly in these early years, since she won't be able to remember what her first word was or what it was like for her to be potty trained. A father can add to the narrative by filling in these early experiences. When your child becomes six or so, you can tell her stories about what she was like as a baby, how she loved to play peekaboo or bounce on

your knee. These playful stories reinforce not only your connection to her, but hers to herself. This aids in identity formation.

Consider This

In his book *Play*, Stuart Brown says, "[Play] shapes the brain and makes animals smarter and more adaptable. In higher animals, it fosters empathy and makes possible complex social groups. For us, play lies at the core of creativity and innovation."

Empathy and Social Skills

During father play, babies and toddlers get a taste of what it feels like to be in the presence of "the other." The infant begins the crucial yet ongoing steps toward otherness, or experiencing people outside of themselves. If you think about it, much of your baby's young life has been merged with her mother. For nine months she was literally living inside her mother and now she is separate and discovering that there are more people in the world than her mother. In a way, her father represents the first social experiment through his play. Through this socializing, for example, a father may pretend to be hurt and the baby or toddler will learn how to empathize with her father.

THE "RULES" OF PLAY

One of the hardest things about playing with infants and toddlers is that they don't play by the rules. It's not about winning. It's not about finishing. It's not even about creating. In fact, it's probably the opposite of all those things. In general, it makes the most sense at this age to think of play as an act of mutual learning and exploration, where you both are free to meander, get lost, find yourselves, connect, detach, and be with each other. Here are ten rules for father play:

1. Make sure you stop when your child starts to express discomfort, annoyance, or pain.
2. Give yourself time to shift gears from work to play and change into comfortable clothes—play clothes.
3. Expect multiple distractions but try to minimize your own lapses in attention. Turn off the BlackBerry, iPhone, and so on, particularly around younger children.
4. Get down on the floor, on your child's level, as much as possible.
5. As children get closer to age three, they use imagination. Feel free to join in. It doesn't have to make sense.
6. Let older children lead as soon as they can (this can start as early as the first year) unless it becomes dangerous or inappropriate.
7. Commit fully to the play and try not to do other things at the same time.
8. Think of yourself as clay and malleable and flexible enough to adapt to your child's world and way of thinking.
9. Sometimes all you need to do is watch. It is important for them to be seen and for you to observe them.
10. Be mindful of the size, strength, and power differential between you and your child.

LET THE GAMES BEGIN

It goes without saying that newborns don't play the same way as three-year-olds. The newborn's attention span is minimal, their hand-eye coordination is spastic, and they can't use their words to express what they need. So, if we revisit the dad who is alone with the baby for the weekend while his wife visits a sick family member . . . how do you play with a baby versus a growing toddler? If she responds to music and rhythms or banging pots and pans, pick her up and dance. If she likes jostling and bouncing, play horsey and gallop her all over the house. If it's gentle swaying that makes her coo, turn your arms into a swing and get swaying.

If you know what makes your child beam, head in that direction. But here are some more ideas for age-appropriate play from your baby's birth to three years. The goal here for you is to start small and build upon prior success. The time requirement is minimal, particularly in the beginning when the primary goal is to allow your baby to get to know your face, become familiar with your voice, and sense your presence. Remember, the learning and discovery curve for young children is huge and you will be able to read a lot about what is going on in your child's head and the connections he's making by simply watching his reactions.

Birth to 3 Months

Newborns are working hard at trying to see and work out their many reflexes. The best time to play is when they are in the Quiet Alert or Active Alert state.

Reflex games. At this stage babies operate primarily on reflex. They do not have much capacity to think and then act. The challenge is to meet them where they are. With seventy-five possible reflexes, you have many options. One of the strongest and most functional is the sucking reflex. With a clean pinky finger and a cleanly cut fingernail, gently place your finger (with the nail facing down against the tongue) in your baby's mouth. Lightly stimulate the roof of the mouth and watch your baby suck. Try to remove your finger and, if you're able, watch your baby suck even harder. You'll be impressed with how strong the muscles are and for how long babies can do this. See if your baby can turn your pinky into a raisin.

Five fingers. As your baby's visual capacity develops you can actually witness her vision improve by holding your hand about ten inches away and watching her track the movement of your fingers. Slowly open your hand, finger by finger, and watch

your baby catch sight of each new finger—she'll be in awe. You've never had such a captivated audience. See how long she can hold visual contact.

Nappin' on Dad. Since most of what a baby does during these early months is sleep, why not catch some Zs together? This can be a great way to connect. It's one of life's joys to have your baby fall asleep on your bare chest. This gives the baby great sensory exposure to your smell, touch, and breathing rhythms. For the hairy-chested dads out there, you might want to throw on a T-shirt or put a burp cloth on you. Your baby may pull your chest hair (and that's not part of the game) as he flexes his grasping skills. For the heavy sleeper, make sure the baby is not vulnerable to falling off your chest or to you rolling over onto him.

Dance. Whether you have a son or daughter this a great time to throw on some of your favorite music and move around. If you are a "bad" dancer, don't worry. Your baby won't know. Babies delight in being up high and swung around very gently.

Reading on Daddy's lap. It's best to use books with hard covers and thick pages. It's more fun and meaningful if you can turn reading into a regular ritual. Even though a newborn can't understand the story, she will enjoy the feeling of cuddling with you and hearing the rhythm of your voice as you read. This is a lifetime thing—soon after her first birthday, your baby will learn to turn the pages, repeat sounds, and finish words for you. And when she is about five, she will even begin to read herself. It's thrilling to witness. (For more on reading, see 9 to 12 months, below.)

3 to 6 Months

They are really coming alive at this age and relating more, seeing more, and moving around more.
A variation of peekaboo. This variation of peekaboo has you putting a large napkin or scarf over your head while saying, "Where's Daddy?" At first your baby won't know what to do, so you'll have to pull the napkin away. After repeated times, he'll catch on and actually pull the napkin away himself. The delight this generates is wonderful to watch. It seems particularly exciting that he can make Daddy appear. Take turns and put the napkin on his head and watch him pull it off with gusto.

Tummy time. Pediatricians regularly recommend giving your baby "tummy time." My wife and I got a lot of pleasure out of this ritual. Place your baby on her tummy and watch what she does. First you'll notice that she does nothing but lie there, but by the sixth month she'll get better at lifting up her head and torso. It's a great workout for back and neck muscles. (Definitely do this before the bowsprit, which follows.) If your baby is getting tired and frustrated, give her a rest and place a foam wedge or pillow under her chest so she's not exerting too much energy.

The bowsprit. When my children reached the age of five months I used to do what became known as the bowsprit. I would hold my son (and later my two daughters) at the top of his thighs, just below his waist, facing out (his back toward me) and slowly start to lean his torso forward so that it was no longer upright. He would resist the pull of gravity and of falling over, arching his back and generating a powerful grin. After repeatedly doing this, his back muscles got so strong he could literally keep his torso parallel with the ground.

Clap, clap, clap. Your baby will imitate you , so if you open your eyes wide, he will as well. If you clap, he will too. Sing the following traditional children's song, do the motions with your hands, and watch your baby try to follow. The lyrics go like this: "Open, shut them, open, shut them, give a little clap clap clap. Open, shut them, open, shut them, put them in your lap lap lap. Creep them, crawl them, creep them, crawl them, right up to your chin chin chin. Open wide your little mouth, but do not let them in. No, do not let them in." You can use this little ditty and finger game up through the second year. (You can purchase music CDs with this and other songs by doing an Internet search.)

Airplane. This starts off with your baby on his belly during tummy time. You may notice that he has outstretched his arms and legs and is flying on his belly. Your job is to add the sound effects. When your baby is more stable, you can lie down on your back and lift your legs, keeping your knees and ankles together. Put your baby on your shins and hold his or her hands. Gently move your legs up and down and buzz like an airplane. Bring your baby in close for the grand finale—a big kiss.

Bounce. Lay your baby down on her back on your bed and, with your hands, gently bounce the bed. She'll jiggle and jostle and crack up. When your baby is a little older and more comfortable on her belly, this will be a great way to help her work on her neck control. And finally, when she is sitting and you are bouncing the bed, she is working on balance. Usually, when she falls over, the cracking up starts all over again.

6 to 9 Months

At this age children are generally kneeling on all fours, rolling over, sitting up, and crawling.

Mirror mirror. Sit him in front of a mirror within reaching distance. Watch how he reaches for himself, fascinated by his own movement. Or pick up your baby, walk by a mirror, and stop and look. Move away and then back into mirror view. My favorite was to start about ten feet away from the mirror, walk closer and closer and closer until we'd zoom to the left or right, just missing the mirror—again, sound effects help.

Tickle time. Babies like to be tickled. The trick (and trust me, it isn't too hard) is finding where their tickle spots are: under the arms, gently squeezing the muscles just above the knee or thigh, alongside the ribs. Make sure you stop when your baby starts to express discomfort or annoyance. Raspberries on the belly are also a great way to get a laugh.

The elevator. With one hand on her chest and the other on her rear, slowly and gently raise your baby above your head and bring

her down. This usually brings a delightful grin. Do this repeatedly and watch for delight or distress. It's important not to toss your baby in the air, despite how fun it can be—the risk of her getting seriously hurt is too great.

Push over. Again on the bed, sit the baby up and put a pillow behind him. Gently push the baby backward until he is resting on the pillow. When he sits up, gently push him down again. He will realize it's a game and get excited for the next chance to topple over. When he gets bigger, you can try this while he's standing—carefully, of course! For really sophisticated players, see if you can blow your baby over while saying, "I'll huff and I'll puff and I'll blow you down!"

Sounding off. Make a sound repeatedly at your baby, something that comes from her own personal repertoire. Repeat the sound, then see if she will repeat it. This is the beginning of verbal communication. Once she does, add to it. Do two sounds, an ooh and a click together. Then try to keep it going . . .

More tummy time. Now stronger than before, your baby will be able to hold himself up without much effort and roll over. Place desirable toys within reach and watch him go get them. This is a sign of precrawling. Another variation on the rollover: Place your baby on the edge of the couch, lying on his back or belly. Place yourself right next to him. Encourage him to roll over into your arms and catch him. Cheer when you grab him and do it all over again.

Fun with blocks. Place two blocks in front of your baby and watch her grab with thumb and forefinger (pincer grasp). Aahh, pure delight. Then place a third block on a mat in front of your baby and watch her think and problem solve. She may lunge forward, pull the mat toward her and, along with it, the block. However she gets it, mission accomplished. Cheer loudly! Her problem is she doesn't have enough room in his hands to hold three blocks. Watch what she does; she is sure to entertain you.

9 to 12 Months

Your baby is working on crawling, standing, talking and cruising.

Reading on Daddy's lap. Board books are best for this age group, because they're made of thick cardboard and hold up better to baby abuse. Some recommendations for this age are:
- Peekaboo books containing hidden objects behind flaps; touch and feel books
- *Pat the Bunny* by Edith Kunhardt
- *Your Personal Penguin* by Sandra Boynton

Round and round the garden. Hold your baby's hand with the palm facing up. Using your index finger to make circular motions on the palm of his hand and say, "Round and round the garden looking for teddy bear." Then, as your fingers walk up his arm and arrive at the underarm, say, "One step, two step, tickle him under there."

The lyricist. This is a great time to make up songs about your baby or about characters or objects in her life. This may not be your thing, but I've noticed some of the most conservative dads really get into this. I know one dad who would sing songs and insert his baby's name in it, while also including other important people into the lyrics. More often than not it provided laughter for him and his wife, but hey, why not? You know the saying: Sing like there's no one listening. The songs can be to the tune of a well-known song, or totally made up.

The crawler. One dad who was just discovering the wonder of play told me about his nine-month-old daughter and her love of being chased, even as a crawler. She so enjoyed exercising her newfound muscles that she would crawl away from him while he said, "I'm going to get you!" She would giggle and crawl frantically as he gently grabbed her heels—sending her into peals of laughter. If he let her get too far away, she'd turn around and wait for her dad to come after her again. What father wouldn't enjoy that game? It's an opportunity to be physical and silly and listen to those great baby laughs. And when your baby starts walking and running, the game can just grow with you.

The jockey. This is best played when your little one's back muscles are good and strong, typically after nine months. Place your baby on your knee, facing you, while securely holding his hands, and gently bounce the baby up and down while doing your best imitation of a horse. Start off slow by saying, "Trot . . . trot . . . trot." Then pick up the pace just a bit by saying, "Canter . . . canter . . . canter." When finally your baby is able to "Gallop, gallop, gallop" really fast, an excited laugh comes out. For extra special effects, blow on his face for a wind effect during the gallop. Play close attention to his discomfort level and be sure to stop if he is not having fun.

The shredder. Need incriminating documents and old magazines shredded? Your nine-month-old is just the one to do it. They love the power and sound associated with tearing and ripping. Give them old magazines to tear up—they probably work better than photocopy paper as they're less likely to cause paper cuts. It's fun for them and fun to watch. Remove sharp objects like staples or paper clips.

Roly poly. This is a great time to roll balls back and forth, sitting on the floor with your legs outstretched. Gentle rolls back and forth really create a wonderful sense of connection and purpose. It sends the message "I can roll this ball to Daddy and Daddy can roll it back"—what power!

Real Dad: Dads Who Play

Matt, 26, reported that as he observed his four-month-old daughter playing, he noticed things about her that he hadn't seen before: the folds in her wrists, the tiny hairs on her ears, and the dimples in her knuckles. Even the act of watching his child, he said, was a very profound experience.

Tony, 45, shared that his twelve-month-old was adept at doing an army crawl, dragging his body with his arm, propping his knee on the ground, and pivoting around and around. Since it was not the most efficient way to get around, Tony thought maybe his son's motor or cognitive skills were delayed. The challenge for Tony was to simply watch and resist the temptation to fix the behavior or worry that something was wrong. Tony discovered that if he arched his back and made a bridge, his son would crawl under him. Tony's careful observations and willingness to adapt made such a moment possible. And, by the way, his son began walking at thirteen months, right on schedule.

Devin, 24, said that his two-year-old girl was more interested in walking around an empty parking lot picking up stones and pebbles than playing in the playground. It confused him until he learned that toddler play at this age is mostly exploratory, not purposeful or goal-directed.

When my two oldest kids were two and four and sharing the same bedroom, I wanted to read books to them but couldn't fit them both on my lap. I would lie down on the floor in between their beds with the lights out and a camping headlight on my head. It was a fun way to read a book. They could both see the pictures and after the book was read I would stretch out my arms and hold both their hands. It was the most precious few moments and a great way to end the day.

12 to 18 Months

Your baby is officially a toddler now and is mastering the skill of walking. Children this age love it when you get down on the floor with them.

Reading on Daddy's lap. Your child should be able to sit long enough for you to read an entire age-appropriate book. As you read, point to pictures, make sounds, ask her where a character is. By now she should be helping you turn the page. It's still best to use board books, as kids this age tend to rip flexible pages. Some personal recommendations include:

- *The Monster at the End of This Book* by Jon Stone
- *Little Gorilla* by Ruth Bornstein
- *Goodnight Moon* by Margaret Wise Brown

Baby doll. If your baby has a dolly that she likes, take the baby and swaddle it in a blanket and hand it to your child. See how she reacts. She might hold it gently or drop it without a care. You may find that she likes to watch you swaddle and take care of her doll or she may get jealous. You are teaching her about caring for something; pat the baby doll gently on her back and rock with her. Don't expect your child to be consistently gentle. She's learning, so praise her for any sign of tenderness you see.

Itsy bitsy spider. This is also called "Teensy Weensy Spider." As you do the hand motions of a spider climbing up a spout, say: "The itsy bitsy spider climbed up the water spout, down came the rain and washed the spider out, out came the sun and dried up all the rain, and the itsy bitsy spider climbed up the spout again." Kids this age are fascinated with the hand gestures. When you are done, ask her if she wants you to do it again and see if she says no or some emphatic form of yes!

This little piggy. Take her big toe between your thumb and index finger (pincer grasp) and say, "This little piggy went to the market." Moving to her next toe, say, "and this little piggy stayed home." Next toe, say, "This little piggy had roast beef," and next toe say, "this little piggy had none" (say this with a sad look and voice). On her final pinky toe say, "But *this* little piggy went WEE WEE WEE all the way home!" as your fingers climb up her legs and torso to tickle her armpit.

Fetch. This is a great learning game as tots make connections between objects and people. Ask your child to give the ball to Mommy (make sure she knows the name of the object and the person). When she does it successfully, praise her, clap, and say, "Yeah, good job!" She will want you to do it again and again. Switch the objects and people for a more sophisticated game.

18 to 24 Months

Your toddler has mastered walking and now he is working hard at talking. The play should be active to match his energy level.

Reading on Daddy's lap. Your child is probably taking an even greater interest when you read age-appropriate books, and it's one of the best investments of "father time" you can make. Some personal recommendations include:

- *Calling All Toddlers* by Francesca Simon
- *The Very Hungry Caterpillar* by Eric Carle

• *Hop on Pop* by Dr. Seuss

Trot trot to Boston. While in a seated position, have your child sit on your lap and face you. Hold his hands and begin to bounce him on your knee, saying: "Trot trot to Boston, trot trot to Lynn, watch out little boy or you might fall in." Spread your legs apart as you say the words *fall in* while holding his hands.

Pillow fort. Using pillows and cushions from beds and couches, build a fort or a secret place to hide. Have it fall apart or pretend that you are the Big Bad Wolf and you've huffed and huffed and you blew the house in.

Hide-and-seek in the tent. Create tents with blankets draped over chairs, hide under them, and play hide-and-seek. Pretend you have no idea where she is and watch her blow her cover every time. Absolutely hilarious.

24 to 30 Months

This is a great age to spend time working on the larger muscle and coordination groups.

Reading on Daddy's lap. Try these titles:

• *A Fly Went By* by Mike McClintock

• *Go, Dog. Go!* by P. D. Eastman

• *How Do Dinosaurs Say Goodnight?* by Jane Yolen

Playground. Anything you can do with a ball, climbing a jungle gym, hanging from bars, and getting pushed on a swing are just what your child needs at this age.

Diaper baseball. No greater time to introduce your son or daughter to America's favorite pastime—baseball. While he is still in diapers and trying to learn hand-eye coordination, breaking out a ball and bat is perfectly acceptable. Grab a soft, cushiony oversize ball and bat and take your time. See if your child can put out his arms and catch the ball. No matter how badly he misses the ball, always say, "*Almost!*" Do this over and over as long as he is interested. And when he catches it, go crazy and say, "*Good catch!*" Teach him how to hold the bat and see if he can hit the ball. Don't force this and don't expect anything too great, but when he connects with the ball it truly is magical.

Potty time. As your child is becoming more and more aware of how to control bowel movement and peeing sensations, you may have her sit on the potty. For boys, place a piece of toilet paper in the toilet and see if they can shoot a urine stream at it. My daughter taught me the "Patty Cake" song (also called "Pat-a-Cake") while sitting on the toilet. Spend some time in there with them and see what comes up. This is an important milestone for you to be present for.

Wrestle. In this game it's important to always lose. Let her push you over, get on top of you, bounce on you, and revel in her strength.

Shoulder time. Going for a walk with your child on your shoulders has few comparisons. It's one of life's joys. Of course, it should go without saying, to play this game with safety in mind.

30 to 36 Months

Play around this age becomes a little more gender oriented. This is partly influenced by family, culture, and DNA.

Reading on Daddy's lap. Don't forget that this is the perfect age to teach children another language. There are many books out there featuring the first hundred words of another language. Or try any of these titles:

• *Sheep in a Jeep* by Nancy E. Shaw
• *Fancy Nancy* by Jane O'Connor
• *Chugga Chugga Choo Choo* by Kevin Lewis

King. I was amazed when my daughter dubbed me a king during one of our playtimes. So I created a kingly voice and told her: "This is all mine: the trees, buildings, hills, oceans, flower, birds and air. It is all mine!" And then I said, "But it's all about the love and it's all about the sharing." She would come running over to me and ask, "King, can I get you anything?" "Why, yes," I said. "Please get me some figs and apples and fruit!" (The king had good manners.) She ran off and pretended to pull those items off a tree. It's the most obedient she'd ever been and I was hooked. We had fun and we continue to play a variation of King to this day (she is now six).

Tickle monster. For this game you need a third person to play the part of tickle monster. While tickle monster is chasing your child around, you play the role of protector. Let her hide under the protective shelter of you as a bridge. You are on all fours and keeping the tickle monster from getting to her. My daughter taught me both King and Tickle Monster and amazed me by dubbing me her king and protector, roles that are archetypically Father.

Nails. Girls might be more interested in this than boys, but either way, let your child paint your nails with kiddie nail polish. Take turns and do her nails. It might get a little messy so put newspaper or paper towels under the hand that is being painted. Also make sure you have nail polish remover. A lot of the play-teaching might focus on how not to make a mess and how to clean up.

Project time. I do not consider myself a handyman at all, but I am able to do a couple of things around the house, like change lightbulbs or put up some hooks to hang coats—simple jobs. Having your child play assistant can be great. At this age your child wants to help and show off that he can do stuff too, and you can teach him about safety and test his fine motor skills. Be extra mindful of small parts and sharp objects.

Co-draw. Try drawing with your child. Co-drawing is great because you both draw together. Get a piece of paper and a marker, pen, or pencil and draw a squiggly line. Then instruct your child to extend the line. Then you add something to the line and so on and so forth. What you end up creating is usually a squiggly mess but it's been created by the both of you.

PRACTICAL QUESTIONS ABOUT FATHER PLAY

When is it okay to take my child to a ballgame? The answer depends on your child's interest, but suffice it to say that you can take him to a game as early as six months. Just remember that you are primarily there to take care of the baby, and don't expect to stay for the whole game. Your whole experience of watching and enjoying a game will not be what it used to be. You probably won't be able to truly enjoy a game with your son or daughter unless he or she takes an interest in the sport, which probably won't be until the age of four or later.

When can I take my child to her first movie or show? When she expresses an interest, but be mindful of pushing too hard. There will be plenty of time for these things in the future. With that said, I contradicted my own advice with my first child when I so badly wanted to take him to his first movie at the age of three. He resisted for reasons I could not figure out; he said he wanted to wait until he was thirty-six years old. I think he was hesitant about the dark room and the size of the theater.

It was an age-appropriate movie and he ended up really liking it. This is a good example of how knowing your child will help you make the judgment call. In retrospect I probably could have waited another year or so, but there was no harm done.

When can I toss my child up into the air? Every pediatrician will tell you *never* and my most protective self will say the same. But I've been doing it with my kids since they were about eight or nine months. I have not dropped them or hurt them. I know it is risky, but it is so much fun; so just be very careful.

Is it harmful to pull my kid up by his arms while holding his hands? Yes. And again, every pediatrician will tell you not to do it. The risk of arm dislocation is pretty high up until the age of two. Certainly refrain from swinging him around.

How important is it to set limits around the TV, computer, and electronic game use? I believe in strict limits for these things, especially at this age. And this comes from having a TV addiction. The thing to be mindful of is how it is promoting or inhibiting your child's social growth. It can lead to serious social isolation if not monitored. If you are going to allow it, have limits and supervise.

A Lifetime Connection

The main goal of play is to let your child explore and learn as much as she can about herself, you, and the world around her. Another goal is to simply *be with* each other and get to know each other. The play that you engage in, whether it be exploring, pouring, pounding, dropping, bouncing, hiding, creating, or destroying, will help solidify your bond.

Whatever way you play, it is guaranteed that it will be unique to you and your child. No other dad will play it like you. What will that spark look like? How will you create it? The above-mentioned games are just a few ideas that will hopefully inspire you to generate some of your own. Allow the spirit to move you and don't be afraid to be spontaneous and silly. Just remember to keep your own expectations within the limits of your child's capabilities and you'll be on your way to some serious fun.

REFLECTION QUESTIONS

1. What play activities does your child enjoy or dislike?
2. How would you describe the difference between the types of play you provide versus the play your partner provides?
3. What do you notice within you when your baby does not want to play? Disappointment, relief, feeling like chopped liver?
4. Based on the play that you and your child engage in, what have you learned about yourself and your child? What observations, assumptions, or projections are you making about your child? For example: She's coordinated; he's smart; she's athletic; he's slow; she's a crybaby.

Fathering and Discipline

The True Meaning of Discipline

It is commonly thought that true discipline begins around the age of two. Why age two? Because now your little one is more engaged and aware and beginning to defy you more. Remember that your child is at the very beginning of learning how to be a responsible, mature person—and you are his teacher.

When you discipline you teach and I will use the words *teach* and *discipline* interchangeably throughout this chapter. This teaching begins as soon as your baby is born and continues throughout his lifespan. There are a variety of ways to teach, for example, in a nurturing, negligent, or aggressive way. As we discipline our children we make them aware that their behavior has reached a limit that is unacceptable to us, to themselves, or to the world in general—sometimes even all three at once.

When you discipline your child it will be helpful to always ask yourself, "What am I teaching?" Think of your rules as boundary definers that must be in place to discipline effectively. As the father you are a critical player in teaching your child about those limits. I am convinced that as we discipline our children, we are in essence training them how to be people. Think of it as people training.

THE GOALS OF DISCIPLINE

Here are what I consider four key reasons to discipline:
• To instill in your child his own internal limit setter. Eventually, your child should be able to predict your response to his behavior.
• To teach your child to respect

herself, her parents, and the world.

- To help your child to be thoughtful and reflective as opposed to reactive and impulsive. The ultimate goal of a well-disciplined (or well-taught) child is not just that he is compliant and behaves in an acceptable manner, but that he will be thoughtful about himself and the world around him and ultimately able to make smart and healthy choices. If we can teach our children to reflect on their behavior, to help them realize that their behavior has an impact on others, themselves, and the world, then we do a huge service to humanity.
- To model what we want to teach and to practice what we preach. Your children are going to mimic you whether you like it or not, so it's important that you model what you want to see in them. They are more likely to respect you if you practice what you preach, so that old line about "do as I say not as I do" is meaningless. The goal is not to be perfect, just earnest.

DIFFERENT DISCIPLINE STYLES

Just as there are different types of dads (see chapter 1), there are different discipline styles. Do you recognize your style here?

The Punitive Disciplinarian

The stereotypical patriarch of the past was a stoic, unfeeling, hard, strict, unbending man who was to be feared more than respected. Mothers in their aprons would threaten their children with the ominous words, "Wait until your father comes home!"

The focus in this style is on obedience through punishment. "Because I said so!" or "I'll give you something to cry about!" may be common phrases uttered by the punitive disciplinarian. Or, instead of words, this type might hit with his fists, belt, or other objects. We now know the harm this method can cause.

The Permissive Disciplinarian

The focus here is on not wanting to upset the child or, in some cases, deferring authority to mom—not wanting to be the "bad guy." "I will not do to my kid what my dad did to me" is often the refrain of men who suffered the rod as children.

The permissive disciplinarian is a more recent phenomenon, a reaction to the harsh discipline styles of the past. This type of disciplinarian is a soft, emasculated, or ineffectual dad who does not discipline his child when he misbehaves. He has disengaged and allows his kids to "run wild."

The Firm and Tender Disciplinarian

Somewhere in between the punitive and permissive disciplinarians lies the ideal, what I call the firm and tender approach. The twenty-first-century dad is attempting to be more integrative in an effort to adjust to widespread shifts in our culture, including dual-income households and an increased cost of living, just to name two. What I mean by being more "integrative" is to possess the classic masculine and feminine traits, to be "both and" as opposed to "either or." To be someone who sets firm limits and consequences but knows how to be tender and comforting too.

This approach is similar to the notion of tough love in that you have two opposites at play—you are both tough on behavior and loving toward feelings. The image that captures this approach best for me is the famous painting by Rembrandt entitled *The Prodigal Son*. If you examine the painting closely, you will see that one hand is tender, feminine, slender, more refined, and characterizes all the stereotypes of the soft and nurturing mother figure, while the other hand is more firm, masculine, bigger with more veins, and connotes all the stereotypes of the hard, strong father figure.

The firm and tender approach requires four things:

1. **You are the boss.** When you became a father you were endowed with authority and power. As Haim Ginott, a child psychotherapist and teacher, wrote in *Teacher and Child*, "As a teacher I possess tremendous power to make a child's life miserable or joyous. I can be a tool of torture or an instrument of inspiration. I can humiliate or humor, hurt or heal. In all situations, it is my response that decides whether a crisis will be escalated or de-escalated, and a child humanized or dehumanized."

   As the quote says, you can use your power to destroy or create. Some of you will shy away from this and some of you will step into it, but from an early age you can make it clear that you are the boss. If you are co-parenting, make it clear to your children that they have two bosses. (Yes, this can be complicated.) It is critical that you and your partner become as unified as possible when it comes to limits, rules, and the values you want to teach. You want your child to end up respecting your authority. At different times in his life, your child may need to fear you, reject you, and idealize you, but in the end you want him to trust you and know that you have his best interests in mind.

   So how do you make it clear to your child that you are the boss? You tell him directly: "I'm the boss. I'm in charge." Around the age of two is a good time to tell him this. When I first told my two-year-old that I was the boss, he said, "No, I'm the boss." Expect your child to push back—that's his job—but make it clear that the buck stops with you. It's very important to establish this early on.

2. **You are the boundary definer.** As the boss it is your job to be the boundary definer or limit setter. For example, a two-year-old is hitting a tennis racquet against a car. One response is to yell, "Don't hit the car with the tennis racquet!" A better response is, "No, we don't hit cars." Immediately follow it up with, "But we can hit balls. Here's a ball; let's see if you can hit it." You establish the boundary in just a few words, and then you offer an alternative. As the boundary

definer you are teaching your child what is permissible and what is not.

One thing that has really helped me in disciplining my kids is to remember how little they know about the ways of the world. This is not their fault; it's just a fact and a function of their age and experience. Since we know more about the ways of the world it is our job to teach them about it by providing a sense of right and wrong and of appropriate risk taking. At this age it is okay for children to view the world as "either or," good or bad. They have a lifetime to learn that the world is gray, messy, and not always fair or orderly. What they need most as they figure this out are boundaries. And it is their parents' role to define those boundaries.

3. **Accept their feelings**. With the firm and tender approach, you accept your child's feelings but not her inappropriate behavior. Keep this phrase in mind: "Comfort the feelings, correct the behavior." Your toddler will not like the boundaries you set and will not always want to accept your authority. When I used to set a limit with my daughter, like the TV needed to be turned off, or it was time to go to bed, or she couldn't have candy right now, she would often get so upset that she would kick or stomp. My response was firm and tender: "You can be mad, but you cannot kick. If you are mad, I want to hear about it. But you are not allowed to kick me or anything else." You want to get the message across that the feelings are valid and acceptable, but the misbehavior is not.

4. **Give and receive forgiveness**. As a teacher and disciplinarian it is critical that you both ask for and grant forgiveness. You are not a perfect teacher—you will make mistakes and lose your cool—and it is important that you model your humanity and admit when you have erred. Likewise your baby or toddler is not perfect and will make many mistakes. It is essential that he learn about his own humanity and be forgiven by you when he falls short.

BENEFITS OF THE FIRM AND TENDER APPROACH

There are many benefits to being regarded as a multidimensional parent. Here are a few:

- Your child will experience a man who is integrated, possessing both traditionally masculine and feminine traits. This is quite exciting in that it helps teach your child how to be a full and well-rounded human being and mitigates some of the gender stereotyping that exists in our society.
- You will be feared and respected, as opposed to just feared or thought of as negligible or a pushover. Eventually you will be seen as someone your child can go to with messy feelings and behaviors.
- By giving and accepting forgiveness, your child will learn how to forgive herself and will affect future choices of mates and friends.

• Over time your child will come to see you as human, a person who has flaws and shortcomings but who is also respected.

These strategies promote a growing mutual respect and trust between you and your child. But they work only when you're consistent in their usage. What's the big deal about consistency? Essentially it means your *yes* means yes and *no* means no. When it comes to parenting, consistency is paramount. You need to back up your words with actions. Parents need to work together and get on a unified page and commit to meaning what you say and saying what you mean.

You must also be aware of your emotional life because, believe it or not, it is your emotional life that contributes to inconsistency. For example, if you feel guilty, that emotion can keep you from setting limits. Be clear about what's a yes, no, and maybe. Know your rules and know what's acceptable. For example, climbing on the furniture, walking across the street, and singing loudly may be acceptable in some households but not in others. Every parent has different tolerance levels, which is okay, just be clear about what yours are.

TIME-OUTS

I'm a believer in time-outs for toddlers. The goal of the time-out technique is to defuse and redirect an escalating situation in an unemotional way, and to teach your toddler to behave without setting a negative example, the way yelling does. It is critical that you not think of a time-out as a punishment. Instead, it's a break from the action. The time-out is a discipline tool used when your child has exhibited unacceptable behavior such as hitting, biting, kicking, spitting, or doing something that puts your child or someone else at risk after you've asked him repeatedly not to do so.

Here's a baker's dozen rules for making time-outs effective:

1. Begin using time-outs around the age of two and use them for as long as they are effective. Don't give up on this strategy too soon. It takes work.

2. Keep in mind that time-outs are not a punishment but a designated amount of time to de-escalate and reflect.

3. Nip the behavior in the bud. In other words, try to implement the time-out before you lose your patience and get angry. Try your best to keep your emotions out of it. Give your child one or two warnings at the most before implementing a time-out.

4. The length of a time-out one minute per year. That means two-year-olds get two minutes, three-year-olds get three minutes, and so on. Use a timer or some formal method of keeping track of time. Before age two, the time-out really isn't an effective technique.

5. Keep your child close during the time-out. You will want to be able to see her so you can make sure she is using the time to calm down and reflect on her behavior rather than engaging in some sort of distraction, like playing with a toy. For this reason, do not send her to her room.

6. Do not expect your child to be particularly good at calming down and using the time-out as it was designed at first. This will take repetition, practice, consistency.

7. The location you use for time-outs should have a neutral name like "time-out area." I do not recommend calling it something like the "naughty corner," because your child may come to think that *she* is inherently naughty or bad, as opposed to her behavior. I realize this may seem like a fine distinction, but you want your child to understand that it is the *behavior* that is unacceptable, not her.

8. Do not interact with your child while he is in a time-out. If he speaks to you, it's best to ignore him until the time-out is over and then explain why there is no talking.

9. Do not allow him to play, look at books, draw, or anything else during a time-out. It should be a true break from all stimulation.

10. When the time-out is complete, get down on your child's level and review why she was there. Be specific but brief: "You were in time-out for hitting. We do not hit. Please do not do it again." As she gets older, ask her if she can name the behavior that put her in time-out. Encourage her to practice apologizing, whether it's to you for disobeying, to her brother, friend, or whomever. Do not expect her to say it like she means it.

11. Offer alternatives. Say something like, "Next time I want you to use your words if you are mad, sad, or scared." As your child gets older, ask him he if he can think of anything that he could do differently next time.

12. Once it's over, shake it off and move on. Give her a hug if she wants one and get back in the game. Do not dwell on the misbehavior.

13. Stick to it. Time-outs are not easy to implement. Be sure he stays in the chair for the allotted time or redirect him back to the chair. (See below.) Time-outs take perseverance, intention, and a belief that they will work.

TIME-OUT Q&A

What if my child leaves the time-out area? This happens a lot and does not mean you should abandon time-outs. Your toddler needs to be directed and taught what is expected of him during time-out. Either bring him back yourself or direct him back to the timeout area. Remember to keep your cool. You may have to do this several times.

What if my child screams at the top of her lungs while in time-out? Let her scream. Let her have her feelings—they are what I call "big feelings." I know this is easier said than done, but you send a message of acceptance (meaning, you accept her feelings) when you allow her to scream. If it's really bothering you, ask her calmly to please stop screaming.

What if time-out just doesn't seem to work for my kid? It may not. Not every kid or parent is the same. I will say, though, before you abandon time-outs, make sure you given them a good, long, concerted effort. Speaking of concerted effort, if you can't give it, then don't do it. It won't work if you are not firm, clear, and committed to it.

Being an engaged dad is hard work. Over the next year, I can almost guarantee you will lose your cool (if you haven't already), scare yourself, or scare your child or partner. Ask her for help, rely on her for relief, think of yourselves as a tag team, and take a breather. When you take your own time-out you are modeling the need to be reflective and not reactive. (For more suggestions on how to prevent blow-ups see chapter 13.) While taking your time-out ask yourself three questions:
1. What do I need to be okay in the short run?
2. Was what I got upset about that important?
3. Do I need to apologize to anyone?

WINNING DISCIPLINE STRATEGIES

If you find yourself barking "No!" so much that it's bugging even you, you might want to consider offering more than just that. Don't get me wrong; the *no* is important. *No* communicates the limit that you as the boundary definer have set, but it's also important to follow it up with something that tells your child that you are on his side, that you are *with* him.

Here's a scenario to demonstrate what I mean: It's Saturday morning. You've had a long week. You've barely seen your kid. You thought it would be nice to run an errand with your two-and-a-half-year-old son even through this errand holds no particular interest for him . . . it's not a kid activity. Upon entering the outdoors your son falls apart and begins wailing, crying, screaming at the top of his lungs and struggling mightily to get out of his stroller. What the heck is going on? There is no magic cure but here are some sound options:

Get down on his level. This is the best position to be in if you want your child to listen to you. You find out that he thought you were going to the park and he is expressing his abject disappointment.

Name the behavior. The behavior you are trying to correct needs to be named for both your child and yourself. The reason: to begin distinguishing at an early age the difference between their behavior and their self-image. For example: "that behavior is bratty" or "that behavior is risky and dangerous".

Name the feeling. Just as children are attached to objects, they are also attached to their feelings. It's hard for them to separate themselves from their emotions. Start with the basics: Is he glad, mad, sad, or scared? This is important—it will give him a greater sense of his identity.

Encourage him to put what he is feeling into words. If he cannot, then do it for him. Tell him that you think he is feeling sad, mad, shy, or scared. If he can say he is sad or mad, great—then you have something to work with. This is a big step and a very important beginning!

Calmly express your emotion. Teach your child that she has an impact on things and people. For example, when she bites, tell her clearly and in no uncertain terms that it hurts when she does that. Or, express your commiseration or empathy. For instance, say, "Oh, I see that you are upset that we can't go to the park. I wish we could go to the park too." Show him your emotion through facial expressions or body language that you too are mad or sad. This is a form of mirroring and can be enormously helpful in de-escalating big feelings.

Offer an alternative and involve him in the solution. Suggest something like, "Hmm, let's think about when we can go to the park. Do you have any ideas?"

Reinforce natural consequences. Be mindful of teaching them what the natural or related consequences are to their misbehavior. For instance, the natural consequence to not eating is that they will be hungry.

You will both need a lot of practice in making this flow and feel like you've come up with plausible solutions . . . but that's what you are there for. After you've heard his suggestions, you can offer an alternative like, "After you take your nap I will talk with Mommy and see if we can take you to the park."

LOSING DISCIPLINE STRATEGIES

It is not an easy thing to discipline your child effectively. It can be so easy to fall into some of the losing strategy traps. Here are just a few:

Shaming. One of the greatest challenges for parents is to discipline in a way that does not cause the child to experience shame. By shame I mean that the child feels as though he is flawed, worthless, or wrong in some *fundamental* way. This is why when we discipline we focus on the behavior that needs correcting, not the feeling or the person. We attempt to separate the behavior from the feeling and person, which is another reason why I discourage blanket statements like "good boy" or "bad boy" but instead recommend getting specific by saying "good sharing" or "bad sharing." This is subtle but incredibly important because the subtle stuff is what tends to be repeated daily and internalized by your child. You may wonder how you can know if you're shaming your kids. Here are some clues:

• You find yourself yelling a lot.
• Your kids are scared of you.
• You reprimand without explaining or reviewing what happened.
• If you find yourself saying *you* a lot in your reprimands.

It is important to remember that you are dealing with a very tender sense of self. Your child's sense of himself may appear strong, but he is truly a fragile work in progress.

Giving too much responsibility. It is very tempting, the older they get, to give children some responsibility. But we must always be mindful of what a child can handle at a particular age. (See chapter 10.) It is not your child's job or responsibility to dictate the plan for the day or tell you what TV show he is going to watch or what food he is going to eat. You are the parent, you are in charge, and you are the boss.

Offering too many choices. Instead of asking an open-ended question like, "What would you like for snack?" ask your child, "Would you like an orange or an apple?" A child is more likely to be able to choose from two or three options rather than from every possible snack option in the pantry.

Becoming the Scary Monster. New fathers are often surprised, scared, or ashamed to report that they have trouble containing their irritability with their children. The irritability may turn into anger, rage, or explosiveness. We all have the capacity of being a Scary Monster. I know, I've been one to my children and it scares them, my wife, and me. I also know that even though I may lose my cool and yell at them, I have the capacity to prevent myself from physically hurting them. And if I do yell, I can—and should!—ask for forgiveness.

Turning a blind eye. It is not uncommon to turn a blind eye on your toddler's misbehavior. Sometimes this is conscious but more often than not it's probably an unconscious reaction stemming from the fact that you haven't been trained to handle misbehavior or that your own "leash" was quite long when you were a child. Either way, if this is you, then you need to develop an antenna, pay close attention, and respond to your toddler's ways.

Negative role modeling. Sometimes we excuse ourselves from the very behavior we are trying to teach to our children not to engage in. They may not see the discrepancy clearly yet, but they will and you'd better have a good explanation for why you don't have to hang your coat up when they do.

Tit-for-tatting. Sometimes it can be tempting to do back to your little one what she has done to you. Don't do this. You are the adult and it's important that you act that way. Your child needs you to be the grown-up in situations that call for discipline. You can express that hitting hurts without inflicting the hurt.

Bribing. Bribing can be a very hard thing for parents to resist. It is a quick and easy way to get your child to behave the way you want him to. But what does it teach? It tends to teach that good behavior equals a treat rather than good behavior makes good sense. It teaches him to negotiate for good behavior.

Avoiding. You may be tempted to distract your baby when she wants something she can't have or you need to take something away from her. Get her to focus on something else instead and presto—it's out of sight, out of mind. It worked then, but your growing toddler has developed what's called object permanence or object constancy, which means she remembers things a little better and won't let go so easily of the object she desires. This is a losing strategy because it prevents your child from dealing with a negative emotion. It also prevents you from helping your child work through a negative emotion.

Taking away privileges. This can be a good strategy when they are around seven or eight. But toddlers are too young to fully understand the concepts of earning privileges and losing them, like television or a toy, for bad behavior. I do believe that if your three-year-old has something in his possession that you do not want him to have, then by all means you should take it away or, ideally, he should be taught to give it to you. Keep in mind that the lost privilege should match the behavior you're trying to correct.

Hitting. This teaches your child how to become a hitter and that it's okay to lose control. It does not model the kind of behavior you want your child to adopt.

Asking for Forgiveness

Before I became a father I used to counsel parents who had been mandated into counseling by New York City's Administration for Children's Services (ACS) for either abuse or neglect toward their children. I remember thinking with great judgment, "How could they have ever done that to their own child?" After becoming a parent I could really understand how one, if not careful, if not trained, if not supported, if not conscious enough, could lose his cool and hurt his child.

Even with all my professional training, and all the love and seriousness with which I take the role of being a dad, I can still lose my temper. I remember vividly a time when I yelled at my six-year-old son in a way that scared him and made him cry. That night as I was putting him to bed I apologized not for what I said but for how I said it. I went on to say that I may need to ask him to forgive me again in the future and then asked the big question: "How many times will you forgive me?" To my surprise, without hesitating, he said, "Seven thousand." I was blown away.

While I don't want to use up all of those seven thousand times, I do want my son to know that even though I may be the boss, the boundary definer, an acceptor of feelings, and a forgiver, I am also human and will make mistakes. As men we do not have to perpetuate the behavior of men who don't acknowledge their mistakes, who don't reflect on their own faults, who don't ask to be forgiven, and who don't take responsibility for their own actions. This can stop with us. And, in fact, one of the big things we are trying to teach our children when we discipline them is to take responsibility for their actions. I believe it is never too early to start modeling this.

I'm not inviting you to blow up at your kids as many times as you want simply because children have large reservoirs of forgiveness. But if you do lose your cool, there are things you can do to prevent it from happening again and you can repair the damage. A simple and clear apology acknowledging what you did is a great place to start.

Consider This

It is normal to sometimes feel like you want to kill your kids. It is not normal to plan and strategize about how to do it. Many joke that 90 percent of parenting is suppressing homicidal tendencies.

RULES TO DISCIPLINE BY

You and your partner may have very different opinions about how to discipline. Maybe one of you came from a home with very few rules while the other was disciplined quite strictly. It's very common for one parent to be the "softie" and the other the "strict tyrant." Whatever your dynamic, you should work hard at coming to a joint understanding and agreement as to what the rules are in your home. This usually means having a discussion as to what is acceptable and what is not for you as parents of this particular toddler. You might find the need to modify the rules as your child grows, but establishing the basics is important and being clear as to why you are shifting the rules is also important.

1. Be thoughtful about how you discipline.
2. Don't expect your child to understand the consequences when he is in the midst of Big Feelings.
3. When his feelings have subsided, try to appeal to his logic and reasoning. This is when he is most teachable. Remember—your newborn learned best when she was in the Quiet Alert state.
4. What you are teaching should be developmentally appropriate. For example, a twenty-four-month-old should not have privileges taken away but should be able to learn something through a time-out if done properly.
5. Consistency benefits both you and your child.
6. Discipline *with* your kids, not *to* your kids. It's a mixture of taking charge, collaborating, joining, mirroring, and problem solving.
7. It's easy to set rules, but it's hard to enforce them. Mean what you say and say what you mean.
8. You may need a time-out too! This can be one of the wisest moves you ever make.
9. As therapist Haim Ginott wrote, "Permit the feeling, not the act."

Common Discipline Issues

Not every problem you encounter with your child is going to merit the same kind or degree of response. Below are some common issues that come up for most parents and some ideas for how you can deal with each one effectively.

Food throwing. Children at this age will do it unknowingly and knowingly. If they do it knowingly, then it needs to be responded to quickly, nipped in the bud with a verbal warning like, "We do not throw food. Please stop." If it continues I would recommend either one more warning or a time-out.

Tantrums in public. There is nothing more embarrassing than the tantrum in a public place. All sense of control that you feel as a man is suddenly attacked by a two-year-old. Your child has thrown himself down on the floor and is screaming at the top of his lungs. You may be thinking something like: "How dare he embarrass me! People are going to think I've done something to hurt him or that I'm a bad father or maybe they will want to call child protective services!"

There are ways to get through a public tantrum:

- Stay calm. Take a deep breath, and reassure yourself that you have done nothing wrong.
- Let him have his big feelings. This is a common way that two-year-olds deal with their negative feelings.
- Make sure he is not hurting himself or others or causing any damage to objects around him. If he is, you will need to step in and stop him.
- Take him away from the public place, though it may interrupt your plans.
- Stick to your guns. The tantrum probably started because you set a limit and said no to something. He will get over it.
- Do not try to reason with a child in the middle of a tantrum. Wait for him to calm down before you talk with him about it.
- Talk about what happened without belaboring the event.
- Keep it private. Do not tell too many people about the tantrum,

especially in front of your child. You want to avoid shaming him.
- Move on. Expect that your child will gain the ability to deal with limits and disappointments and let it go.

What if we were as patient and understanding with our toddlers as we were with our infants? We don't expect much from our infants because we know how dependent and helpless they are. What if we were as patient with our school-age children as we were with our toddlers? Our patience wears thinner as our children get older. Remind yourself: (1) Children need to rebel, resist, and refuse in order to become who they are meant to be, and (2) As a parent, you are in the process of becoming too and your patience, or lack thereof, tells you something about yourself—be curious about what that is.

Splitting. No, this isn't about your marriage. It's when your child expresses a preference—"I want Mommy!" or "I want Daddy!" She may exclaim this as she stretches out her arms, and makes the unwanted parent feel . . . well, unwanted. This is very common and it's okay for your child to express a preference for one parent over the other (commonly called splitting). If her preference is expressed as a response to discipline or not getting her way she may go to Mommy to see if she gets a different answer. Make sure you and your partner are on the same page about what the limit was; even if you don't agree with the limit it's important that you support each other. Assess whether or not your child's preference can be granted. If it can without too much of a hitch, then let her have her preference. If she cries, wails, or screams because her preference can't be granted, that's okay. Let her have her feelings. You want to avoid changing things too drastically or rewarding tantrums.

Sharing. Sharing is hard for toddlers. A primary way that children relate to the world is through objects and the attachments they form to those objects. The special meaning they place on an object may seem insignificant to us, but if you ever try to take a shovel away from a two-year-old who has been digging in the sand, forget about it. Comedian Brian Regan does a riff about a father and a son walking together and the kid loses a balloon that was tied to his wrist. The kid freaks out and cries uncontrollably. The father says, "What are you crying for? It's just a balloon." Regan goes on to explain, in a very funny way, that the only way to understand what the kid might be going through is to have the father experience what it would feel like if his wallet started floating away. He'd freak out too!

Biting, hitting, kicking. A clear and decisive consequence needs to occur here. Whether it's a simple *no*, a time-out, or a removal from the situation is a judgment call. The reason kids of this age (and older) bite, hit, or kick is because they are feeling great frustration or excitement. They generally do not fully understand the impact they are having on the other person. Your goal is to teach them to communicate with words.

Sleep training. It is very common for two-year-olds to begin showing signs that they are ready to transition to a toddler bed, like climbing out of their cribs. It's a big step. The new sense of freedom is exciting and hard to contain. If you are not going to allow your toddler to sleep with you, you both need to commit to that decision. It will mean one of you (or both of you on alternating shifts) will be getting up in the middle of the night with your little guy and redirecting him back to his own bed as soon as possible. The more you let him sleep with you the more he will want to sleep with you. If you are okay with that, fine. Just be sure that you and your partner have both committed to allowing it or not allowing it.

Consider This

Negative behaviors can be spun into positive outcomes. For example, if your child is disobedient, ornery, sassy, or whatever you want to call it, try to reframe your view so that you celebrate or honor that part of your child. In other words, a stubborn child could also be described as decisive and independent.

Firm on Behavior, Tender with Feelings

In these early years you are a godlike figure, bigger than life to your child. As fathers, we must take this idealization seriously. We need to remember how much power we have over our children and how much damage we can do as a result. That's one of the reasons why it's so important to allow your child to see you as human. A common fear for a father is that if his child sees him as human (that is, flawed or weak), then he'll lose credibility as a disciplinarian. This does not have to be the case.

The firm and tender approach toward discipline can help show that, while you are bigger than life to your child, you're also fair and humble. The approach emphasizes being firm with behavior and tender with feelings. It also emphasizes admitting when you're wrong and taking a break when you need one. Through discipline, you are trying to do some very big things, like teach your child

to become the person he is meant to be and want him to be. No one said it was an easy task, but it's certainly worth the trouble.

REFLECTION QUESTIONS

1. Do you gravitate toward a particular kind of discipline? For example, are you firm yet loving? Do you regularly turn a blind eye? Or are you the "do as I say not as I do" type?
2. Whom do you model yourself after when it comes to discipline? If you can't think of a specific person, describe the characteristics you honor in a disciplinarian.
3. Take a negative behavior in your child and find a positive trait in it. What do you come up with? Is it a trait you or your partner shares with your child?

Consider This

You are living in a world of mostly "have to" and your toddler is living in a world of "want to."

Expecting and Managing Big Feelings

The first three years of fathering can be fraught with emotions coming from all sides. The emotions can range from pure delight and joy to intense feelings of anxiety, sadness, or rage. There is no avoiding the emotional ups and downs of being a dad. There are, however, healthy ways of managing those feelings and that is what this chapter will help you do.

Let me begin by saying that emotions can be messy, confusing, and hard to figure out. For example, you may have wondered: How can I be so delighted with this child and yet resentful that I don't have as much freedom? Or how can I love my partner so much yet be so irritable and judgmental with her when she doesn't give me attention? Likewise, how can I be so harsh (angry/critical) with

myself when I fail or come up short or let people down when I know I'm doing my best under the circumstances?

Making sense of opposing feelings or thoughts is often the challenge and learning to do this well will help you minimize the messiness. It is possible to decipher emotions, respond to them prudently, and tune into their importance. This chapter will name, normalize, and help you manage some of the big feelings that you, your baby, and your partner might feel over the course of your child's first three years with a particular focus on months twenty-four to thirty-six.

Real Men Have Feelings

It's important to remember that all big emotions are there for good reason. Let's deal with what feelings might come up for you and how knowing them will help you be a better dad. Your challenge, as new dad, is to get comfortable or at least familiar with your own emotions—not an easy thing for some men to do. As Sean Elder wrote in "The Emperor's New Woes," a *Psychology Today* (March/ April 2005) article on marriage and fatherhood: "To care about someone else's feelings you have to be in touch with your own, and getting in touch with your feelings is not something [men have] been raised to think of as essential, or even admirable."

We, as a society, admire great thinkers, not great feelers. Yet it's awareness of feelings that will help you tend to your baby and partner the best way possible. Haim Ginott, the pioneering parent educator and child therapist, said it this way: "While we are not free to choose the emotions that arise in us, we are free to choose how and when to express them, provided we know what they are. That is the crux of the problem. Many people (especially men) have been educated out of knowing what their feelings are." The following will give you a sense of what they are.

THE FOUR BIG FEELINGS

When you are in doubt about what you feel, ask yourself if it's one of these four basic emotions: sad, mad, glad, or scared. These are certainly not the only emotions in the human experience but a good place to start when first getting comfortable with your own. You may notice that three out of four of the emotions are "negative" and therefore harder to express. Who wants to feel anger, sadness, or fear? We would all much rather feel happiness.

1. **Sad**. Derivatives can be disappointed, tired, bummed, bored, lazy, depressed. Usually focused on the past.
2. **Mad**. Derivatives can be irritable, frustrated, angry, enraged, annoyed, resentful. Usually focused on the past.
3. **Glad**. Derivatives can be happy, delighted, proud, pleased, content. Usually present focused, but could be past or future as well.
4. **Scared**. Derivatives can be nervous, anxious, jealous, fearful, afraid, worried. Usually focused on something that will happen in the future.

LEARNING HOW TO "DO" FEELINGS

It might be helpful to think of the first couple of years of fatherhood as an intensive crash course in feelings. While this may be true, many men don't "do" feelings. I know this both as a man and as a therapist who works with men. When asked what they're feeling, the typical man (myself included) will tell you what he thinks. The distinction between feelings and thoughts is not clear for many men. You may be an excellent critical or strategic thinker, a skill you've honed daily at your workplace, or perhaps you are a doer, all about action and making things happen. And who has time to feel when there is so much to do?

Most babies and mothers, however, are all about feelings, so it's important to become fluent in the language of emotion. The more you can increase your awareness of emotions, the more you will be able to figure out how to help those around you, not to mention yourself. Once you're able to accurately discern emotions, then you will be able to decide how to respond, if at all.

When we suppress, minimize, or deny our emotions or block those we trust from what we are feeling it can damage ourselves and our relationships. I am not encouraging you to dwell on the emotions, but to become good at feeling and naming them and to be curious about what they might be telling you. I've had a number of dads in my practice come to the realization that they felt depressed, a feeling they wanted to deny or find a quick fix to. Unfortunately there is such shame and weakness associated with feelings of depression and a clinical diagnosis of depression that it can prevent men from getting help and cause unnecessary suffering. But when they named it and were honest with themselves and me, we were then able to do something about it. For some men, doing something about it means increasing their self-care strategies,

such as physical exercise, and for others it may mean taking medication. Here are some tips to help you do feelings:

- **Grant yourself permission.** The first step is to allow yourself to experience the feeling. Try to pay attention to how you experience your feelings and what happens in your body. For example, when you are happy, how does that manifest itself? Or when you are sad, what happens?

- **Name it.** There is great power in naming a feeling. Sometimes in the act of naming it, it can even dissipate. The four big feelings, remember, are: sad, mad, glad, and scared. Again, pay attention to what's happening in your body—heart rate, blood pressure, ability to concentrate, and so on—and how your mood affects bodily function.

- **Wait and see.** Sometimes action is required and sometimes just letting the feeling inform and move through you is what's called for. For example, your fifteen-month-old daughter is climbing on a piece of furniture and you begin feeling anxious and worried that she might fall and hurt herself. You watch and wait to see how she balances herself. She doesn't do so well, so you respond or take action by helping her get down. Generally, the best decisions are made when emotions are low, especially when the emotion is anger.

- **Stop, breathe, think.** This is a proven technique that even the kids show *Blues Clues* endorses and teaches. This is best used when you are angry. As you start to feel yourself boiling over, stop, breathe, and shift into thinking mode. While you are thinking, ask yourself a variety of questions like: How important is this? Am I at risk? Is someone else at risk? Why am having such a strong reaction? Like it or not, our behavior is often dictated by the emotions we feel.

- **Show and tell.** If you are unable to express your feelings to your child while you're in the moment, save them for later, after some reflection. By telling and showing your children your emotions, you are teaching them (1) that it is human and normal to have feelings, (2) that they have an impact on you, and (3) that it is important to express feelings verbally. Children learn how to be empathic when they see us having feelings.

> ## Real Dad
>
> *"I didn't realize that my ritual of holding my son in my arms before I put him down for bed wasn't just helping him fall asleep; it was healing me, too. For the first five years of my life, my mother suffered from depression and relied on others to take care of me. It occurred to me then how much not being held by my mother had wounded me."*
>
> —Stephen, 36

Unexpressed Negative Feelings

As I've mentioned, many dads don't "do" feelings. This can be of great consequence and prevents men from taking care of themselves. Feelings that go unexpressed can cause heightened emotional buildup, leading to resentments or even physical illness. For example, those who have chronic bouts of anger are at higher risk of developing cardiac failure and other diseases.

It should be noted that whether you defend yourself against emotions or express them too much, the goal is to manage your emotional health. Often times our defenses operate unconsciously, meaning we are not fully aware of it. One of the first tasks is to become aware of what defenses—and we all use them—you use to fend off emotion. The most common forms of defense against feelings are to:

- **Deny or minimize.** You are miraculously rid of the

problem—for now. The thinking is: "If the feeling doesn't exist then neither does the problem."

- **Avoid or distract.** This technique is common and often very subtle. The thinking is if you change the subject or divert your attention—"Hey, how about those Jets?"—maybe the unwanted feeling will go away.

- **Fix it quick.** I often encourage the men I work with to slow down and try to understand the issue or what it is that they are feeling before they fix it. You can't properly fix something before you've identified it. If you stay with the feeling long enough, and really listen to it, it will inform you and guide you to a solution.

- **Approach with sarcasm or humor.** While humor can be very helpful in managing negative emotions, it can also prevent necessary feelings from getting expressed. Ask someone you trust if he thinks your humor or sarcasm feels defensive.

WHY WE HAVE FEELINGS

Whether the feelings are coming from you, your partner, or your child, feelings are information. Emotions tell you when something is up—not necessarily good or bad, just up.

Your Feelings

The challenge is often to stay with a feeling long enough to listen to what it is telling you. Do you or your family need something? For example, a dad who has an intense work schedule and moves at a frenetic pace recently came into my office, which operates at an intentionally slower pace. Within minutes he sinks into the chair and observes within himself what he describes as exhaustion and dizziness. We talk and stay with the feeling long enough to realize that he is, indeed, exhausted.

The feeling tells him that he doesn't have too many opportunities in his life to downshift, to just sit and talk. It also tells him that he needs to get some rest. Now whether or not he will be able to do that is a different story—his work is intense and he, his partner, and his two-year-old were all battling colds. You might be wondering, well, what good is it to know what we feel if we can't do anything about it?

There's always something you can do about it, even if it's just to cut yourself some slack, pick yourself up by your bootstraps, understand why you are being irritable, or get some sleep (catnaps can be great sources of renewal).

Remember, feelings are information. Listen to them.

Your Partner's Feelings

Becoming a mother is a major life event that brings about shifts in a woman's hormones, identity, and schedule, just to name a few. These shifts are probably the biggest in her life. Motherhood comes with a lot of big feelings, both positive and negative.

For starters, the hormonal changes can be very radical and real and affect women differently. Some women respond to the changes in their hormones by getting depressed, others find their moods elevated, and still others experience minimal changes in mood. Second, a woman who had a well-established career may mourn the satisfaction her career brought her when she becomes a mother. Third, but certainly not finally, the practical demands of mothering bring real changes in her schedule. Whether she's home full time with the baby or returns to work full time or tries to balance both, as a mother this very practical adjustment can bring up all sorts of feelings. For example, your partner may have had a regular routine and a lot of power and responsibility, and now, as a mom, she spends her days talking very little with adults, with erratic nightly feedings, and sometimes foregoing even a basic grooming regimen.

Being comfortable with and sensitive to your partner's emotions is critically important. This means understanding and accepting her emotions, which is obviously easier said than done. You may not always understand the cause or know how to fix things, but you can become interested in and accepting of your partner's emotions. Sometimes that's all that's called for.

RESPONDING TO BIG FEELINGS

Listen, Listen, Listen

Train yourself to be quiet and just listen. This can be difficult. Men have often been trained to "don't just sit there; do something." But the goal here is to understand as much as possible about what is going on for her. "At times of strong emotions there is nothing as comforting and helpful as a person who listens and understands," wrote Haim Ginott in his book *Between Parent and Child.*

Be Curious and Interested

"Tell me more" is the stance to take. You want to get the message across that you are genuinely interested and curious. You and your partner are a team committed to creating a happy family. Together you can do anything.

Mirror, Mirror

This means voluntarily telling your partner what you see or what you hear when you listen. This can be music to her ears. You might say something like, "You sound really frustrated" or, "You look really beautiful—I love watching you nurse the baby."

Help as Needed

"How can I help?" is a question you should get used to asking. It is very common to assume, based on all that good listening you just did, that you know what she needs or that she doesn't need anything. We all know what can happen when we assume. Sometimes that assumption can be accurate and sometimes it is wildly off the mark.

Real Mom

Sharon was very nervous about becoming a mother. She had been left to fend for herself when she was a child and, as a result, she had a hard time relying on people. She was concerned that she would perpetuate the pattern and inflict the same things onto her kids.

After her baby was born, she discovered that she was wonderful at nurturing. Her awareness of her mother's ways made Sharon very conscious of her own mothering. This left her feeling more hopeful and excited about being a mom.

YOUR CHILD'S FEELINGS: CRYING

How can such a little being create such excruciating noise? Initially you might consider their cries cute. Later, as they throw tantrums (and not all babies or toddlers do), you might find it very hard to listen to. Babies and toddlers will have big feelings, and your job is to work with them to try to regulate and soothe those feelings. By the beginning of their third year, children should have acquired some soothing skills of their own.

Here are some tips for getting comfortable with your child's emotions:

• Know that crying is his primary way of communicating until he develops words.
• Expect her feelings to change frequently.

• It helps to have your own emotions in check or under control in order to help your child deal with his.
• Try to name what your child is feeling using one of the four primary emotions: sad, mad, glad, and scared.
• Say to yourself, "Whatever my child feels, I can handle it. Bring it on!"

Common psychological wisdom and research has told us over the years that crying is a natural and healthy expression of feelings that in most cases can be cathartic for the crier. But a recent study suggests that the cathartic effects of crying are only effective for those who have parents who respond compassionately. Those who have parents who are mostly nonresponsive, irritated, or bothered by the crying were essentially taught that crying was not a good option for expressing their feelings.

It's vitally important that fathers learn how to respond to crying because "crying, for a child," says Judith Kay Nelson, psychotherapist and author of *Seeing Through the Tears: Crying and Attachment*, "is a way to beckon the caregiver, to maintain proximity and use the caregiver to help regulate mood or negative arousal." You don't have to respond to every cry with a rush of sympathy and consoling, but it is important to pay attention to how you react or respond to crying. How you respond over the years will influence how your child thinks men act in response to a show of feelings. It can be a challenge to decipher what your baby is crying about. Is he tired, hungry, uncomfortable, or just letting off some steam? How should you respond? You will likely find yourself confused, uncomfortable, and sometimes quite distressed about what your little one is trying to say and how to help. Here are some possible reasons for that cry:

- **Attention.** You know the cry has to do with attention when you give him attention and the crying stops. By the way, there is nothing inherently manipulative or wrong about a child needing attention.
- **Separation.** When your baby has formed attachments to people, places, and things and then those things are taken away, whether it be a pacifier, her mommy, or the park, crying and screaming can follow. She will get over it. Young children tend to have their feelings and then move on.
- **Discomfort or pain.** This cry may be quiet at first and then become loud and a clear communication that your child is experiencing a pain of some sort. It may be due to a rash on his bottom, teething, or a fall and bump on his head.
- **Tiredness.** This cry tends to be less enthusiastic and is generally accompanied by yawns—a dead giveaway.
- **Hunger.** This is often a whiny cry and perhaps a little more difficult to discern. Again, you'll know she was crying due to hunger if it stops once she has been fed.
- **Colic.** This is often indicated by inconsolable crying, usually in the evening and nighttime. The causes are not completely known but experts suspect that it is abdominal pain due to intestinal gas. This condition almost always

> ## Real Dad
>
> *"I worried that my three-year-old son, Brandon, was too sensitive. He cried at the drop of a hat. I thought of how other boys would destroy him—I was bullied as a child, and I did't want to raise a wimp. But finally, I had to remember that my son is not me, and what happened to me will not necessarily happen to my son."*
>
> —Jeffrey, 38

goes away by the end of the third month. Try the following: (1) Swaddle, keeping your baby in a womblike setting; (2) Rock, move and pace, lifting your baby up and down in a slow elevator-like fashion; (3) Take breaks—this can be very stressful on both of you; and (4) Consult with your pediatrician.

TIP

Avoid labeling your child names like "a crier," "impatient," "spoiled," or "a fighter," as these perceptions only get reinforced. Labels don't give your child a chance to grow beyond the (often hastily made) perception.

TIP

Many times what you feel is a by-product of what your child feels. It's what therapists call "induced feelings." So if you find yourself feeling intense anger, impatience, or irritability, perhaps your child is feeling the same thing.

Big Feelings Happen

You, your partner, and your child will all experience big feelings occasionally. National Football League head coach Eric Mangini has a policy for his players that I think is worth considering. He says that a player has five seconds to express his big feelings—positive or negative—and then he has to move on, otherwise it will affect his play. You, your partner, and your child will likely need more time than that, but the point is a good one—feel the feeling, let it move through you, be with it and see what it tells you, and then move on to the next thing.

REFLECTION QUESTIONS

1. What emotion(s) related to fatherhood have surprised you?

2. How do you typically express feelings of impatience, frustration, anger, and rage? Do you fight or flee, express it, or deny it?

3. What were you taught about how to deal with emotions? Sometimes we learn just through watching and witnessing. What did you learn from your parents about emotions? How were your emotions responded to?

4. With respect to feelings, how might you be repeating what you were taught? How might you be doing things differently than what you were taught?

5. How do you handle your baby's crying?

Afterword

Your child is three and you have just closed the chapter on this part his or her life. How will she reflect back on these years? What will he remember? Probably not too much, but one thing is sure. You are in the process of developing a trusting, connected relationship. Hopefully this book has helped you make that connection since it really is worth making and has implications for how you and your child will live the rest of your lives. If you haven't made the connection or the bond, what will you do? Time has not run out. You still have opportunities.

- Make a commitment to begin today. Spend regular time together, just the two of you.
- The next few years are fun, because your child will engage in more collaborative play. Join in the fun.
- Make your interests known to your child, whether it's music, art,

a particular sport, or something else. Invite him in and show him your world, whether it's work or hobbies.
- Be curious about her interests. Let her show what she did in preschool. Visit her preschool.

In just a few years your child will be starting grade school, and, once that happens, he will spend considerably more time out of your orbit. This is the best time to have a real influence on your child, perhaps, before others begin to exert their influence. And while you are far from being an empty nester you are sending your little boy or girl out into the world. And there will probably never be a time again when you are so strongly at the center of her world. Don't let time go by without making your positive presence felt.

As this book comes to an end I look back on what I've covered and tried to do. The original goal was to promote and encourage your involvement in your first child's life and help you navigate the emotional and practical challenges. I've covered a lot of territory, and by now you have some experience under your belt.

I was telling a friend the other day that bringing this book to fruition is my version of giving birth. I may still have mother envy, but I have labored and brought forth something that will hopefully help some new dads.

Much like a father, I've wondered if I have allowed you enough space to grow and allowed your own process to unfold. While I wanted to instruct in this book and give specific information on what to do when, I also wanted to give you the freedom to experiment and play with what works best for you. This is your process, your narrative as a father that is being created and it is very personal to you. The combination of information, active things you can do, and Reflection Questions at the end of each chapter were designed to be your guide, not your dictator, along the way.

PERSONAL REFLECTIONS

At the age of six, I remember being in the presence of my father. The smell of Barbasol on his cleanly shaven face, the thoroughbred strength of his neck. I liked to examine him, take him in with all my senses—my eyes, hands, nose—and play with his ear or sniff the starch of his Brooks Brothers shirts. He was big. I was small.

That's what I thought big dads felt like. As I examined him I noticed he put his socks on differently than I did. He had to hoist one leg up onto his knee and put his socks on sideways. Why couldn't he just bend over and put them on like I did? He was big. I was small. That's what I thought big dads did. Then there were Saturday mornings when all I wanted to do was play with him and all he seemed to want to do was what big dads do, rake the leaves, mow the lawn, pay the bills. Thank God I wasn't a big dad, there was too much fun to be had. And then I turned seventeen and learned that he was no longer committed to my mother, he had had enough of their thirty-year marriage for many complicated reasons.

I now have the smell of Edge shaving cream on my face, a leg I have to hoist before I can pull up my socks, and chores to do. I walk, not in my father's footsteps but pretty close behind and often right alongside them. He is not perfect. I am not perfect. But we love each other deeply. He has helped me become the man and dad that I am today. He came to visit me and my family a couple of weekends ago and we had a sleepover. My kids could not get enough of him. My wife and I could not get enough of him. He's able to be a dad now in ways he couldn't before.

LEGACY REFLECTIONS

It's natural for men to wonder what they will leave behind and how they will be remembered by their children. If all goes according to plan, your kids will outlive you. What part of you, what part of your teachings, what part of your love do you want your children to retain? Many dads want their children to:

- Love hard—God, themselves, others, and nature.
- Play hard—at sports, hobbies, and friendship.
- Work hard—with a strong work ethic and ability to persevere through tough times.
- Rest well—knowing when to stop, breathe, and think through their options.
- Forgive themselves and others—to be tender.
- Be grateful—know that what they have is not to be taken for granted.
- Be happy.

SAMPLE LEGACY LETTER

As you wonder about what sort of legacy you are leaving your children, consider writing them a letter. It's something that they will not only appreciate someday and probably keep for the rest of their lives to help remember you by, but it's also an important exercise for you. It will help you think about what kind of father you are and how to measure up against the father you hope to be. Feel free to modify it to suit your needs.

Dear Son or Daughter,

In my life I was mostly _____

_____ with how I lived. I wished I had done more_____

_____ with my time. I have some regrets but many more things that I am proud of. One of the things I am most proud of is having you in my life. You have showed me how to _____

_____. I will never forget the day when you/we_____

_____. You taught me how to_____

_____ and for that I am forever grateful. When I leave this earth I will hopefully leave you with the knowledge that I loved you, that your mother loved you, and that our combined love sustains you. I also want to leave behind a few things for you. These are things that cannot be identified in a will or placed in a box. These are memories that I have and they are:

1)_____

_____

_____

_____

2)_____

_____

_____

_____

3)_____

_____

_____

4)_____

_____

_____

5)_____

_____

_____

_____

Love,
Dad

Looking Forward

The father-child relationship can be fraught with pain, absence, abuse, disappointment, and neglect. The so-called "sins" of a father are said to last generations. Perhaps you had a poor relationship with your father. Perhaps your father is dead and repairing things is impossible. Maybe you have no desire to repair things; perhaps they are beyond repair. These scenarios are real, so what's a new dad to do? You have two choices: (1) do nothing, or (2) do something. If you want to do something, here are just a few options to consider:

• Men's Leadership Alliance (MLA) is a charitable nonprofit organization dedicated to inspiring authentic manhood. Their nondenominational programs are meant to address the needs of men and their journey through life. MLA offers father-son retreats as well as retreats for adult men. Visit their Web site at www.mensleadershipalliance.org.

• Get into therapy or some other healing process and ask—even insist—your father to be a part of it.

REFLECTION QUESTIONS

1. Have you and your partner prepared a will?
2. How do you want to be remembered by your child?
3. What type of legacy would you like to leave your child?

I hope these questions have helped lead you to some answers, about what's most important to you, about what kind of father you are, about how good you are at some aspects of fathering and how you can improve in others. I hope you'll keep reflecting on these things all along your journey.

Index

Acceptance and denial, 9–10
Amniocentesis, 27
Apgar score, 45
Baby's room, readying, 9, 30–31, 32
Biophysical profile, 31
Birthing. *See* Delivery of baby; Labor
Birth plan, 18, 28, 31, 33, 34, 45
Biting, hitting, kicking, 145, 173, 181
Blood pressure, 23, 43, 45, 47, 185
Bottle-feeding, 57, 67, 92–93, 94, 96
Brazelton approach, 64
Breastfeeding, 17, 67, 74, 82
Breastmilk, 94
Breech birth, 43, 45
Carriers and transporters, 99–100
Cesarean section (c-section), 18, 43–44
Changes. *See also* Finances; Priorities;
    Relationship with partner; Schedule
    in her, 12–13
    sense of purpose, 77–78
    in you, 10–12
    in your home, 14–15
Checklists
    for bringing baby home, 37
    for expectant dads, 34
    for outings with baby, 102–103
Child care, 16, 17
Chorionic villus sampling (CVS), 23
Circumcision care, 68–69
Circumcision decision, 29, 32, 129
Cleaning babies, 68–69
Clothing and accessories, 16, 17, 88–92
Cognitive skills, 59–60, 114–115, 150–151
Colic, 59, 190
College, planning for, 16
Co-parenting, 134–137
CPR, infant, 69–70, 119
Crawling, 18, 54, 56, 90, 101, 115, 161, 162, 163
Creative outlets and being creative, 127–128
Crying
    child's feelings and, 189–190
    deciphering different cries, 59
    differences in approaches to, 135
    emotional/psychological development and
        responses and, 58–59, 112–113, 149–150
    possible reasons for, 59, 190
    responding to, 58, 59, 66, 189–190
    soothing strategies, 66
Decision making
    co-parenting and, 134–137
    who delivers baby, 18
    your role in doctor visits, 13, 18
Delivery of baby, 35–47. *See also* Hospital or
birthing center; Labor
    common questions about, 42–46
    deciding on ob-gyn or midwife, 18
    difficult, dealing with, 45
    getting prepared for, 35
    key questions for informed decision
        making, 46
    location of, 19
    other relevant decisions, 28–29
    pain management considerations, 28, 44
    reflection questions, 47
    who will be present, 19
    your roles, 36–37
Denial and acceptance, 9–10
Development
    Brazelton approach, 64
    cognitive skills, 59–60, 114–115, 150–151
    concerns, 63, 118–119, 153
    emotional and psychological, 58–59,
        112–113, 149–150
    family events impeding, 154
    language skills, 61–62, 116–117, 151–152
    milestone definitions, 55
    "normal," 54–55
    physical and behavioral, 55–57, 108–111,
        145–148
    social skills, 62, 117–118, 152–153
    typical newborn baby states, 52–53
    by year. *See* Year 1; Year 2; Year 3
Diapers
    changing, 68, 69
    cloth vs. plastic, 17
    cost of, 17
    saving on, 17
Discipline, 169–182
    about: overview of, 169
    asking for forgiveness and, 178
    common issues, 179–181
    firm and tender approach, 170–174, 182
    goals of, 169–170
    losing strategies, 176–178
    reflection questions, 182
    rules to guide, 179
    styles, 170–172
    tempering the *No*, 175–176
    timeout Q & A, 174–175
    for toddlers, 112
Doctor visits. *See also* Prenatal care and tests
    child medical concerns, 69–70, 119–120
    picking pediatrician and, 69
    your role in, 13, 18, 26
Doulas, 18, 28, 29, 33
Driven Dads, 6

Electronic Fetal Monitoring (EFM), 46
Emergencies
    birth-related, 42–43
    common injuries, 120
    family emergency plan, 121
    infant CPR, 69–70, 119
Emotional and psychological development,
    58–59, 112–113, 149–150
Emotions and feelings, 7–10, 183–191
    about: overview of, 183
    acceptance and denial, 9–10
    big four feelings, 184
    dealing with openly, 7
    fear of change, 11–12. See also Changes
    how to "do" feelings, 184–186
    "induced feelings" and, 59
    negative, 8, 186–187
    positive, 8
    postpartum depression (PPD) and, 71–72
    psychic shifts, 77
    reasons for feelings, 187–188
    reflection questions, 191
    responding to Big Feelings, 188, 191
    typical thoughts during pregnancy, 33
    unexpressed negative, 186–187
    of your child, 189–190. See also Crying
    yours and your partner's, 187–188
Epidurals, 19, 43, 44, 46
Episiotomy, 44

False labor, 38–39
Family events, impeding development, 154
Family (extended) and friends, 82–83
Fatherhood and parenting. See also Discipline;
    Playtime; Preparing for fatherhood; specific
    topics
    co-parenting and, 134–137
    differences in co-parenting and, 135–137
    duties and fathering instincts, 84–86
    later years, reflections, and legacy, 193–196
    valuable communication techniques,
        136–137
Feeding. See Food
Feelings. See Emotions and feelings
Finances
    changes in, 15–17
    money-saving tips, 16–17
    overview of added costs, 15–17
First birthday, 73–74
Food
    cost of, 16, 17
    feeding and soothing supplies, 92–96
    feeding baby, 56, 67, 78, 83, 84, 96, 111. See
        also Breastfeeding
    formula, 95
Forgiveness, asking for, 178
Furniture. See Gear and furniture

Gear and furniture, 87–104
    about: overview of, 87
    assembling, 32
    cost of, 16
    furniture and accessories, 96–99
    reflection questions, 104
    resources, 103–104
    what you need/don't need, 88–103
Gender expectations, 135
Genetic counseling, 19
Glucose tolerance test, 27, 31
Good Enough Dads, 6–7

Hand-me-downs, 17
Heart, monitoring, 46
Height and weight, 63, 118, 153
Holding baby, 64–66. See also Swaddling
Home
    changes in, 14–15
    sharing job responsibilities, 83–84
    things to learn before returning from
        hospital, 46
Hospital or birthing center
    choosing, 19
    dealing with staff, 45
    emergency situations and, 42–43
    length of stay at, 42
    parking car at, 36
    pre-registering at, 36
    staying overnight in, 29
    things needed at, 37–38
    things to learn before leaving, 46, 66
    touring, 31
    when to leave for, 42

Induced labor, 45–46
Infidelity, 72–73
Insurance, health, 16, 42
IV (intravenous) bag, 46

Job responsibilities, sharing, 83–84. See also
    Work

Labor
    active, signs, 40
    difficult, dealing with, 45
    early, signs, 39–40
    false, 38–39
    induced, 45–46
    stage 1 (labor and dilation), 39–41
    stage 2 (birthing stage), 41
    stage 3 (placental stage), 41–42
    transition, signs, 40–41
Language skills, 61–62, 116–117, 151–152
Legacy reflections and letter, 194–196
Listening skills, 136–137

Medical care. *See* Doctor visits; Emergencies
Medicines, 110, 120
Milestones. *See* Development
Miscarriage, 12, 22, 23, 24–25, 26, 27
Motor skills. *See* Development

Newborns. *See also* Year 1 (0 to 12 months)
  cognitive skills, 59–60
  complete dependence of, 52
  emotional and psychological development,
    58–59
  emotional/behavioral states, 52–53
  language skills, 61–62
  meeting development needs, 53–54
  milestone definitions, 55
  "normal" development, 54–55
  observing, 70
  physical and behavioral development,
    55–57
  playtime, 158–160
  primary (BIG FIVE) needs of, 51–52
  social skills, 62
  weight and height, 63
Nonstress test, 31–32

Observing baby, 70
Outing supplies, 102–103
Outlets. *See* Self-care
Overprotective Dads, 6

Pacifiers, 56, 94, 103, 153
Pain management considerations, 28, 44
Partner. *See also* Relationship with partner;
  Supporting partner
  changes in, 12–13
  feelings of, 187–188
  returning to work, 81
  things to take to hospital, 38
Pediatrician, picking, 69. *See also* Doctor visits
Perfect Dads, 6
Physical and behavioral development, 55–57,
  108–111, 145–148
Physical outlets and getting physical, 128–129
Pitocin, 44, 45, 46
Playtime
  about: overview of, 155–156
  age-specific suggestions, 158–166
  benefits of, 156–157, 167–168
  common impediments to, 156
  lifetime connection through, 167–168
  practical questions about, 166–167
  reflection questions, 168
  rules of, 158–159
Postbirth decisions and considerations, 29
Postpartum depression (PPD), 71–72
Potty training, 92, 148, 149, 154, 165
Preeclampsia, 23, 43, 45

Pregnancy
  changes during. *See* Changes
  men denying then accepting their
    experience of, 9–10, 11
  support during. *See* Supporting partner;
    Trimesters (finding your role)
  sympathetic, 10
  telling others about, 23, 29–30
Prenatal care and tests. *See also specific tests*
  being involved with, 13, 26–27
  first trimester (weeks 1 to 13), 23–25
  second (weeks 14 to 24), 26–29
Preparing for fatherhood. *See also* Delivery of
  baby; Finances
  about: overview of, 2–3
  coping with change. *See* Changes;
    Emotions and feelings
  decision making, 18–19
  expectant dad's checklist, 34
  reflection questions, 20
  types of dads and, 5–7
Priorities. *See also* Schedule; Self-care
  adjusting expectations and setting, 80–83
  competing needs and, 79
  sharing job responsibilities, 83–84
  trying to do everything, 75–83

Real Dad stories, 25, 26, 27, 32, 43, 44, 66, 70,
  74, 80, 128, 163, 186, 190
Regressive behavior, 154
Relationship with partner, 131–139. *See also*
  Sex and intimacy
  changes in, 13–14, 27–28, 78, 132
  children deepening, 13–14
  children ruining, 14
  co-parenting and, 134–137
  cost of unhealthy marriage, 138
  differences in co-parenting and, 135–137
  focusing on, 131–137
  intentional acts to strengthen, 132–134
  prioritizing, 81
  reflection questions, 138–139
  strong marriage, 139
  valuable communication techniques, 136–137
  wondering, wandering, and infidelity, 72–73
Reluctant Dads, 6
Rh factor screening, 24
Roles you play. *See* Your roles

Safety gear, 98. *See also* Carriers and
  transporters
Safety precautions, 6, 68, 97, 119
Schedule
  changing routines, 27–28
  reflection questions, 86
  time for baby, 82
  time management, 76–77, 80

Self-care, 123–130
    about: overview of, 123–124
    creative outlets and being creative,
        127–128
    dad therapy benefits, 127
    outlets required for, 124
    physical outlets and getting physical,
        128–129
    reasons for outlets, 124–125
    reflection questions, 130
    social outlets and socialization, 125–127
    spiritual outlets and questions, 129
Separation, saying good-bye, 114
Sex and intimacy
    after birth of baby, 72–73, 82, 133
    during pregnancy, 12, 27–28
Sleeping
    changes for you, 78, 79
    child, 53, 56, 65, 67–68, 71, 110–111, 124, 159
    furniture and accessories, 96–99
    training, 181
Social outlets and socialization (dad), 125–127
Social skills (child), 62, 117–118, 152–153
Sonogram. See Ultrasound (sonogram)
Spiritual outlets and questions, 129
Splitting, 180–181
Stage 3 (placental stage), 41–42
Standing, 57
Supporting partner
    during pregnancy, 13. See also Trimesters
        (finding your role)
    sharing job responsibilities, 83–84
Swaddling, 46, 59, 64, 66, 190
Swaddling blankets and wraps, 90, 94–95
Sympathetic pregnancy, 10

Tantrums, 150, 180, 189
Tests. See Prenatal care and tests; specific tests
Toddlers. See Year 2 (12 to 24 months)
Toys, 100–102
Traditions, 135
Travel. See Carriers and transporters; Outing
    supplies
Trimesters (finding your role), 21–34
    about: overview of, 21, 22; reflection
        questions, 34
    first (weeks 1 to 13), 22–25
    second (weeks 14 to 24), 25–30
    third (weeks 25 to 40), 30–33
Types of dads, 5–7

Ultrasound (sonogram), 13, 24, 25, 26, 31
Umbilical cord care, 68
Unconscious Dads, 6

Walking, 57, 108, 109, 113, 115, 164
Water breaking, 42
Weight and height, 63, 118, 153
When Men Are Pregnant (Shapiro), 12–13
Work. See also Schedule
    balancing time/energy at, 76–77, 80
    checking flexibility of schedule, 31
    partner returning to, 81

Year 1 (0 to 12 months), 51–74. See also
    Newborns
    about: overview of, 50
    cleaning, 68–69
    fatherhood challenges, 70–73
    fear of hurting baby, 70–71
    holding and swaddling, 64–66. See also
        Swaddling
    medical care, 69–70
    milestone definitions, 55
    playtime, 158–163
    primary needs, 64–73
    reflection questions, 74, 121–122
    sleeping, 67–68
Year 2 (12 to 24 months)
    about: overview of, 106
    cognitive skills, 114–115
    emotional and psychological development,
        112–113
    language skills, 116–117
    milestone definitions, 108
    "normal" development, 107–108
    physical and behavioral development, 108–111
    playtime, 164–165
    social skills, 117–118
    toddlerproofing, 119
    weight and height, 118
Year 3 (24 to 36 months)
    about: overview of, 142
    cognitive skills, 150–151
    emotional development, 149–150
    family events and regressive behavior, 154
    language skills, 151–152
    not-so-terrible twos, 143–144
    physical and behavioral development, 145–148
    playtime, 165–166
    reflection questions, 154
    social skills, 152–153
    weight and height, 153
Your father, v, 11–12, 77, 78, 139, 196
Your roles. See also Fatherhood and parenting;
    Work
    delivery day, 36–37
    during pregnancy. See Trimesters (finding
        your role)
    sharing job responsibilities, 83–84